Growth in Mathematics

PURPLE

TEST DESIGN AND EVALUATION

WILLIAM A. MEHRENS
Professor of Educational Measurement
  and Evaluation
Michigan State University
East Lansing, Michigan

ERIC M. GORDON
Assistant Professor of Education
Michigan State University
East Lansing, Michigan

SPECIAL DESIGN FOR INSTRUCTION

JOSEPH F. LOUGHMAN
Art Director
Center for Curriculum Development
New York, New York

Center for Curriculum Development
New York

Growth in Mathematics

PURPLE

CURRICULUM AND WRITING

DAVID W. WELLS
Director of Instruction
   and Mathematics Education
Oakland Schools
Pontiac, Michigan

JANET S. ABBOTT
Coordinator of Mathematics
Chula Vista City School District
Chula Vista, California

MARYANNE E. YACONO
Executive Editor, Elementary Mathematics
Center for Curriculum Development
New York, New York
formerly Mathematics Teacher
Fair Lawn, New Jersey

ROBERT L. SPENCE
Vice President
Center for Curriculum Development
New York, New York
formerly Chairman, Mathematics Department
Haddon Heights, New Jersey

RESEARCH AND CRITIQUE

GEORGE A. SPOONER
Professor of Mathematics
Central Connecticut State College
New Britain, Connecticut

LESLIE S. BEATTY
formerly Mathematics Consultant
Chula Vista City School District
Chula Vista, California

LOLA J. MAY
Mathematics Consultant
Winnetka Public Schools
Winnetka, Illinois

Harcourt Brace Jovanovich
New York   Chicago   San Francisco   Atlanta   Dallas   *and*   London

CRITICAL READERS

BARBARA BRANCH
Mathematics Consultant for the
    Central Area of Memphis City Schools
Memphis, Tennessee

JAMES DAVIS
Coordinator of Mathematics and
    Specialized Curriculum Services
Clayton County Board of Education
Jonesboro, Georgia

LOUISE GEMAKE
Mathematics Supervisor
Community School District 4
New York, New York

MARJORIE JACKSON
Junior High Mathematics Consultant
Indianapolis Public Schools
Indianapolis, Indiana

DR. RONALD MASSIE
Mathematics Consultant
Lincoln Public Schools
Lincoln, Nebraska

TAYE M. MATOI
Parent
Los Angeles, California

TRUDY NAPOLILLO
Mathematics Coordinator
South Stickney School District #111
Burbank, Illinois

DR. M. M. OHMER
Dean, College of Sciences
Nicholls State University
Thibodaux, Louisiana

MARY SCHNEIDER
Fifth Grade Teacher
Pleasant Ridge School
Cincinnati, Ohio

DR. IRENE ST. CLAIR
formerly Director of Mathematics Program
    for the State of Texas (Levels K-8)
Austin, Texas

DR. HAZEL WAGNER
Director of the Criterion-Reference
    Testing Program
Research and Evaluation Department
Chicago Board of Education
Chicago, Illinois

JOYCE WHITE
Mathematics Supervisor
Cobb County Schools
Marietta, Georgia

MARY FRANCES WILLINGHAM
Fifth Grade Teacher
Summit Drive Elementary School
Greenville, South Carolina

PHOTOGRAPH ACKNOWLEDGMENTS   *Cover:* J. Alex Langley, DPI   *Text:* O. Buitrago and E. Maristany; Harbrace.
                                page 199, New York Public Library, Picture Collection.
ART ACKNOWLEDGMENTS   *Text:* M. Haller, D. Crews, and M. Vivo.
TECHNICAL ILLUSTRATIONS AND MECHANICAL PRODUCTION: Pencils Portfolio, Inc.

PRINTED IN THE UNITED STATES OF AMERICA

ISBN 0-15-351281-4

Contents

Marks Along the Nile

Birds are eating the grain in the field.
Nefer and Abu chase the birds away.
They make a record of how many they chase.
They make marks in the sand.

They make this mark for each bird.

When they have made ten marks,
they smooth over the sand.
They make this mark for ten.

When they have made ten of these,
they smooth over the sand again.
They make this mark for one hundred.

Here are marks they made. Read the numbers they name.

| | | | ∩|| ∩∩∩||||| 9∩∩|||||||
  4   12   35   126

What number do these marks name?

1. ||| 2. ||||||| 3. ∩||||| 4. ∩∩∩|||||||

5. 9   6. 9∩|| 7. 9∩∩∩| 8. 99∩∩∩|||||

Grouping by Tens

We use ten symbols to name numbers.
The symbols are **digits.**   0 1 2 3 4 5 6 7 8 9

We use ten digits because we group by tens.

1 one   **1 ten**   **1 hundred**   **1 thousand**
          (ten ones)   **(ten tens)**   **(ten hundreds)**

Which digits do you see below the blocks?

1 thousand   **3 hundreds**   **5 tens**   **2 ones**

— **try these** —

Write the digits.
1.

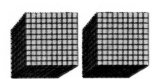 

_?_ thousands   _?_ hundreds   _?_ tens   _?_ ones

2

now do these

Make a chart like the one at the right.
Look at the blocks to complete the chart.

	thousands	hundreds	tens	ones
2.	1	3	2	4
3.				
4.				
5.				
6.				
7.				
8.				
9.				

3

Expanded Notation

We use **numerals** to name numbers.

To name 458, we group by hundreds, tens, and ones.

Then we add.

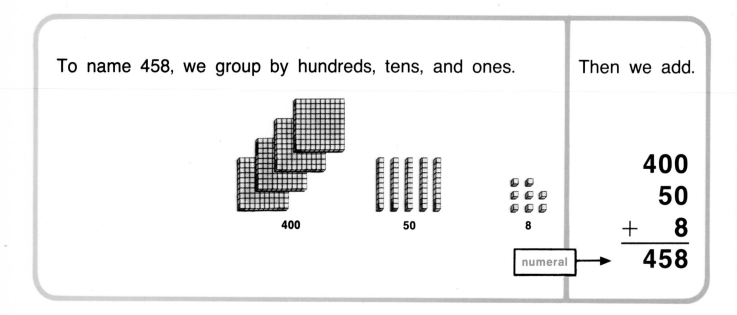

400

50

+ 8

458

To name 2375, we group by thousands, hundreds, tens, and ones.

Then we add.

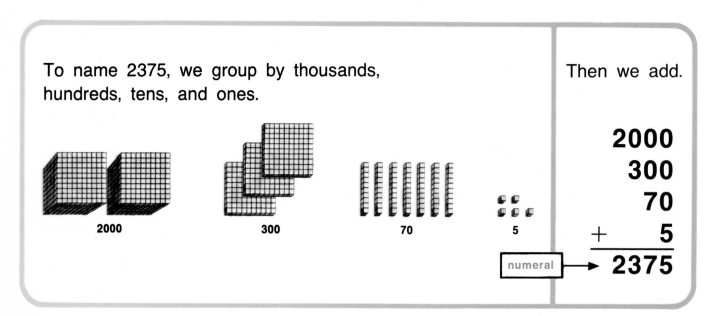

2000

300

70

+ 5

2375

4

Write the numeral.

1. 200
    60
 +   7
 ───

2. 500
    80
 +   3
 ───

3. 3000
    600
     20
 +   4
 ────

4. 9000
    400
 +   1
 ────

5. 4000
 +   6
 ────

Write an addition example like those shown above for the sum.

6. 378   7. 937   8. 406   9. 5821   10. 2940

Write the numeral.

11. 100
     70
 +   4
 ───

12. 300
     50
 +   6
 ───

13. 7000
     300
      10
 +   9
 ────

14. 6000
       50
 +   2
 ────

15. 5000
     400
 +   10
 ────

Write an addition example like those shown above for the sum.

16. 594   17. 862   18. 703   19. 916   20. 250

21. 2486   22. 9730   23. 3504   24. 4375   25. 5443

26. 6075   27. 8300   28. 4077   29. 9002   30. 3080

THE COOKIE CUTTER

I cut cookies for the fair—
2000 round and 400 square
And 60 quickly and 5 with care.
How many cookies have I there?

5

Place Value

A digit in different places names different numbers.
In the ones place, the 5 names the number 5.
In the tens place, the 5 names the number 50.
In the hundreds place, the 5 names the number 500.

What number does the 5 name in the thousands place?
What number does the 5 name in the ten-thousands place?
What number does the 5 name in the hundred-thousands place?

hundred thousands 10 × 10,000	ten thousands 10 × 1000	thousands 10 × 100	hundreds 10 × 10	tens 10 × 1	ones 1
					5
				5	0
			5	0	0
		5	0	0	0
	5	0	0	0	0
5	0	0	0	0	0

**Each place in a numeral has a value
ten times the value of the place at its right.**

6

What number does the 3 name in the numeral?

hundred thousands	ten thousands	thousands	hundreds	tens	ones
1.		5	3	4	2
2.	6	8	4	3	7
3. 5	1	3	6	0	2
4. 3	4	7	9	6	8
5. 8	3	5	4	2	1

now do these

In what place is the red digit?

6. 142   **7.** 476,103   **8.** 52,188   **9.** 942,581

10. 3768   **11.** 4636   **12.** 753,214   **13.** 76,894

What number does the red digit name?

14. 142   **15.** 476,103   **16.** 52,188   **17.** 942,581

18. 3768   **19.** 4636   **20.** 753,214   **21.** 76,894

In which numeral does the 3 name the greater number?

22. 3256 or 2356   **23.** 10,316 or 11,237

24. 1372 or 4613   **25.** 347 or 103

26. 743,621 or 436,107   **27.** 54,013 or 79,365

Write in order from least to greatest.

28. 6759, 8327, 5904   **29.** 5863, 5214, 5064

30. 1936, 1950, 1942   **31.** 3483, 3480, 3489

7

Millions

The distance between the Sun and the Earth
is about one hundred forty-nine million,
five hundred ninety thousand kilometers.

Millions Period			Thousands Period			Ones Period		
hundred millions	ten millions	millions	hundred thousands	ten thousands	thousands	hundreds	tens	ones
1	4	9	5	9	0	0	0	0

Commas are used to separate the **periods.**
They make the numeral easier to read.

Read the numeral. ⟶ **149 million, 590 thousand**
Write the numeral. ⟶ **149,590,000**

Here is the numeral for another large number.

24,617,938

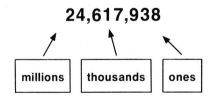

Read the numeral. ⟶ **24 million, 617 thousand, 938**

Read the numeral.

1. 46,172   2. 94,625   3. 212,874

4. 6,371,192   5. 18,721,965   6. 783,192,841

now do these

Write the digits that are in the millions period.

7. 52,175,983   8. 197,461,803   9. 906,142,111

Write the digits that are in the thousands period.

10. 29,362   11. 14,739,156   12. 874,396,172

Name 100 more.

13. 762   14. 14,800   15. 29,609

Name 1000 more.

16. 29,421   17. 472,600   18. 1,721,840

Name 1,000,000 more.

19. 7,421,836   20. 19,201,964   21. 536,199,400

THINK ABOUT IT

Suppose you have a job.
You earn $4.00 an hour.
You work 7 hours a day.
You work 5 days a week.
You work 50 weeks a year.
It would take over 140 years
to earn a million dollars.

9

Billions

The distance between the Sun and the planet Neptune
is about four billion, four hundred ninety-eight million,
one hundred thousand kilometers.

Billions Period			Millions Period			Thousands Period			Ones Period		
hundred billions	ten billions	billions	hundred millions	ten millions	millions	hundred thousands	ten thousands	thousands	hundreds	tens	ones
		4	4	9	8	1	0	0	0	0	0

Read the numeral. ⟶ **4 billion, 498 million, 100 thousand**
Write the numeral. ⟶ **4,498,100,000**

Here is the numeral for another large number.

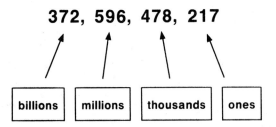

372, 596, 478, 217

billions   millions   thousands   ones

Read the numeral. ⟶ **372 billion, 596 million, 478 thousand, 217**

Read the numeral.

1. 7,116,295,101   2. 8,000,671,842   3. 24,172,000,142

4. 19,764,963,400   5. 162,792,100,631   6. 834,117,345,104

now do these

Write the digits that are in the billions period.

7. 4,421,834,112   8. 82,147,632,109   9. 326,963,147,197

Write the digits that are in the millions period.

10. 3,471,327,502   11. 194,372,114   12. 17,942,324,163

Name 1000 more.

13. 142,764,000   14. 965,173,040,174   15. 62,437,852

Name 1,000,000 more.

16. 726,371,425   17. 10,475,429,471   18. 99,400,000

Name 1,000,000,000 more.

19. 432,000,000,000   20. 72,416,349,146   21. 763,142,973,761

THINK ABOUT THIS

Have you ever counted how many breaths
you take in one minute?
About how many do you think you take
in one hour? in one day?
Did you know that to take one billion breaths
you would have to live for more than one hundred years?
Doesn't that leave you breathless?

11

Comparing Numbers

56 is greater than 42.

56 > 42

42 is less than 56.

42 < 56

Use > or < to make a true sentence.

2,467,598 ● 3,728,641

Think:
2 million is less than 3 million.
So,

2,467,598 < 3,728,641

Use > or < to make a true sentence.

4,586,298 ● 4,574,375

Think:
Same number of millions.
Same number of hundred thousands.
Compare the ten thousands. 8 > 7
So,

4,586,298 > 4,574,375

Write > or <.

1. 696 ● 642

2. 4634 ● 4684

3. 27,421,046 ● 27,542,017

4. 316,475,326 ● 471,304,129

— now do these

Write > or <.

5. 714,832 ● 629,421

6. 302,175 ● 418,727

7. 643,721 ● 642,819

8. 138,924 ● 139,410

9. 572,118 ● 572,374

10. 892,904 ● 892,409

11. 4,721,925 ● 8,365,147

12. 3,725,109 ● 2,406,118

13. 2,177,824 ● 2,275,132

14. 9,421,372 ● 9,392,174

15. 7,640,000 ● 7,690,104

16. 5,379,101 ● 5,378,204

17. 8,432,831 ● 8,432,381

18. 6,424,803 ● 6,525,803

STATE THE ORDER

During one census, these populations were reported by ten states.
List the states in order from the least to the greatest number of people.

State	Population	State	Population
Alaska	304,000	New York	18,384,000
California	20,007,000	North Dakota	620,000
Indiana	5,202,000	Tennessee	3,937,000
Maryland	3,938,000	Texas	11,236,000
Michigan	8,890,000	Wyoming	334,000

Approximations

Ulysses S. Grant was elected president in 1872.
He received 3,597,070 votes.
His opponent, Horace Greeley, received 2,834,079 votes.

Approximations are easier to think about.
These are approximations to the nearest hundred thousand.
  Grant   → 3,600,000 (3,597,070 is nearer to 3,600,000 than to 3,500,000.)
  Greeley → 2,800,000 (2,834,079 is nearer to 2,800,000 than to 2,900,000.)

Which hundred is nearest to 325?

For 325, the approximation to the nearest hundred is 300.

Which thousand is nearest to 4826?

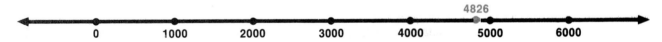

For 4826, the approximation to the nearest thousand is 5000.

Which ten thousand is nearest to 175,000?

175,000 is halfway between 170,000 and 180,000.
In such cases, we agree to use the greater approximation.
For 175,000, use 180,000 as the approximation to the nearest ten thousand.

try these

What is the nearest ten?

1.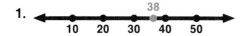

2.

What is the nearest hundred?

3.

4.

now do these

Write the approximation to the nearest ten.

5. 61   **6.** 143   **7.** 794   **8.** 1939

Write the approximation to the nearest hundred.

9. 496   **10.** 547   **11.** 4854   **12.** 16,925

Write the approximation to the nearest thousand.

13. 35,121   **14.** 17,721   **15.** 172,914   **16.** 29,571

Write the approximation to the nearest ten thousand.

17. 26,410   **18.** 83,572   **19.** 115,721   **20.** 4,398,194

BE A REPORTER

You are a reporter in 1904.
You must write a story about the presidential election.
In the story, you are to approximate the votes to
the nearest hundred thousand.
What approximations will you use?

A. Theodore Roosevelt 7,628,834
B. Alton B. Parker 5,084,491

Test

Write the numeral.

1. 200
    50
  + 3
    (p. 4)

2. 400
  + 8
    (p. 4)

3. 6000
    70
  + 4
    (p. 4)

4. 8000
  + 9
    (p. 4)

What number does the red digit name?

5. 5831 (p. 6)   6. 27,304 (p. 6)   7. 857,921 (p. 6)   8. 463,880 (p. 6)

9. In which numeral does the 5 name the greater number?   1358 or 1583 (p. 6)

Write in order from least to greatest.

10. 4218, 4281, 4258 (p. 6)   11. 7392, 7489, 7399 (p. 6)

Name 1000 more.

12. 84,369 (p. 8)   13. 8,412,053 (p. 8)

Name 1,000,000 more.

14. 5,718,293 (p. 8)   15. 423,662,498 (p. 8)

Name 1,000,000,000 more.

16. 847,000,000,000 (p. 10)   17. 36,523,000,000 (p. 10)

Write > or <.

18. 11,486 ● 12,000 (p. 12)   19. 27,402 ● 27,399 (p. 12)

20. 8,743,911 ● 8,744,203 (p. 12)   21. 16,656,492 ● 16,595,837 (p. 12)

Write the approximation to the nearest hundred.

22. 811 (p. 14)   23. 6235 (p. 14)   24. 8471 (p. 14)   25. 26,450 (p. 14)

Write the approximation to the nearest thousand.

26. 6342 (p. 14)   27. 32,456 (p. 14)   28. 87,964 (p. 14)   29. 830,500 (p. 14)

Write the approximation to the nearest ten thousand.

30. 32,456 (p. 14)   31. 58,423 (p. 14)   32. 291,899 (p. 14)   33. 6,555,293 (p. 14)

16

Roman Numerals

The ancient Romans used these symbols to name numbers.

I	V	X	L	C	D	M
1	5	10	50	100	500	1000

Their system was not a place-value system.
They added or subtracted the values of the symbols.

Symbol	Operation	Decimal Numeral
III	1 + 1 + 1	3
XI	10 + 1	11
IX	10 − 1	9
MDLX	1000 + 500 + 50 + 10	1560
MDXL	1000 + 500 + (50 − 10)	1540

What number is named?

1. II

2. VI

3. IV

4. XVI

5. XXIII

6. XXXVII

7. XL

8. LX

9. LXXVI

10. CCXIII

11. CCCLXV

12. DCXXI

13. MMCCXII

14. MDCLXVI

15. MDCXLIV

Here is an important year in our history. What happened that year?

MDCCLXXVI

2 Addition

Addition

8 star ships are on a
trip to Alpha Centauri.
6 other star ships join them.
How many star ships are there in all?

When two or more groups are joined,
you use **addition** to find how many in all.

$$8 + 6 = 14$$

You can use a number line to find sums.

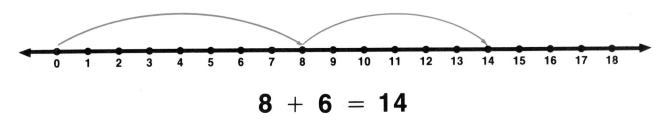

$$8 + 6 = 14$$

Here are two ways to show addition.

addend ⟶ **8**

addend ⟶ **+6**

8 + 6 = 14 ⟵ sum ⟶ **14**

Add.

1. $9 + 9 =$ ___?___

2. $7 + 7 =$ ___?___

3. $6 + 8 =$ ___?___

4. $4 + 6 =$ ___?___

5. $9 + 4 =$ ___?___

6. $7 + 5 =$ ___?___

7. $\begin{array}{r} 6 \\ +5 \\ \hline \end{array}$

8. $\begin{array}{r} 5 \\ +8 \\ \hline \end{array}$

9. $\begin{array}{r} 8 \\ +6 \\ \hline \end{array}$

10. $\begin{array}{r} 4 \\ +8 \\ \hline \end{array}$

11. $\begin{array}{r} 6 \\ +7 \\ \hline \end{array}$

12. $\begin{array}{r} 9 \\ +7 \\ \hline \end{array}$

now do these

Add.

13. $\begin{array}{r} 6 \\ +9 \\ \hline \end{array}$

14. $\begin{array}{r} 4 \\ +7 \\ \hline \end{array}$

15. $\begin{array}{r} 7 \\ +8 \\ \hline \end{array}$

16. $\begin{array}{r} 6 \\ +6 \\ \hline \end{array}$

17. $\begin{array}{r} 8 \\ +5 \\ \hline \end{array}$

18. $\begin{array}{r} 9 \\ +8 \\ \hline \end{array}$

19. $\begin{array}{r} 8 \\ +9 \\ \hline \end{array}$

20. $\begin{array}{r} 8 \\ +7 \\ \hline \end{array}$

21. $\begin{array}{r} 4 \\ +9 \\ \hline \end{array}$

22. $\begin{array}{r} 7 \\ +6 \\ \hline \end{array}$

23. $\begin{array}{r} 9 \\ +5 \\ \hline \end{array}$

24. $\begin{array}{r} 7 \\ +4 \\ \hline \end{array}$

25. $\begin{array}{r} 5 \\ +9 \\ \hline \end{array}$

26. $\begin{array}{r} 5 \\ +7 \\ \hline \end{array}$

27. $\begin{array}{r} 8 \\ +8 \\ \hline \end{array}$

28. $\begin{array}{r} 5 \\ +6 \\ \hline \end{array}$

29. $\begin{array}{r} 8 \\ +4 \\ \hline \end{array}$

30. $\begin{array}{r} 9 \\ +6 \\ \hline \end{array}$

Solve the problem.

In 1935, what was the cost of

31. an ice cream pop and a dish of ice cream?

32. a candy bar and a cola?

33. a dish of ice cream and a cola?

34. a pretzel and an ice cream cone?

PRICES
COLA   5¢
CANDY BAR   5¢
PRETZEL   2¢
ICE CREAM CONE 5¢
ICE CREAM POP 5¢
Dish of ICE CREAM 7¢

19

Properties of Addition

Compare the sums.

$$9 + 5 = 14 \qquad 5 + 9 = 14$$

**You can add two numbers in either order.
The sum is always the same.**

Compare the sums.

The numbers named inside the parentheses are added first.

$$(5 + 3) + 7 = ? \qquad 5 + (3 + 7) = ?$$
$$8 \quad + 7 = 15 \qquad 5 + \quad 10 \quad = 15$$

**You can group addends differently.
The sum is always the same.**

Compare the sums.

$$4 + 0 = 4 \qquad 0 + 6 = 6 \qquad 0 + 0 = 0$$

**When one of two addends is 0,
the sum equals the other addend.**

20

Add.

1. $9 + 8 = \underline{\ ?\ }$

2. $8 + 9 = \underline{\ ?\ }$

3. $0 + 7 = \underline{\ ?\ }$

4. $(8 + 2) + 7 = \underline{\ ?\ }$

5. $8 + (2 + 7) = \underline{\ ?\ }$

6. $(7 + 0) + 9 = \underline{\ ?\ }$

now do these

Add.

7. $8 + 7 = \underline{\ ?\ }$

8. $7 + 8 = \underline{\ ?\ }$

9. $9 + 9 = \underline{\ ?\ }$

10. $6 + 9 = \underline{\ ?\ }$

11. $9 + 6 = \underline{\ ?\ }$

12. $8 + 8 = \underline{\ ?\ }$

13. $9 + 7 = \underline{\ ?\ }$

14. $7 + 9 = \underline{\ ?\ }$

15. $7 + 7 = \underline{\ ?\ }$

16. $(2 + 8) + 8 = \underline{\ ?\ }$

17. $2 + (8 + 8) = \underline{\ ?\ }$

18. $(7 + 3) + 5 = \underline{\ ?\ }$

19. $(4 + 6) + 7 = \underline{\ ?\ }$

20. $4 + (6 + 7) = \underline{\ ?\ }$

21. $7 + (8 + 2) = \underline{\ ?\ }$

22. $(6 + 7) + 8 = \underline{\ ?\ }$

23. $6 + (7 + 8) = \underline{\ ?\ }$

24. $9 + (6 + 6) = \underline{\ ?\ }$

Write $=$, $>$, or $<$.

25. $3 + 7 \ \bigcirc\ 7 + 3$

26. $4 + 2 \ \bigcirc\ 5 + 2$

27. $3 + 7 \ \bigcirc\ 2 + 7$

28. $8 + 5 \ \bigcirc\ 9 + 5$

29. $6 + 7 \ \bigcirc\ 7 + 6$

30. $8 + 7 \ \bigcirc\ 9 + 7$

31. $5 + (5 + 7) \ \bigcirc\ (5 + 5) + 7$

32. $6 + 0 \ \bigcirc\ 0 + 9$

33. $(8 + 6) + 3 \ \bigcirc\ 8 + (6 + 3)$

34. $(4 + 3) + 9 \ \bigcirc\ 4 + (2 + 9)$

35. $1 + 8 \ \bigcirc\ 0 + 8$

36. $8 + (5 + 9) \ \bigcirc\ (8 + 3) + 9$

A Rule Machine

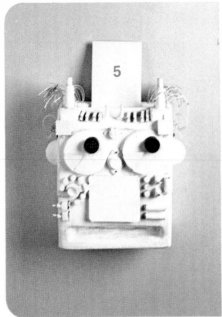  

Put a number
into Amazo.
Call it the **input.**

Amazo uses a **rule.**
This time the rule
is "Add 3."
Amazo adds 3 to
the input.

Out comes a number.
Call it the **output.**
It is the sum
of the input and 3.

---

try these

1. The table shows some inputs and a rule.
   List the outputs.
   (The first one is done for you.)

ADD 5

INPUT	OUTPUT
3	8
7	?
9	?
6	?

List the outputs.

2. ADD 8

INPUT	OUTPUT
9	?
6	?
7	?
4	?

3. ADD 2

INPUT	OUTPUT
7	?
6	?
8	?
9	?

4. ADD 9

INPUT	OUTPUT
3	?
7	?
5	?
6	?

5. ADD 3

INPUT	OUTPUT
9	?
7	?
8	?
6	?

6. ADD 7

INPUT	OUTPUT
3	?
8	?
4	?
9	?

7. ADD 4

INPUT	OUTPUT
8	?
7	?
9	?
6	?

8. ADD 6

INPUT	OUTPUT
7	?
5	?
4	?
8	?

9. ADD 1

INPUT	OUTPUT
8	?
9	?
7	?
6	?

10. ADD 5

INPUT	OUTPUT
4	?
5	?
8	?
6	?

WHAT IS THE RULE?

Study the pairs of inputs and outputs.
Then write the rule that was used.

A. ?

INPUT	OUTPUT
7	16
6	15
8	17
9	18

B. ?

INPUT	OUTPUT
6	13
9	16
7	14
8	15

C. ?

INPUT	OUTPUT
9	17
7	15
6	14
8	16

23

quick check

See how well you know your facts.
Drive around the track nine times.

The first time add 1 to each number.
The second time add 2.
The third time add 3,
and so on.
The last time, you will add 9.
Try to do it without making a mistake.

Have a friend check you.
Write down any facts you miss.
Study them.
Then try again.

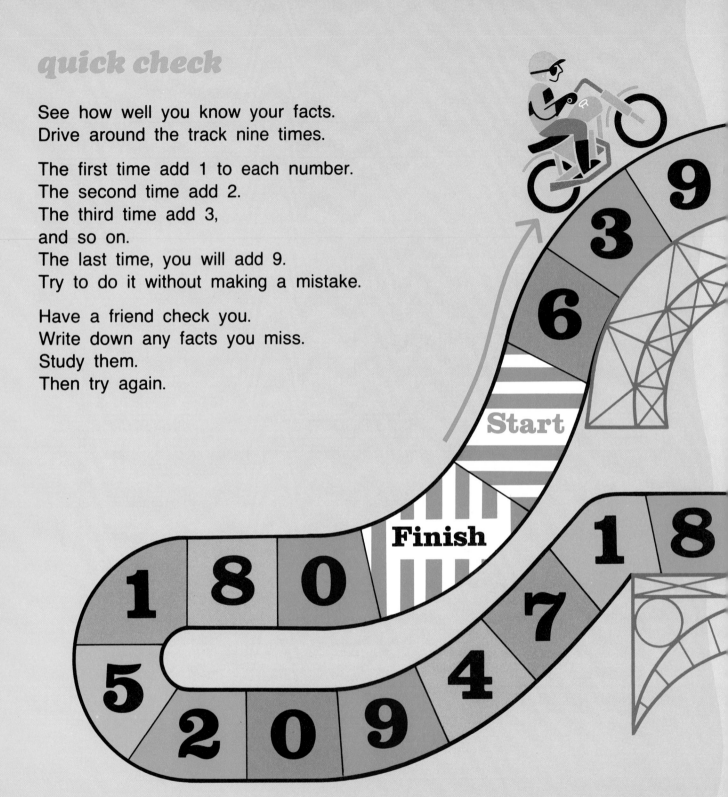

24

Estimating Sums

Boiling Springs

Bean Blossom

Biggerville

It is 28 kilometers from Boiling Springs to Bean Blossom.
It is 45 kilometers from Bean Blossom to Biggerville.
About how far is it from Boiling Springs to Biggerville?

You can add the nearest tens to estimate sums.

Numbers	Nearest Tens
28 $\longrightarrow$	30
$+45$ $\longrightarrow$	$+50$
	80

The distance is **about** 80 kilometers.

For some problems, you can add the nearest hundreds.

Numbers	Nearest Hundreds
637 $\longrightarrow$	600
$+250$ $\longrightarrow$	$+300$
	900

Estimate. Use the nearest tens.

1. 85
   +67

2. 93
   +27

3. 72
   +53

4. 64
   +69

5. 59
   +92

6. 31
   +94

— now do these —

Estimate. Use the nearest tens.

7. 45
   +59

8. 82
   +44

9. 73
   +29

10. 92
    +37

11. 55
    +85

12. 62
    +53

13. 52
    +67

14. 67
    +83

15. 35
    +85

16. 72
    +49

17. 82
    +33

18. 67
    +38

19. 85
    +83

20. 92
    +47

21. 64
    +44

22. 55
    +77

23. 73
    +69

24. 35
    +73

Estimate. Use the nearest hundreds.

25. 243
    +852

26. 478
    +625

27. 738
    +365

28. 923
    +501

29. 753
    +750

30. 532
    +465

31. 493
    +910

32. 805
    +916

33. 259
    +167

34. 483
    +729

35. 351
    +650

36. 445
    +465

37. 928
    +650

38. 575
    +525

39. 432
    +864

40. 927
    +721

41. 725
    +767

42. 925
    +943

Adding Greater Numbers

Add 364 and 125.

Step 1	Step 2	Step 3
364 +125 9	364 +125 89	364 +125 489
Add the ones.	Add the tens.	Add the hundreds.

You can check by adding up.

Step 1	Step 2	Step 3
9 364 +125 489	89 364 +125 489	489 364 +125 489
Add the ones.	Add the tens.	Add the hundreds. Compare the sums.

---

try these

Add.

1. 600
+527

2. 513
+845

3. 907
+362

4. 715
+ 12

5. 367
+622

6. 456
+ 43

28

now do these

Add.

7. 423
+965

8. 872
+917

9. 283
+116

10. 425
+773

11. 845
+400

12. 867
+302

13. 823
+610

14. 525
+943

15. 927
+ 11

16. 705
+ 63

17. 9123
+5456

18. 6264
+6031

19. 5342
+8136

20. 8002
+ 783

21. 6301
+ 648

22. 8040
+ 736

23. 2468
+ 21

24. 6597
+ 302

25. 6543
+ 26

26. 4700
+ 89

27. 42,530
+81,304

28. 36,917
+92,031

29. 41,235
+ 3,624

30. 92,045
+96,303

31. 31,420
+ 7,009

Solve the problem.

32. There are 425 gumballs in one machine.
There are 363 in another.
How many gumballs are there in all?

33. There are 124 pieces of licorice.
52 more are put into the jar.
How many pieces are there in all?

34. There are 1316 gumdrops.
There are 242 mints.
How many candies are there in all?

29

Renaming

Sometimes you must rename when adding.
You know that ten ones make one ten.

Count the tens and ones.   Make another ten.   Write the numeral.

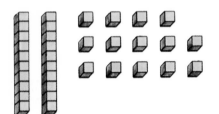   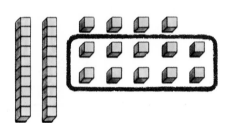

2 tens   14 ones ⟶ 3 tens   4 ones ⟶ 34

─── **try these** ───────────────

Copy and complete.

1. 4 tens 16 ones ⟶ 5 tens 6 ones ⟶ _?_

2. 8 tens 19 ones ⟶ 9 tens _?_ ones ⟶ _?_

3. 5 tens 14 ones ⟶ _?_ tens _?_ ones ⟶ _?_

4. 7 tens 11 ones ⟶ _?_ tens _?_ one ⟶ _?_

5. 3 tens 10 ones ⟶ _?_ tens _?_ ones ⟶ _?_

30

now do these

Write the numeral.

6. 6 tens 12 ones

7. 3 tens 15 ones

8. 8 tens 14 ones

9. 5 tens 17 ones

10. 4 tens 16 ones

11. 7 tens 19 ones

12. 2 tens 15 ones

13. 5 tens 12 ones

14. 6 tens 13 ones

15. 3 tens 14 ones

16. 4 tens 17 ones

17. 7 tens 16 ones

18. 8 tens 19 ones

19. 9 tens 18 ones

20. 4 tens 10 ones

21. 17 tens 13 ones

22. 18 tens 10 ones

23. 15 tens 17 ones

24. 25 tens 10 ones

25. 34 tens 16 ones

26. 47 tens 13 ones

27. 52 tens 11 ones

28. 30 tens 14 ones

29. 64 tens 12 ones

30. 29 tens 10 ones

31. 88 tens 18 ones

32. 40 tens 19 ones

AMAZO

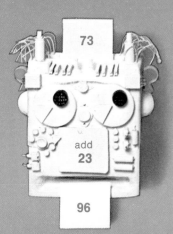

Copy and complete.

A.

ADD 23

INPUT	OUTPUT
73	96
55	?
62	?
34	?
86	?

B.

ADD 134

INPUT	OUTPUT
854	988
632	?
261	?
745	?
943	?

31

Addition with Renaming

Renaming once.

Step 1	Step 2	Step 3
$$\begin{array}{r} 532 \\ +296 \\ \hline 8 \end{array}$$	$$\begin{array}{r} 1 \\ 532 \\ +296 \\ \hline 28 \end{array}$$	$$\begin{array}{r} 1 \\ 532 \\ +296 \\ \hline 828 \end{array}$$
Add the ones.	Add the tens. Write the 2. Remember the 1.	Add the hundreds.

Renaming more than once.

Step 1	Step 2	Step 3
$$\begin{array}{r} 1 \\ 765 \\ +189 \\ \hline 4 \end{array}$$	$$\begin{array}{r} 1\,1 \\ 765 \\ +189 \\ \hline 54 \end{array}$$	$$\begin{array}{r} 1\,1 \\ 765 \\ +189 \\ \hline 954 \end{array}$$
Add the ones. Write the 4. Remember the 1.	Add the tens. Write the 5. Remember the 1.	Add the hundreds.

Copy and complete.

1. $\overset{1}{2}37$
   $+526$
   $\overline{63}$

2. $\overset{1}{3}65$
   $+462$
   $\overline{27}$

3. $\overset{11}{5}89$
   $+67$
   $\overline{6}$

4. $\overset{11}{7}08$
   $+396$
   $\overline{4}$

5. $\overset{11}{}89$
   $+964$
   $\overline{3}$

Add.

6. 437
   $+371$

7. 659
   $+286$

8. 605
   $+397$

9. 26
   $+964$

10. 967
    $+877$

Add.

11. 235
    $+346$

12. 646
    $+627$

13. 773
    $+52$

14. 578
    $+662$

15. 478
    $+314$

16. 653
    $+154$

17. 792
    $+322$

18. 99
    $+202$

19. 303
    $+958$

20. 576
    $+632$

21. 769
    $+232$

22. 477
    $+235$

23. 88
    $+735$

24. 404
    $+896$

25. 89
    $+942$

26. 1672
    $+3758$

27. 923
    $+1079$

28. 1348
    $+526$

29. 3579
    $+2461$

30. 9876
    $+8765$

31. $59{,}765$
    $+61{,}327$

32. $60{,}989$
    $+70{,}598$

33. $67{,}905$
    $+21{,}495$

34. $87{,}502$
    $+4{,}639$

35. $53{,}421$
    $+659$

33

Column Addition

Sometimes there are more than two addends.

Step 1	Step 2	Step 3

Step 1

```
  2
 372
 164
 278
+ 96
───
   0
```

Add the ones.
Write the 0.
Remember the 2.

Step 2

```
 3 2
 372
 164
 278
+ 96
────
  10
```

Add the tens.
Write the 1.
Remember the 3.

Step 3

```
 3 2
 372
 164
 278
+ 96
────
 910
```

Add the hundreds.

---

try these

Copy and complete.

```
    1 2              1 2                1                  2                 2
1.  407         2.   659          3.    94          4.   856          5.   245
    609              38                 659              759               965
   +786             +346              +723              234               347
   ────             ────             ─────             +123               895
     02               43                 6                 2             +234
                                                        ────             ────
                                                                           6
```

34

now do these

Add.

6.　28
　　　 9
　+96
　───
　　113

7.　97
　　　5
　+18
　───
　　116

8.　　6
　　62
　+31
　───
　　99

9.　27
　　88
　+18
　───
　　133

10.　95
　　　63
　　+22
　　───
　　　180

11.　72
　　83
　+952
　────
　　　7

12.　282
　　493
　+597
　────
　　1172

13.　294
　　378
　+181
　────
　　853

14.　289
　　493
　+571
　────
　　1453

15.　172
　　283
　+491
　────
　　946

16.　4075
　　2786
　+3457
　─────
　　10318

17.　5403
　　2798
　+1273
　─────
　　9474

18.　7049
　　 279
　+6732
　─────
　　14060

19.　　28
　　8982
　+5403
　─────

20.　4093
　　3798
　　 29
　+4006
　─────

21.　　8
　　35
　　17
　+ 9
　───

22.　　48
　　260
　　　3
　+ 49
　────

23.　　53
　　42
　　994
　+897
　────

24.　596
　　847
　　243
　+2796
　─────

25.　303
　　708
　　104
　+1189
　─────

26.　56
　　20
　　86
　　49
　+53
　───

27.　　7
　　69
　　325
　　479
　+625
　────

28.　375
　　　8
　　42
　　89
　+972
　────

29.　　49
　　425
　　27
　　189
　+1256
　─────

30.　509
　　402
　　47
　　1189
　+4567
　─────

35

too much information

To solve a mystery, a detective must find the facts.
To solve a problem, you must be a good detective.
To answer a question, you must find only the facts you need.

Find the facts you need to answer this question.

Question: <u>How many cookies disappeared</u>?

Facts: Two groups of scouts went camping.
There were 75 scouts in the two groups.
They camped for 14 days.
One group brought 225 cookies.
The other brought 155 cookies.
One day, the scouts went swimming.
When they returned, the cookies were gone.

These are the facts you need:
One group brought 225 cookies.
The other brought 155 cookies.
You add to find the answer.
380 cookies disappeared.

Which facts do you need to answer the question?

1. <u>How many cookies in all</u>?
Parents visited the 75 scouts on Sunday.
More than 20 of them brought cookies.
They brought 250 oatmeal cookies.
They also brought 165 sugar cookies.

2. <u>How many parents visited the scouts</u>?
The parents visited for 4 hours.
Some traveled more than 50 kilometers.
There were 25 fathers and 27 mothers.
8 sisters and 7 brothers also visited.

Answer the question. Use only the facts you need.

3. How many lanterns went out?
   27 lanterns went out at 9 P.M.
   No more went out for 30 minutes.
   Then 13 more lanterns went out.
   The whole camp was dark.

4. How many woke up before 7 A.M.?
   24 scouts woke up at 5:30 A.M.
   25 more woke up before 6 A.M.
   15 more woke up between 6 A.M. and 7 A.M.
   The rest woke up before 7:30 A.M.
   The first ones awake saw 4 raccoons.

5. How many cookie wrappers did they find?
   5 scouts found cookie wrappers on the ground.
   They found 6 wrappers near the flagpole.
   They found 12 between the flagpole and the woods.
   They found 3 more wrappers in the woods.
   They told 2 scout leaders about their discovery.

6. How many raccoons did they find?
   The scouts discovered that 80 more cookies were missing.
   7 scouts followed the trail of cookie wrappers.
   In the woods, they found a raccoon family.
   There were 2 adult raccoons and 3 baby raccoons.
   They had found the cookie thieves.

Problem-solving Help 37

Test

Add.

1. $8 + 5 = \underline{\ ?\ }$ (p. 18)

2. $6 + 9 = \underline{\ ?\ }$ (p. 18)

3.
$$\begin{array}{r} 7 \\ +4 \\ \hline \end{array}$$
(p. 18)

4. $(8 + 2) + 4 = \underline{\ ?\ }$ (p. 20)

5. $7 + (5 + 5) = \underline{\ ?\ }$ (p. 20)

6. $(4 + 3) + 6 = \underline{\ ?\ }$ (p. 20)

7.
$$\begin{array}{r} 6351 \\ + 406 \\ \hline \end{array}$$
(p. 28)

8.
$$\begin{array}{r} 923 \\ + 74 \\ \hline \end{array}$$
(p. 28)

9.
$$\begin{array}{r} 3048 \\ + 21 \\ \hline \end{array}$$
(p. 28)

10.
$$\begin{array}{r} 36{,}410 \\ +62{,}185 \\ \hline \end{array}$$
(p. 28)

11.
$$\begin{array}{r} 68{,}000 \\ + 896 \\ \hline \end{array}$$
(p. 28)

12.
$$\begin{array}{r} 856 \\ + 73 \\ \hline \end{array}$$
(p. 32)

13.
$$\begin{array}{r} 441 \\ +329 \\ \hline \end{array}$$
(p. 32)

14.
$$\begin{array}{r} 97 \\ +648 \\ \hline \end{array}$$
(p. 32)

15.
$$\begin{array}{r} 2486 \\ +4815 \\ \hline \end{array}$$
(p. 32)

16.
$$\begin{array}{r} 23{,}710 \\ +34{,}894 \\ \hline \end{array}$$
(p. 32)

17.
$$\begin{array}{r} 6 \\ 13 \\ +89 \\ \hline \end{array}$$
(p. 34)

18.
$$\begin{array}{r} 481 \\ 397 \\ + 68 \\ \hline \end{array}$$
(p. 34)

19.
$$\begin{array}{r} 6082 \\ 1304 \\ 695 \\ +1180 \\ \hline \end{array}$$
(p. 34)

20.
$$\begin{array}{r} 29 \\ 476 \\ 300 \\ + 8 \\ \hline \end{array}$$
(p. 34)

21.
$$\begin{array}{r} 811 \\ 359 \\ 617 \\ 260 \\ +4112 \\ \hline \end{array}$$
(p. 34)

Write $=$, $>$, or $<$.

22. $6 + 4 \;\bullet\; 4 + 6$ (p. 20)

23. $1 + 6 \;\bullet\; 0 + 6$ (p. 20)

24. $(3 + 8) + 9 \;\bullet\; (3 + 9) + 9$ (p. 20)

25. $1 + (3 + 8) \;\bullet\; (1 + 2) + 8$ (p. 20)

bonus

Solve the problem.

26. There are 16 red bicycles.
There are 27 blue bicycles.
How many bicycles are there in all?
(p. 32)

27. There are 250 fifth graders at the picnic.
There are 187 sixth graders.
How many students are there in all?
(p. 32)

Calendar Sums

Look at the 2 by 2 square
on the calendar.
Add along the diagonals.

$9 + 17 = \underline{\ ?\ }$
$16 + 10 = \underline{\ ?\ }$

What do you notice?
Try it with other squares.

Choose a 3 by 3 square
from the calendar.
Add along the diagonals.

$10 + 18 + 26 = \underline{\ ?\ }$
$24 + 18 + 12 = \underline{\ ?\ }$

Add the middle column.
Add the middle row.

$11 + 18 + 25 = \underline{\ ?\ }$
$17 + 18 + 19 = \underline{\ ?\ }$

What do you notice?
Try it with other squares.

Choose a 4 by 4 square.
Add along the diagonals.
Are the sums the same?

Can you find any rows or
columns that have that same sum?

Add the numbers shown
in the four corners.

$7 + 10 + 28 + 31 = \underline{\ ?\ }$

Add the numbers shown
in the middle.

$15 + 16 + 22 + 23 = \underline{\ ?\ }$

What do you notice?
Try this with other calendars.

March

	1	2	3	4	5	6
7	8	9	10	11	12	13
14	15	16	17	18	19	20
21	22	23	24	25	26	27
28	29	30	31			

10	11	12
17	18	19
24	25	26

7	8	9	10
14	15	16	17
21	22	23	24
28	29	30	31

3 Subtraction

When to Subtract

Subtract to find how many are left.
Fred has 7 dollars.
He spends 3 dollars.
How many does he have left?
7 − 3 = ?

Subtract to find how many more you need.
Carmela needs 7 dollars.
She has earned 3 dollars.
How many more does she need?
3 + ? = 7 or 7 − 3 = ?

Subtract to compare.
Joan has 7 dollars.
Carole has 3 dollars.
How many more does Joan have?
7 − 3 = ?

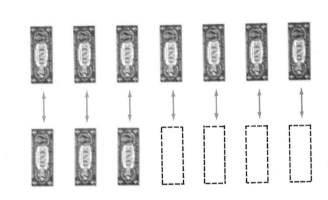

Here are two ways to show subtraction.

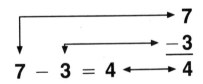

7 − 3 = 4

40

Subtract.

1. $9 - 5 = \underline{\ ?\ }$
2. $15 - 7 = \underline{\ ?\ }$
3. $14 - 6 = \underline{\ ?\ }$

4. $11 - 2 = \underline{\ ?\ }$
5. $18 - 9 = \underline{\ ?\ }$
6. $13 - 5 = \underline{\ ?\ }$

7. $16 - 8$
8. $17 - 9$
9. $13 - 7$
10. $14 - 5$
11. $13 - 4$
12. $15 - 6$

Subtract.

13. $12 - 3$
14. $13 - 8$
15. $11 - 2$
16. $16 - 9$
17. $15 - 7$
18. $14 - 6$

19. $12 - 4$
20. $18 - 9$
21. $13 - 6$
22. $14 - 7$
23. $13 - 5$
24. $14 - 8$

25. $10 - 2$
26. $15 - 9$
27. $17 - 8$
28. $16 - 7$
29. $11 - 3$
30. $12 - 6$

Use the number line.
Complete the sentence.

31.

$8 - 5 = \underline{\ ?\ }$

32.
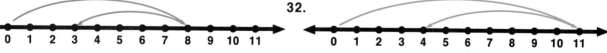
$11 - 7 = \underline{\ ?\ }$

33.
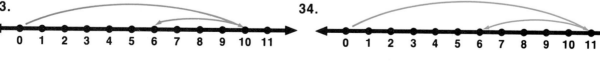
$10 - 4 = \underline{\ ?\ }$

34.

$11 - 5 = \underline{\ ?\ }$

41

Related Facts

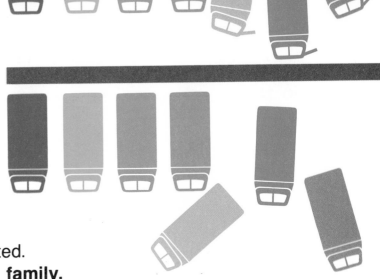

4 trucks are at the loading dock.
3 more drive up.
How many are there now?

4 + 3 = 7

3 drive away.
How many are there now?

7 − 3 = 4

Addition and subtraction are related.
4, 3, and 7 belong to a **number family.**

4 + 3 = 7   **7 − 3 = 4**

3 + 4 = 7   **7 − 4 = 3**

A number family is a group of related facts.

---

try these

Write the other related fact.

1. 7 + 3 = 10   2. 5 + 9 = 14   3. 7 + 6 = 13   4. 3 + 8 = 11
    3 + 7 = 10   9 + 5 = 14   13 − 6 = 7   11 − 8 = 3
    10 − 3 = 7   14 − 9 = 5   13 − 7 = 6   11 − 3 = 8

Use the three numbers. Write four related facts.

5. 3, 5, 8   6. 9, 4, 13   7. 5, 7, 12   8. 6, 4, 10

42

now do these

Write four related facts.

9. 7, 4, 11

10. 3, 7, 10

11. 8, 4, 12

12. 3, 9, 12

13. 6, 9, 15

14. 2, 8, 10

15. 7, 8, 15

16. 9, 7, 16

17. 5, 8, 13

18. 9, 2, 11

19. 6, 8, 14

20. 9, 8, 17

Find the missing number.

21. $9 + \underline{\ ?\ } = 10$

22. $5 + \underline{\ ?\ } = 13$

23. $\underline{\ ?\ } + 9 = 14$

24. $\underline{\ ?\ } + 8 = 13$

25. $\underline{\ ?\ } + 5 = 12$

26. $8 + \underline{\ ?\ } = 17$

27. $15 - 7 = \underline{\ ?\ }$

28. $15 - 8 = \underline{\ ?\ }$

29. $16 - 7 = \underline{\ ?\ }$

30. $11 - 7 = \underline{\ ?\ }$

31. $13 - 9 = \underline{\ ?\ }$

32. $11 - 6 = \underline{\ ?\ }$

33. $14 - 7 = \underline{\ ?\ }$

34. $12 - 4 = \underline{\ ?\ }$

35. $16 - 8 = \underline{\ ?\ }$

36. $12 - 6 = \underline{\ ?\ }$

37. $11 - 5 = \underline{\ ?\ }$

38. $18 - 9 = \underline{\ ?\ }$

CROSSING THE BRIDGE

4862 Kilograms

4685 Kilograms

4793 Kilograms

Load Limit 9500 Kilograms

All of these trucks should not be on the bridge at the same time. Why?

Which two can be on the bridge at the same time?

43

quick check

To subtract well, you must know your facts.
Study your facts.   Then make the journey.
Can you make the whole trip without a mistake?

UPSTREAM

Use canoe number 9.
(Subtract 9 from each number.)
Then try it with canoe 8.

OVER THE MOUNTAIN

Drive truck number 7.
(Subtract 7 from each number.)
Then try it with truck 6.

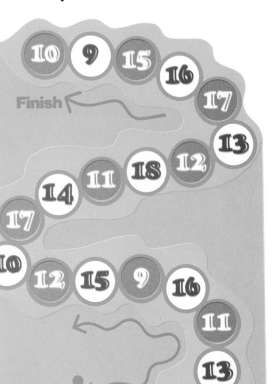

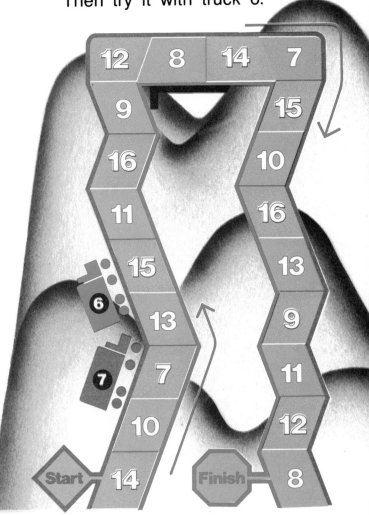

44

ACROSS THE DESERT

Ride camel number 5.
(Subtract 5 from each number.)
Then try it with camel 4.

THROUGH THE WOODS

Ride horse number 3.
(Subtract 3 from each number.)
Then try it with horse 2.

45

Estimating Answers

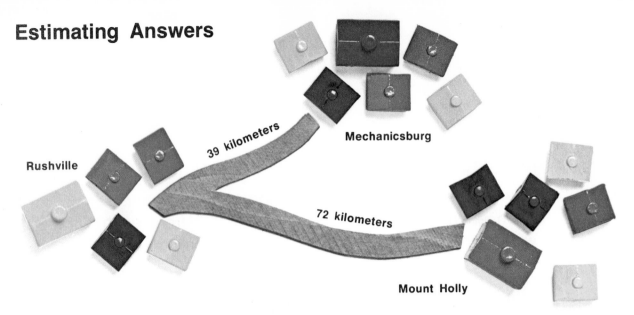

Rushville

39 kilometers

Mechanicsburg

72 kilometers

Mount Holly

About how much farther is it from Rushville to Mount Holly than from Rushville to Mechanicsburg?

You can subtract the nearest tens to estimate answers.

Numbers		Nearest Tens
72	→	70
−39	→	−40
		30

It is about 30 kilometers farther.

For some problems, you can subtract the nearest hundreds.

Numbers		Nearest Hundreds
750	→	800
−482	→	−500
		300

46

Estimate. Use the nearest tens.

1. 94	2. 78	3. 59	4. 64	5. 35	6. 57
−75	−64	−29	−35	−23	−18

now do these

Estimate. Use the nearest tens.

7. 35	8. 34	9. 48	10. 69	11. 87	12. 92
−24	−19	−35	−38	−36	−43

13. 63	14. 72	15. 79	16. 57	17. 83	18. 69
−39	−33	−35	−29	−42	−24

Estimate. Use the nearest hundreds.

19. 593	20. 835	21. 927	22. 450	23. 469	24. 693
−143	−524	−543	−256	−138	−522

25. 457	26. 634	27. 629	28. 695	29. 283	30. 727
−342	−219	−350	−457	−142	−243

PATTERNS

Each number is 5 greater than the number named before it. What are the next two numbers?

7	12	17	?	?

What are the next two numbers in the pattern?

A.
3	27	51	?	?

B.
4	40	76	?	?

C.
201	305	409	?	?

D.
400	532	664	?	?

Subtracting Greater Numbers

Subtract 134 from 579.

Step 1	Step 2	Step 3
$$\begin{array}{r} 579 \\ -134 \\ \hline 5 \end{array}$$	$$\begin{array}{r} 579 \\ -134 \\ \hline 45 \end{array}$$	$$\begin{array}{r} 579 \\ -134 \\ \hline 445 \end{array}$$
Subtract the ones.	Subtract the tens.	Subtract the hundreds.

Check your answer.
You subtracted 134. So, now add 134 to your answer.
You should be back where you started.

Problem

$$\begin{array}{r} 579 \\ -134 \\ \hline 445 \end{array}$$

These should be the same.

Check

$$\begin{array}{r} 445 \\ +134 \\ \hline 579 \end{array}$$

try these

Subtract. Check your answer.

1. $$\begin{array}{r} 247 \\ -223 \\ \hline \end{array}$$
2. $$\begin{array}{r} 794 \\ -653 \\ \hline \end{array}$$
3. $$\begin{array}{r} 877 \\ -574 \\ \hline \end{array}$$
4. $$\begin{array}{r} 197 \\ -\ 92 \\ \hline \end{array}$$
5. $$\begin{array}{r} 989 \\ -902 \\ \hline \end{array}$$
6. $$\begin{array}{r} 536 \\ -\ 20 \\ \hline \end{array}$$

48

now do these

Subtract.

7. 965 −543	8. 799 −592	9. 964 −423	10. 635 − 24	11. 358 −323
12. 676 −432	13. 549 −245	14. 194 − 83	15. 987 − 43	16. 763 −732
17. 3985 −3473	18. 5780 −2630	19. 8873 −8252	20. 9579 −5459	21. 6345 −2335
22. 1858 − 823	23. 9459 − 245	24. 6845 − 240	25. 1579 − 26	26. 2379 − 278
27. 13,598 − 2,354	28. 78,879 −43,539	29. 14,375 − 7,232	30. 46,576 −32,565	31. 87,943 − 501

PATTERNS

Each number is five less than the number named before it. What are the next two numbers?

25	20	15	?	?

What are the next two numbers in the pattern?

A.
49	46	43	?	?

B.
97	77	57	?	?

C.
879	769	659	?	?

D.
999	988	977	?	?

49

Renaming

Sometimes you must rename before subtracting.

Remember:
One ten makes ten ones.

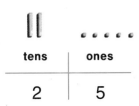

tens	ones
2	5

Rename:
Show one fewer ten
and ten more ones.

tens	ones
₁2	₁₅5

₁2 ₁₅5

Remember:
One hundred makes ten tens.

hundreds	tens	ones
4	2	6

Rename:
Show one fewer hundred
and ten more tens.

hundreds	tens	ones
₃4	₁₂2	6

₃4 ₁₂2 6

---

try these

Copy. Rename: Show one fewer ten and ten more ones.

1.

tens	ones
4	8

2.

tens	ones
5	0

3.

tens	ones
6	3

4. 31   **5.** 60   **6.** 42   **7.** 19   **8.** 26   **9.** 17

50

now do these

Copy. Rename: Show one fewer ten and ten more ones.

10.

tens	ones
1	3

11.

tens	ones
2	3

12.

tens	ones
2	0

13.

tens	ones
3	5

14.

tens	ones
8	4

15.

tens	ones
9	9

16. 27   17. 10   18. 40   19. 68   20. 11   21. 84

22. 55   23. 92   24. 49   25. 77   26. 30   27. 23

Copy. Rename: Show one fewer hundred and ten more tens.

28.

hundreds	tens	ones
3	7	4

29.

hundreds	tens	ones
2	3	2

30.

hundreds	tens	ones
3	1	3

31.

hundreds	tens	ones
3	0	6

32.

hundreds	tens	ones
1	6	7

33.

hundreds	tens	ones
3	2	3

34. 212   35. 404   36. 345   37. 867   38. 521   39. 698

40. 182   41. 114   42. 600   43. 903   44. 750   45. 439

Subtraction with Renaming

Subtract 26 from 83.

Step 1

$$
\begin{array}{r}
{\scriptstyle 7\ 13} \\
\cancel{83} \\
-\ 26 \\
\hline
\end{array}
$$

Look at the ones.
6 is greater than 3.
Rename: Show one fewer
ten and ten more ones.

Step 2

$$
\begin{array}{r}
{\scriptstyle 7\ 13} \\
\cancel{83} \\
-\ 26 \\
\hline
7 \\
\end{array}
$$

Subtract the ones.

Step 3

$$
\begin{array}{r}
{\scriptstyle 7\ 13} \\
\cancel{83} \\
-\ 26 \\
\hline
57 \\
\end{array}
$$

Subtract the tens.

Subtract 274 from 857.

Step 1

$$
\begin{array}{r}
857 \\
-\ 274 \\
\hline
3 \\
\end{array}
$$

Look at the ones.
No need to rename.
Subtract the ones.

Step 2

$$
\begin{array}{r}
{\scriptstyle 7\ 15} \\
8\cancel{5}7 \\
-\ 274 \\
\hline
83 \\
\end{array}
$$

Look at the tens.
Rename: Show one fewer
hundred and ten more
tens. Subtract the tens.

Step 3

$$
\begin{array}{r}
{\scriptstyle 7\ 15} \\
8\cancel{5}7 \\
-\ 274 \\
\hline
583 \\
\end{array}
$$

Subtract the hundreds.

Copy and complete.

1. $\overset{8\ 12}{\cancel{92}}$
-69
$\overline{3}$

2. $\overset{8\ 13}{\cancel{93}}$
-87
$\overline{6}$

3. $\overset{7\ 14}{\cancel{84}}$
-35
$\overline{9}$

4. $\overset{5\ 11}{\cancel{661}}$
-326
$\overline{5}$

5. $\overset{6\ 12}{727}$
-386
$\overline{41}$

Subtract.

6. 34
-26
$\overline{}$

7. 51
$-\ 7$
$\overline{}$

8. 90
-39
$\overline{}$

9. 604
-563
$\overline{}$

10. 469
$-\ 89$
$\overline{}$

Subtract.

11. 36
-29

12. 51
-29

13. 74
-38

14. 63
-54

15. 50
-24

16. 295
-158

17. 247
$-\ 29$

18. 890
-368

19. 462
-355

20. 320
$-\ 19$

21. 716
-683

22. 563
-473

23. 728
$-\ 78$

24. 710
-370

25. 509
$-\ 73$

26. 7254
-5037

27. 2467
$-\ 358$

28. 6913
-1722

29. 4727
-3144

30. 6736
$-\ 686$

31. $16,309$
$-10,198$

32. $14,264$
$-\ 3,065$

33. $20,327$
$-10,062$

34. $44,210$
$-43,020$

35. $59,753$
$-59,746$

53

Renaming More Than Once

Step 1	Step 2	Step 3
	12	12
2 15	6 2̸ 15	6 2̸ 15
7̸3̸5	7̸3̸5	7̸3̸5
−168	−168	−168
7	67	567
Look at the ones. Rename: Show one fewer ten and ten more ones. Subtract the ones.	Look at the tens. Rename: Show one fewer hundred and ten more tens. Subtract the tens.	Subtract the hundreds.

try these

Copy and complete.

	12 5 2̸ 15		14 3 4̸ 12		13 6 3̸ 10		11 5 1̸ 13		11 4 1̸ 12		12 7 2̸ 10
1.	6̸3̸5̸	2.	4̸5̸2̸	3.	7̸4̸0̸	4.	6̸2̸3̸	5.	5̸2̸2̸	6.	8̸3̸0̸
	−357		−278		−376		− 27		−476		− 97
	78		74		4		6		6		3

Subtract.

7.	572	8.	492	9.	462	10.	654	11.	438	12.	720
	−377		−295		−283		− 95		−239		− 87

54

now do these

Subtract.

13. 435 −147	**14.** 547 −258	**15.** 623 −245	**16.** 326 −147	**17.** 623 − 57
18. 430 − 49	**19.** 841 −449	**20.** 552 − 87	**21.** 173 − 88	**22.** 220 −137
23. 224 −187	**24.** 527 −429	**25.** 851 − 57	**26.** 895 −497	**27.** 835 −236
28. 4837 −1904	**29.** 9456 −6830	**30.** 7500 −6600	**31.** 8475 −4665	**32.** 6329 − 501
33. 9470 − 873	**34.** 4360 − 750	**35.** 5214 −1567	**36.** 3780 − 796	**37.** 2411 − 897

Solve the problem.

38. 646 rock records were sold.
85 classical records were sold.
How many more rock records were sold?

39. There are 367 rock records.
75 are on sale.
How many are not on sale?

40. There are 241 jazz records.
67 are sold.
How many jazz records are left?

41. There are 436 country-western albums.
There are 188 folk-music albums.
How many more country-western albums are there?

55

Zero in Subtraction

Step 1

$$
\begin{array}{r}
8\ \ 10 \\
\cancel{9}\ \cancel{0}\ 5 \\
-\ 2\ 4\ 7 \\
\hline
\end{array}
$$

7 is greater than 5. You must rename. There are 0 tens. Rename: Show one fewer hundred and ten more tens.

Step 2

$$
\begin{array}{r}
9 \\
8\ \cancel{10}\ 15 \\
\cancel{9}\ \cancel{0}\ \cancel{5} \\
-\ 2\ 4\ 7 \\
\hline
8
\end{array}
$$

Rename: Show one fewer ten and ten more ones. Subtract the ones.

Step 3

$$
\begin{array}{r}
9 \\
8\ \cancel{10}\ 15 \\
\cancel{9}\ \cancel{0}\ \cancel{5} \\
-\ 2\ 4\ 7 \\
\hline
5\ 8
\end{array}
$$

Subtract the tens.

Step 4

$$
\begin{array}{r}
9 \\
8\ \cancel{10}\ 15 \\
\cancel{9}\ \cancel{0}\ \cancel{5} \\
-\ 2\ 4\ 7 \\
\hline
6\ 5\ 8
\end{array}
$$

Subtract the hundreds.

Step 1

$$
\begin{array}{r}
7\ \ 10 \\
\cancel{8}\ \cancel{0}\ 0 \\
-\ 3\ 7\ 6 \\
\hline
\end{array}
$$

6 is greater than 0. You must rename. There are 0 tens. Rename: Show one fewer hundred and ten more tens.

Step 2

$$
\begin{array}{r}
9 \\
7\ \cancel{10}\ 10 \\
\cancel{8}\ \cancel{0}\ \cancel{0} \\
-\ 3\ 7\ 6 \\
\hline
4
\end{array}
$$

Rename: Show one fewer ten and ten more ones. Subtract the ones.

Step 3

$$
\begin{array}{r}
9 \\
7\ \cancel{10}\ 10 \\
\cancel{8}\ \cancel{0}\ \cancel{0} \\
-\ 3\ 7\ 6 \\
\hline
2\ 4
\end{array}
$$

Subtract the tens.

Step 4

$$
\begin{array}{r}
9 \\
7\ \cancel{10}\ 10 \\
\cancel{8}\ \cancel{0}\ \cancel{0} \\
-\ 3\ 7\ 6 \\
\hline
4\ 2\ 4
\end{array}
$$

Subtract the hundreds.

try these

Copy and complete.

1.
$$\begin{array}{r}
\overset{9}{\underset{5\ \cancel{10}\ 10}{\cancel{6}\ \cancel{0}\ \cancel{0}}} \\
-\ 2\ 7\ 5 \\
\hline
2\ 5
\end{array}$$

2.
$$\begin{array}{r}
\overset{9}{\underset{3\ \cancel{10}\ 13}{\cancel{4}\ \cancel{0}\ 3}} \\
-\ 2\ 4\ 9 \\
\hline
5\ 4
\end{array}$$

3.
$$\begin{array}{r}
\overset{9}{\underset{7\ \cancel{10}\ 10}{\cancel{8}\ \cancel{0}\ \cancel{0}}} \\
-\ \ \ 9\ 5 \\
\hline
5
\end{array}$$

4.
$$\begin{array}{r}
\overset{9}{\underset{6\ \cancel{10}\ 10}{\cancel{7}\ \cancel{0}\ \cancel{0}}} \\
-\ 6\ 9\ 3 \\
\hline
7
\end{array}$$

5.
$$\begin{array}{r}
\overset{9}{\underset{4\ \cancel{10}\ 16}{\cancel{5}\ \cancel{0}\ \cancel{6}}} \\
-\ 4\ 0\ 9 \\
\hline
7
\end{array}$$

Subtract.

6.
$$\begin{array}{r} 400 \\ -307 \\ \hline \end{array}$$

7.
$$\begin{array}{r} 608 \\ -\ 99 \\ \hline \end{array}$$

8.
$$\begin{array}{r} 502 \\ -376 \\ \hline \end{array}$$

9.
$$\begin{array}{r} 800 \\ -\ 42 \\ \hline \end{array}$$

10.
$$\begin{array}{r} 900 \\ -816 \\ \hline \end{array}$$

now do these

Subtract.

11.
$$\begin{array}{r} 500 \\ -327 \\ \hline \end{array}$$

12.
$$\begin{array}{r} 800 \\ -702 \\ \hline \end{array}$$

13.
$$\begin{array}{r} 600 \\ -\ 14 \\ \hline \end{array}$$

14.
$$\begin{array}{r} 700 \\ -603 \\ \hline \end{array}$$

15.
$$\begin{array}{r} 900 \\ -693 \\ \hline \end{array}$$

16.
$$\begin{array}{r} 602 \\ -439 \\ \hline \end{array}$$

17.
$$\begin{array}{r} 712 \\ -624 \\ \hline \end{array}$$

18.
$$\begin{array}{r} 409 \\ -\ 43 \\ \hline \end{array}$$

19.
$$\begin{array}{r} 302 \\ -207 \\ \hline \end{array}$$

20.
$$\begin{array}{r} 500 \\ -207 \\ \hline \end{array}$$

21.
$$\begin{array}{r} 4700 \\ -2723 \\ \hline \end{array}$$

22.
$$\begin{array}{r} 1500 \\ -\ 707 \\ \hline \end{array}$$

23.
$$\begin{array}{r} 9604 \\ -5328 \\ \hline \end{array}$$

24.
$$\begin{array}{r} 2700 \\ -\ 338 \\ \hline \end{array}$$

25.
$$\begin{array}{r} 3403 \\ -\ 249 \\ \hline \end{array}$$

AMAZO

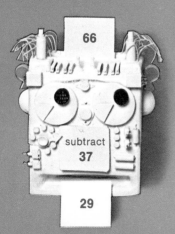

Copy and complete.

A. SUBTRACT 37

INPUT	OUTPUT
66	29
152	?
275	?
84	?
493	?

B. SUBTRACT 183

INPUT	OUTPUT
344	161
476	?
565	?
633	?
857	?

57

Amounts of Money

Add amounts of money as if you were adding whole numbers.
Remember to write the dollar sign and the cents point in the answer.

Step 1	Step 2	Step 3	Step 4
1 $52.67 + 14.98 —— 5	1 1 $52.67 + 14.98 —— 65	1 1 $52.67 + 14.98 —— 7 65	1 1 $52.67 + 14.98 —— $67.65

Subtract amounts of money as if you were subtracting whole numbers.
Remember to write the dollar sign and the cents point in the answer.

Step 1	Step 2	Step 3	Step 4
2 15 $87.35 − 21.49 —— 6	12 6 2 15 $87.35 − 21.49 —— 86	12 6 2 15 $87.35 − 21.49 —— 5 86	12 6 2 15 $87.35 − 21.49 —— $65.86

---

try these

Add.

1. $1.27
+ 1.48

2. $1.29
+ 3.87

3. $4.80
+ 2.60

4. $15.93
+ 17.82

5. $28.95
+ 32.67

Subtract.

6. $4.09
− 2.96

7. $10.00
− 6.75

8. $3.03
− 1.96

9. $26.00
− 14.99

10. $7.45
− 4.08

58

now do these

Add.

11. $3.89
    + 7.65

12. $8.76
    + 1.98

13. $3.06
    + .97

14. $37.83
    + 25.19

15. $4.87
    + 2.68

16. $ .32
       1.23
    + 4.92

17. $3.04
       2.07
    + 3.97

18. $9.95
       3.42
    + 1.27

19. $16.92
      10.45
    +   .71

20. $43.08
       1.43
    + 78.96

Subtract.

21. $18.66
    − 9.77

22. $9.62
    − 4.87

23. $3.86
    − 1.87

24. $9.00
    − 3.45

25. $13.42
    − 10.89

26. $7.25
    − 4.58

27. $3.53
    − 1.85

28. $5.82
    − 3.94

29. $12.00
    − 9.09

30. $42.09
    − 14.72

31. $39.27
    − 6.19

32. $46.05
    − 23.89

33. $15.70
    − 12.38

34. $43.00
    − 39.19

35. $87.00
    − 7.65

I HAVE A PROBLEM

Decide: Add or Subtract.
Then solve the problem.

	Beans	Asparagus	Corn
Brand A	$.49	$.78	$.46
Brand B	$.43	$.91	$.33

A. Sharon buys 1 can of beans and 1 can of corn. She buys the least expensive brand of each. How much does she spend in all?

B. Carla buys 1 can each of beans, asparagus, and corn. She buys Brand A. How much does she spend?

C. Gary has $10.00. He buys the least expensive can of asparagus. How much does he have left?

D. Ron has $8.46. He buys the most expensive can of corn. How much does he have left?

59

making change

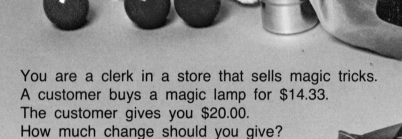

You are a clerk in a store that sells magic tricks.
A customer buys a magic lamp for $14.33.
The customer gives you $20.00.
How much change should you give?

Start with the cost, $14.33.
Count on to reach $20.00.

Start	$14.33
2 pennies	14.35
1 nickel	14.40
1 dime	14.50
2 quarters	15.00
5 dollars	20.00

What coins and bills should you give in change?

1. A magic slipper costs $12.88.
You are given $15.00.

Start	$12.88
_?_ pennies	12.90
_?_ dime	13.00
_?_ dollars	15.00

2. A ring trick costs $6.77.
You are given $10.00.

Start	$ 6.77
_?_ pennies	6.80
_?_ dimes	7.00
_?_ dollars	10.00

60 *Problem-solving Help*

Copy the chart.
Show how many of each coin and bill
you should give in change.
Exercises 3 and 4 are done for you.

	Cost	Given	(penny)	(nickel)	(dime)	(quarter)	$1	$5
3.	$14.86	$20.00	4		1			1
4.	$ 3.29	$ 5.00	1		2	2	1	
5.	$17.81	$20.00						
6.	$14.42	$15.00						
7.	$12.95	$20.00						
8.	$ 4.03	$ 5.00						
9.	$ 2.25	$ 5.00						
10.	$ 6.50	$10.00						
11.	$ 5.63	$10.00						
12.	$18.85	$20.00						
13.	$ 7.78	$10.00						
14.	$ 2.66	$10.00						

Test

Find the missing number.

1. $6 + \underline{\,?\,} = 11$ (p. 42)   2. $\underline{\,?\,} + 3 = 12$ (p. 42)   3. $\underline{\,?\,} + 6 = 14$ (p. 42)

Subtract.

4. $16 - 8 = \underline{\,?\,}$ (p. 40)   5. $13 - 4 = \underline{\,?\,}$ (p. 40)   6. $11 - 9 = \underline{\,?\,}$ (p. 40)

7.
$$\begin{array}{r} 658 \\ -240 \\ \hline \end{array}$$
(p. 48)

8.
$$\begin{array}{r} 4213 \\ -212 \\ \hline \end{array}$$
(p. 48)

9.
$$\begin{array}{r} 563 \\ -48 \\ \hline \end{array}$$
(p. 52)

10.
$$\begin{array}{r} 725 \\ -334 \\ \hline \end{array}$$
(p. 52)

11.
$$\begin{array}{r} 62{,}817 \\ -50{,}395 \\ \hline \end{array}$$
(p. 52)

12.
$$\begin{array}{r} 218 \\ -149 \\ \hline \end{array}$$
(p. 54)

13.
$$\begin{array}{r} 635 \\ -286 \\ \hline \end{array}$$
(p. 54)

14.
$$\begin{array}{r} 7443 \\ -4258 \\ \hline \end{array}$$
(p. 54)

15.
$$\begin{array}{r} 8320 \\ -670 \\ \hline \end{array}$$
(p. 54)

16.
$$\begin{array}{r} 600 \\ -183 \\ \hline \end{array}$$
(p. 56)

17.
$$\begin{array}{r} 8207 \\ -453 \\ \hline \end{array}$$
(p. 56)

18.
$$\begin{array}{r} 5900 \\ -2373 \\ \hline \end{array}$$
(p. 56)

19.
$$\begin{array}{r} \$37.00 \\ -18.30 \\ \hline \end{array}$$
(p. 58)

20.
$$\begin{array}{r} \$35.04 \\ -12.68 \\ \hline \end{array}$$
(p. 58)

21.
$$\begin{array}{r} \$84.00 \\ -4.62 \\ \hline \end{array}$$
(p. 58)

Add.

22.
$$\begin{array}{r} \$5.32 \\ +1.63 \\ \hline \end{array}$$
(p. 58)

23.
$$\begin{array}{r} \$11.95 \\ +36.17 \\ \hline \end{array}$$
(p. 58)

24.
$$\begin{array}{r} \$8.72 \\ 2.14 \\ +3.86 \\ \hline \end{array}$$
(p. 58)

25.
$$\begin{array}{r} \$.64 \\ 11.92 \\ +36.41 \\ \hline \end{array}$$
(p. 58)

bonus

Solve the problem.

26. You have $6.00.
    You spend $1.98.
    How much do you have left?
    (p. 58)

27. You have 36 cookies.
    You eat 9.
    How many do you have left?
    (p. 52)

62

Under the Cards

Some digits are hidden.

Since 5 + 8 = 13,
the digit under ■ is 3.

Since 7 + 8 = 15,
the digit under ■ is 8.

```
  4 7 2 5
+ 3 ■ 6 8
---------
  8 5 9 ■
```

Which digits are hidden?

1.
```
  2 0 7
+ 5 ■ 9
-------
■ 1 6
```

2.
```
  1 0 7 9
+ 1 9 3 2
---------
■ ■ 1 1
```

3.
```
  4 0 3 5
+ 6 0 9 9
---------
1 0 ■ 3 ■
```

4.
```
    2 6 2
      7 2
+   3 2 ■
---------
  ■ 6 0
```

5.
```
  9 ■ 4
  2 9 2
+ 1 7 5
-------
1 3 7 ■
```

Some digits are hidden.

Since 6 − 1 = 5,
the digit under ■ is 6.

Since 12 − 4 = 8,
the digit under ■ is 8.

```
  7 2 4 ■
- 2 4 3 1
---------
  4 ■ 1 5
```

Which digits are hidden?

6.
```
  5 4 ■
-   6 3
-------
■ 8 3
```

7.
```
  6 ■ 5
- 5 6 1
-------
  7 ■
```

8.
```
  9 1 1 3
- 7 2 0 8
---------
  1 ■ ■ 5
```

9.
```
  9 5 0 ■
- 4 3 0 3
---------
  5 1 ■ 7
```

10.
```
  1 5 3 ■
-   9 7 4
---------
  ■ 5 9
```

Like Clockwork

The lever on this wheel moves.
It moves in the same direction
as the hands on a clock.
It can stop in any of six positions.

Now look at some moves the lever can make.

Start at 0.   Move 4.   Stop at 4.

Here is another.

Start at 3.   Move 5.   Stop at 2.

Copy and complete the chart.

Start at	0	0	1	1	2	4	4	5	3	3	2	5
Move	3	7	4	6	8	9	10	12	8	10	16	15
Stop at	?	?	?	?	?	?	?	?	?	?	?	?

Where Will It Land?

The frog starts at 0. It hops by twos.

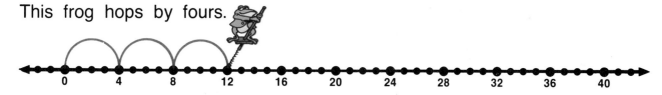

After 5 hops it will land on 10.
Where will it land after 7 hops?   after 9 hops?

This frog hops by threes.

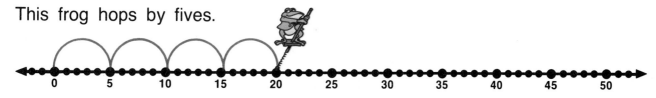

After 4 hops it will land on 12.
Where will it land after 6 hops?   after 8 hops?

This frog hops by fours.

After 3 hops it will land on 12.
Where will it land after 4 hops?   after 7 hops?

This frog hops by fives.

After 4 hops it will land on 20.
Where will it land after 6 hops?   after 9 hops?

Multiplication

There are 5 packages.
There are 8 in each package.
How many are there in all?

You can add to find the answer.

$$8 + 8 + 8 + 8 + 8 = 40$$

When the addends are all the same, you can multiply.

$$5 \times 8 = 40$$

There are 40 in all.

Here are two ways to show multiplication.

$$\begin{array}{r} 8 \\ \times 5 \\ \hline 40 \end{array}$$ ← factor
← factor $\longrightarrow$ $5 \times 8 = 40$
← product

try these

Find the product.

1. $8 \times 6 = \underline{}$ 2. $6 \times 7 = \underline{}$ 3. $9 \times 6 = \underline{}$

4. $3 \times 8 = \underline{}$ 5. $5 \times 6 = \underline{}$ 6. $4 \times 7 = \underline{}$

Multiply.

7. $\begin{array}{r} 8 \\ \times 9 \\ \hline \end{array}$ 8. $\begin{array}{r} 7 \\ \times 8 \\ \hline \end{array}$ 9. $\begin{array}{r} 6 \\ \times 7 \\ \hline \end{array}$ 10. $\begin{array}{r} 9 \\ \times 6 \\ \hline \end{array}$ 11. $\begin{array}{r} 8 \\ \times 4 \\ \hline \end{array}$ 12. $\begin{array}{r} 9 \\ \times 3 \\ \hline \end{array}$

now do these

Multiply.

13. $\begin{array}{r} 8 \\ \times 8 \\ \hline \end{array}$ 14. $\begin{array}{r} 6 \\ \times 7 \\ \hline \end{array}$ 15. $\begin{array}{r} 6 \\ \times 9 \\ \hline \end{array}$ 16. $\begin{array}{r} 6 \\ \times 6 \\ \hline \end{array}$ 17. $\begin{array}{r} 9 \\ \times 4 \\ \hline \end{array}$ 18. $\begin{array}{r} 9 \\ \times 7 \\ \hline \end{array}$

19. $\begin{array}{r} 9 \\ \times 5 \\ \hline \end{array}$ 20. $\begin{array}{r} 7 \\ \times 7 \\ \hline \end{array}$ 21. $\begin{array}{r} 9 \\ \times 8 \\ \hline \end{array}$ 22. $\begin{array}{r} 8 \\ \times 6 \\ \hline \end{array}$ 23. $\begin{array}{r} 9 \\ \times 9 \\ \hline \end{array}$ 24. $\begin{array}{r} 8 \\ \times 5 \\ \hline \end{array}$

25. $\begin{array}{r} 5 \\ \times 7 \\ \hline \end{array}$ 26. $\begin{array}{r} 6 \\ \times 4 \\ \hline \end{array}$ 27. $\begin{array}{r} 5 \\ \times 5 \\ \hline \end{array}$ 28. $\begin{array}{r} 7 \\ \times 3 \\ \hline \end{array}$ 29. $\begin{array}{r} 5 \\ \times 4 \\ \hline \end{array}$ 30. $\begin{array}{r} 4 \\ \times 4 \\ \hline \end{array}$

AMAZO

Copy and complete.

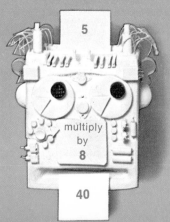

A. MULTIPLY BY 8	
INPUT	OUTPUT
5	40
7	?
3	?
2	?
4	?

B. MULTIPLY BY 9	
INPUT	OUTPUT
5	45
3	?
6	?
4	?
9	?

67

Properties of Multiplication

Compare the products.

$$8 \times 7 = 56 \qquad\qquad 7 \times 8 = 56$$

**You can multiply two numbers in either order.
The product is always the same.**

Compare the products.
The numbers named inside the parenthesis are multiplied first.

$$(3 \times 2) \times 5 = \; ? \qquad\qquad 3 \times (2 \times 5) = \; ?$$
$$6 \quad\; \times 5 = 30 \qquad\qquad 3 \times \quad 10 \quad = 30$$

**You can group factors differently.
The product is always the same.**

Compare the products.

$$7 \times 1 = 7 \qquad 1 \times 4 = 4 \qquad 6 \times 1 = 6 \qquad 1 \times 1 = 1$$

**When one of two factors is 1,
the product equals the other factor.**

Compare the products.

$$4 \times 0 = 0 \qquad 0 \times 6 = 0 \qquad 9 \times 0 = 0 \qquad 0 \times 0 = 0$$

**When a factor is 0,
the product is 0.**

Multiply.

1. $9 \times 6 = \underline{?}$

2. $6 \times 9 = \underline{?}$

3. $8 \times 1 = \underline{?}$

4. $(3 \times 3) \times 2 = \underline{?}$

5. $3 \times (3 \times 2) = \underline{?}$

6. $(2 \times 0) \times 9 = \underline{?}$

now do these

Multiply.

7. $6 \times 8 = \underline{?}$

8. $8 \times 6 = \underline{?}$

9. $7 \times 1 = \underline{?}$

10. $4 \times 9 = \underline{?}$

11. $9 \times 4 = \underline{?}$

12. $1 \times 4 = \underline{?}$

13. $(4 \times 1) \times 6 = \underline{?}$

14. $4 \times (1 \times 6) = \underline{?}$

15. $(2 \times 3) \times 8 = \underline{?}$

16. $(3 \times 2) \times 2 = \underline{?}$

17. $3 \times (2 \times 2) = \underline{?}$

18. $9 \times (2 \times 4) = \underline{?}$

19. $(5 \times 1) \times 6 = \underline{?}$

20. $5 \times (1 \times 6) = \underline{?}$

21. $(3 \times 3) \times 4 = \underline{?}$

Write $=$, $>$, or $<$.

22. $2 \times 4 \;\bullet\; 4 \times 2$

23. $5 \times 3 \;\bullet\; 4 \times 3$

24. $6 \times 4 \;\bullet\; 6 \times 5$

25. $5 \times 7 \;\bullet\; 7 \times 6$

26. $8 \times 5 \;\bullet\; 5 \times 6$

27. $7 \times 4 \;\bullet\; 4 \times 7$

Is the product zero? Write YES or NO.

28. $5 \times 6 \times 1$

29. 49×0

30. $3 \times 0 \times 18$

31. $64 \times 7 \times 0$

32. $7 \times 89 \times 2$

33. 475×0

69

quick check

See how well you know your facts.
Drive around the track nine times.

The first time multiply each number by 1.
The second time multiply by 2.
The third time by 3,
and so on.
The last time, you will multiply by 9.
Try to do it without a mistake.

Have a friend check you.
Write down any facts you miss.
Study them.
Then try again.

70

Multiplying Tens, Hundreds, and Thousands

If you can multiply ones, then you can multiply tens.

$$\begin{array}{r} 4 \\ \times 3 \\ \hline 12 \end{array} \qquad \begin{array}{r} 4 \textbf{ tens} \\ \times 3 \\ \hline 12 \textbf{ tens} \end{array} \qquad \begin{array}{r} 40 \\ \times\ \ 3 \\ \hline 120 \end{array}$$

If you can multiply ones, then you can multiply hundreds.

$$\begin{array}{r} 7 \\ \times 5 \\ \hline 35 \end{array} \qquad \begin{array}{r} 7 \textbf{ hundreds} \\ \times 5 \\ \hline 35 \textbf{ hundreds} \end{array} \qquad \begin{array}{r} 700 \\ \times\ \ \ \ 5 \\ \hline 3500 \end{array}$$

If you can multiply ones, then you can multiply thousands.

$$\begin{array}{r} 6 \\ \times 4 \\ \hline 24 \end{array} \qquad \begin{array}{r} 6 \textbf{ thousands} \\ \times 4 \\ \hline 24 \textbf{ thousands} \end{array} \qquad \begin{array}{r} 6\,000 \\ \times\ \ \ \ \ 4 \\ \hline 24{,}000 \end{array}$$

---

try these

Multiply.

1. $\begin{array}{r} 70 \\ \times\ \ 8 \\ \hline \end{array}$
2. $\begin{array}{r} 80 \\ \times\ \ 5 \\ \hline \end{array}$
3. $\begin{array}{r} 600 \\ \times\ \ \ 9 \\ \hline \end{array}$
4. $\begin{array}{r} 700 \\ \times\ \ \ 7 \\ \hline \end{array}$
5. $\begin{array}{r} 8000 \\ \times\ \ \ \ \ 6 \\ \hline \end{array}$

72

now do these

Multiply.

| 6. 80 × 9 | 7. 50 × 6 | 8. 50 × 9 | 9. 80 × 8 | 10. 70 × 3 |

| 11. 900 × 5 | 12. 700 × 9 | 13. 900 × 7 | 14. 700 × 6 | 15. 900 × 8 |

| 16. 600 × 7 | 17. 900 × 9 | 18. 400 × 6 | 19. 600 × 8 | 20. 200 × 7 |

| 21. 7000 × 7 | 22. 6000 × 6 | 23. 7000 × 5 | 24. 8000 × 7 | 25. 3000 × 8 |

| 26. 8000 × 4 | 27. 4000 × 9 | 28. 2000 × 6 | 29. 7000 × 4 | 30. 6000 × 3 |

Solve the problem.

31. A flea is 3 millimeters long.
It can jump 100 times its length.
How far can it jump?

32. A caterpillar on a tree is
4 centimeters long.
The height of the tree is
200 times that length.
What is the height of the tree?

33. One bee has 5 eyes.
How many eyes are on 20 bees?

34. An ant in the driveway is
4 millimeters long.
The driveway is 2000 times
as long.
How long is the driveway?

73

Add to Find the Product

The elevation of Cheaha Mountain
in Alabama is 734 meters.
The elevation of Mount Elbert
in Colorado is 6 times as high.
What is the elevation of Mount Elbert?

$$734$$
$$\times\ \ \ 6$$

Here is a way to find the product.
Multiply the ones, the tens, and the hundreds.
Add your answers.

$$6 \times 734 = (6 \times 4) + (6 \times 30) + (6 \times 700)$$

You can show your work this way.

Step 1	Step 2	Step 3	Step 4
734 × 6 ——— 24	734 × 6 ——— 24 180	734 × 6 ——— 24 180 4200	734 × 6 ——— 24 180 4200 ———— 4404
Multiply the ones.	Multiply the tens.	Multiply the hundreds.	Add the answers.

Copy and complete.

1. 84	2. 235	3. 789	4. 23	5. 532	6. 406
× 4	× 5	× 3	× 5	× 6	× 5
16	25	27	15	12	30
320	150	240	100	180	0
	1000	2100		3000	2000

Multiply.

7. 87	8. 32	9. 23	10. 32	11. 67	12. 55
× 2	× 9	× 4	× 6	× 4	× 5

Multiply.

13. 456	14. 654	15. 609	16. 256	17. 786	18. 204
× 3	× 6	× 4	× 7	× 7	× 8

19. 423	20. 975	21. 435	22. 398	23. 468	24. 579
× 9	× 6	× 8	× 7	× 5	× 8

25. 658	26. 706	27. 864	28. 597	29. 245	30. 687
× 2	× 7	× 4	× 3	× 8	× 6

quick check

Multiply.

1. 90	2. 300	3. 700	4. 4000	5. 9000
× 7	× 8	× 5	× 5	× 9

6. 34	7. 86	8. 312	9. 456	10. 807
× 2	× 9	× 3	× 3	× 5

A Shorter Way

Some pirates bury
6 treasure chests.
In each chest there
are 27 pieces
of jewelry.
How many pieces
are there in all?

Step 1

$$\overset{4}{27} \times 6 \over 2$$

Multiply the ones.
$6 \times 7 = 42$
Write the 2.
Remember the 4.

Step 2

$$\overset{4}{27} \times 6 \over 162$$

Multiply the tens.
$6 \times 2 = 12$
Add the 4.
Write 16.

There are 162 pieces of jewelry.

There are 243 pieces of gold in each chest. There are 6 chests.
How many pieces of gold are there in all?

Step 1

$$\overset{1}{243} \times 6 \over 8$$

Multiply the ones.
$6 \times 3 = 18$
Write the 8.
Remember the 1.

Step 2

$$\overset{2\,1}{243} \times 6 \over 58$$

Multiply the tens.
$6 \times 4 = 24$
Add the 1.
Write the 5.
Remember the 2.

Step 3

$$\overset{2\,1}{243} \times 6 \over 1458$$

Multiply the hundreds.
$6 \times 2 = 12$
Add the 2.
Write 14.

There are 1458 pieces of gold.

76

Copy and complete.

1. 87
   × 9
   ———
   3
   (small 6 above)

2. 23
   × 6
   ———
   8
   (small 1 above)

3. 38
   × 8
   ———
   4
   (small 6 above)

4. 234
   × 7
   ———
   8
   (small 22 above)

5. 532
   × 5
   ———
   0
   (small 11 above)

6. 905
   × 5
   ———
   5
   (small 2 above)

Multiply.

7. 68
   × 6
   ———

8. 79
   × 9
   ———

9. 86
   × 7
   ———

10. 346
    × 6
    ———

11. 354
    × 4
    ———

12. 423
    × 8
    ———

now do these

Multiply.

13. 78
    × 8
    ———

14. 67
    × 5
    ———

15. 45
    × 4
    ———

16. 203
    × 5
    ———

17. 457
    × 7
    ———

18. 546
    × 3
    ———

19. 906
    × 9
    ———

20. 576
    × 2
    ———

21. 894
    × 5
    ———

22. 579
    × 8
    ———

23. 239
    × 7
    ———

24. 608
    × 3
    ———

25. 893
    × 4
    ———

26. 452
    × 9
    ———

27. 907
    × 6
    ———

28. 365
    × 3
    ———

29. 486
    × 7
    ———

30. 486
    × 8
    ———

TREASURE HUNT

Which would you rather find?
    4 bags of pirates' treasure with
260 pieces of silver in each
            or
5 bags of pirates' treasure with
168 pieces of silver in each.

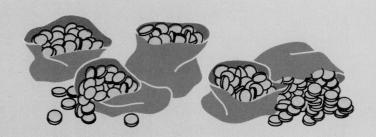

77

Multiplying Greater Numbers

It is 3486 kilometers between Cleveland, Ohio, and San Francisco, California. A salesperson flew this distance 4 times. How many kilometers did she fly?

Step 1	Step 2	Step 3	Step 4
$\begin{array}{r} \overset{\scriptstyle 2}{3486} \\ \times\ \ \ 4 \\ \hline 4 \end{array}$	$\begin{array}{r} \overset{\scriptstyle 32}{3486} \\ \times\ \ \ 4 \\ \hline 44 \end{array}$	$\begin{array}{r} \overset{\scriptstyle 132}{3486} \\ \times\ \ \ 4 \\ \hline 944 \end{array}$	$\begin{array}{r} \overset{\scriptstyle 132}{3486} \\ \times\ \ \ 4 \\ \hline 13,944 \end{array}$
Multiply the ones.	Multiply the tens.	Multiply the hundreds.	Multiply the thousands.

The salesperson flew 13,944 kilometers.

78

Copy and complete.

1. $\begin{array}{r} \overset{356}{2468} \\ \times \quad 8 \\ \hline 744 \end{array}$
2. $\begin{array}{r} \overset{45}{3079} \\ \times \quad 6 \\ \hline 474 \end{array}$
3. $\begin{array}{r} \overset{264}{3286} \\ \times \quad 7 \\ \hline 02 \end{array}$
4. $\begin{array}{r} \overset{3\ 2}{4605} \\ \times \quad 5 \\ \hline 25 \end{array}$
5. $\begin{array}{r} \overset{344}{2345} \\ \times \quad 9 \\ \hline 5 \end{array}$

Multiply.

6. $\begin{array}{r} 5347 \\ \times \quad 4 \\ \hline \end{array}$
7. $\begin{array}{r} 4986 \\ \times \quad 3 \\ \hline \end{array}$
8. $\begin{array}{r} 5842 \\ \times \quad 6 \\ \hline \end{array}$
9. $\begin{array}{r} 7905 \\ \times \quad 8 \\ \hline \end{array}$
10. $\begin{array}{r} 4579 \\ \times \quad 7 \\ \hline \end{array}$

now do these

Multiply.

11. $\begin{array}{r} 9732 \\ \times \quad 5 \\ \hline \end{array}$
12. $\begin{array}{r} 9746 \\ \times \quad 4 \\ \hline \end{array}$
13. $\begin{array}{r} 8007 \\ \times \quad 9 \\ \hline \end{array}$
14. $\begin{array}{r} 4659 \\ \times \quad 6 \\ \hline \end{array}$
15. $\begin{array}{r} 3568 \\ \times \quad 7 \\ \hline \end{array}$

16. $\begin{array}{r} 9487 \\ \times \quad 4 \\ \hline \end{array}$
17. $\begin{array}{r} 9843 \\ \times \quad 5 \\ \hline \end{array}$
18. $\begin{array}{r} 6009 \\ \times \quad 9 \\ \hline \end{array}$
19. $\begin{array}{r} 9849 \\ \times \quad 3 \\ \hline \end{array}$
20. $\begin{array}{r} 4328 \\ \times \quad 9 \\ \hline \end{array}$

21. $\begin{array}{r} 78{,}009 \\ \times \quad 4 \\ \hline \end{array}$
22. $\begin{array}{r} 16{,}892 \\ \times \quad 8 \\ \hline \end{array}$
23. $\begin{array}{r} 42{,}479 \\ \times \quad 7 \\ \hline \end{array}$
24. $\begin{array}{r} 36{,}789 \\ \times \quad 9 \\ \hline \end{array}$
25. $\begin{array}{r} 19{,}753 \\ \times \quad 5 \\ \hline \end{array}$

MONEY AND MULTIPLYING

A ticket for one flight costs $172.50.
How much would 3 tickets cost?
(Multiply amounts of money as if you
were multiplying whole numbers.
Remember to write the dollar sign and
the cents point in the answer.)

$\begin{array}{r} \overset{2\ 1}{\$172.50} \\ \times \qquad 3 \\ \hline \$517.50 \end{array}$

The 3 tickets would cost $517.30.

What would be the cost of

A. 4 tickets? **B.** 6 tickets? **C.** 7 tickets? **D.** 9 tickets?

Multiplying by Tens and Hundreds

Look for a pattern.

$$
\begin{array}{r} 12 \\ \times 10 \\ \hline 120 \end{array}
\qquad
\begin{array}{r} 12 \\ \times 20 \\ \hline 240 \end{array}
\qquad
\begin{array}{r} 12 \\ \times 30 \\ \hline 360 \end{array}
\qquad
\begin{array}{r} 12 \\ \times 40 \\ \hline 480 \end{array}
$$

When multiplying by tens, write 0 in the ones place.
Then multiply by the number of tens.

Step 1	Step 2
$\begin{array}{r} 37 \\ \times 50 \\ \hline 0 \end{array}$	$\begin{array}{r} 37 \\ \times 50 \\ \hline 1850 \end{array}$
Write zero.	Multiply by 5.

Look for a pattern.

$$
\begin{array}{r} 12 \\ \times 100 \\ \hline 1200 \end{array}
\qquad
\begin{array}{r} 12 \\ \times 200 \\ \hline 2400 \end{array}
\qquad
\begin{array}{r} 12 \\ \times 300 \\ \hline 3600 \end{array}
\qquad
\begin{array}{r} 12 \\ \times 400 \\ \hline 4800 \end{array}
$$

When multiplying by hundreds, write a 0 in the ones place and
in the tens place. Then multiply by the number of hundreds.

Step 1	Step 2
$\begin{array}{r} 37 \\ \times 500 \\ \hline 00 \end{array}$	$\begin{array}{r} 37 \\ \times 500 \\ \hline 18{,}500 \end{array}$
Write two zeros.	Multiply by 5.

try these

Multiply the number by 10.

1. 7   2. 18   3. 46   4. 70   5. 84   6. 32

Multiply the number by 100.

7. 7   8. 18   9. 46   10. 70   11. 84   12. 32

Multiply.

13. 42
    ×30

14. 61
    ×70

15. 86
    ×40

16. 53
    ×300

17. 78
    ×400

18. 25
    ×700

now do these

Multiply.

19. 89
    ×90

20. 67
    ×50

21. 50
    ×30

22. 29
    ×60

23. 24
    ×50

24. 35
    ×40

25. 40
    ×90

26. 37
    ×40

27. 35
    ×80

28. 68
    ×70

29. 23
    ×90

30. 52
    ×20

31. 38
    ×600

32. 56
    ×400

33. 48
    ×800

34. 86
    ×500

35. 60
    ×300

36. 23
    ×900

37. 57
    ×700

38. 67
    ×600

39. 69
    ×800

40. 40
    ×400

41. 35
    ×900

42. 74
    ×200

43. 34
    ×500

44. 49
    ×700

45. 20
    ×800

46. 38
    ×400

47. 20
    ×700

48. 81
    ×500

81

Multiplying by Tens and Ones

Each carton contains 36 books.
How many books are in 24 cartons?

Step 1	Step 2	Step 3
$$\begin{array}{r} 36 \\ \times 24 \\ \hline 144 \end{array}$$	$$\begin{array}{r} 36 \\ \times 24 \\ \hline 144 \\ 720 \end{array}$$	$$\begin{array}{r} 36 \\ \times 24 \\ \hline 144 \\ 720 \\ \hline 864 \end{array}$$
Multiply by 4.	Multiply by 20.	Add the products.

There are 864 books.

Each carton contains 144 paperback books.
How many paperback books are in 36 cartons?

Step 1	Step 2	Step 3
$$\begin{array}{r} 144 \\ \times\ 36 \\ \hline 864 \end{array}$$	$$\begin{array}{r} 144 \\ \times\ 36 \\ \hline 864 \\ 4320 \end{array}$$	$$\begin{array}{r} 144 \\ \times\ 36 \\ \hline 864 \\ 4320 \\ \hline 5184 \end{array}$$
Multiply by 6.	Multiply by 30.	Add the products.

There are 5184 paperback books.

82

try these

Copy and complete.

1. 78	2. 86	3. 42	4. 806	5. 465	6. 870
×98	×67	×56	× 97	× 84	× 73
624	602	252	5642	1860	2610
7020	5160	2100	72540	37200	60900

Multiply.

7. 69	8. 87	9. 56	10. 357	11. 723	12. 865
×16	×39	×34	× 82	× 56	× 32

now do these

Multiply.

13. 76	14. 76	15. 69	16. 89	17. 68	18. 80
×43	×25	×67	×46	×69	×59

19. 208	20. 608	21. 807	22. 507	23. 650	24. 390
× 73	× 48	× 78	× 64	× 23	× 42

25. 568	26. 968	27. 149	28. 865	29. 327	30. 572
× 42	× 17	× 27	× 92	× 65	× 48

TAKE CARE OF THAT BOOK

A textbook costs $7.46.
There are 24 students.
How much will it cost to buy
textbooks for all 24 students?

83

Multiplying Greater Numbers

A box weighs 2348 grams.
How much do 84 boxes weigh?

Step 1	Step 2	Step 3
$\begin{array}{r} 2348 \\ \times\ \ 84 \\ \hline 9392 \end{array}$	$\begin{array}{r} 2348 \\ \times\ \ 84 \\ \hline 9392 \\ 187840 \end{array}$	$\begin{array}{r} 2348 \\ \times\ \ 84 \\ \hline 9392 \\ 187840 \\ \hline 197,232 \end{array}$
Multiply by 4.	Multiply by 80.	Add the products.

The 84 boxes weigh 197,232 grams.

try these

Copy and complete.

1. $\begin{array}{r} 9753 \\ \times\ \ 45 \\ \hline 48765 \\ 390120 \end{array}$
2. $\begin{array}{r} 6089 \\ \times\ \ 29 \\ \hline 54801 \\ 121780 \end{array}$
3. $\begin{array}{r} 2479 \\ \times\ \ 37 \\ \hline 17353 \\ 74370 \end{array}$
4. $\begin{array}{r} 6802 \\ \times\ \ 82 \\ \hline 13604 \\ 544160 \end{array}$
5. $\begin{array}{r} 8239 \\ \times\ \ 64 \\ \hline 32956 \\ 494340 \end{array}$

Multiply.

6. $\begin{array}{r} 6432 \\ \times\ \ 54 \end{array}$
7. $\begin{array}{r} 8045 \\ \times\ \ 55 \end{array}$
8. $\begin{array}{r} 7168 \\ \times\ \ 75 \end{array}$
9. $\begin{array}{r} 4301 \\ \times\ \ 73 \end{array}$
10. $\begin{array}{r} 9876 \\ \times\ \ 54 \end{array}$

now do these

Multiply.

11. 9006 × 49	12. 4978 × 63	13. 2843 × 39	14. 4398 × 55	15. 8794 × 74
16. 5723 × 68	17. 7650 × 70	18. 6789 × 48	19. 6587 × 25	20. 6875 × 73
21. 6835 × 27	22. 5946 × 63	23. 7008 × 89	24. 4697 × 46	25. 3297 × 52
26. 7945 × 73	27. 5907 × 28	28. 3485 × 60	29. 4753 × 48	30. 8640 × 30
31. 8794 × 16	32. 3482 × 90	33. 8940 × 45	34. 4978 × 17	35. 5368 × 32

YOU CAN DO IT TOO

Many students in the U.S.A. graduate from high school. 94,883 graduated in 1900. About 32 times as many will graduate in 1980. How many will that be?

Multiplying by Hundreds, Tens, and Ones

Every day a plane flies 729 kilometers from
Kansas City, Missouri, to Indianapolis, Indiana.
How many kilometers are flown on this route
in one year (365 days)?

Step 1	Step 2	Step 3	Step 4
729	729	729	729
×365	×365	×365	×365
3645	3645	3645	3645
	43740	43740	43740
		218700	218700
			266,085
Multiply by 5.	Multiply by 60.	Multiply by 300.	Add the products.

266,085 kilometers are flown in one year.

try these

Copy and complete.

1. 432	2. 430	3. 234	4. 320	5. 402	6. 409
×657	×650	×507	×456	×736	×607
3024	21500	1638	1920	2412	2863
21600	258000	117000	16000	12060	245400
259200			128000	281400	

Multiply.

7. 432	8. 312	9. 900	10. 123	11. 543	12. 467
×302	×214	×456	×203	×926	×234

now do these

Multiply.

13. 320	14. 780	15. 348	16. 647	17. 427	18. 806
×403	×680	×627	×432	×806	×274

19. 423	20. 234	21. 312	22. 512	23. 313	24. 429
×143	×203	×241	×298	×422	×508

25. 746	26. 313	27. 615	28. 530	29. 622	30. 813
×825	×693	×981	×705	×234	×543

31. 923	32. 543	33. 317	34. 418	35. 726	36. 700
×904	×742	×419	×378	×480	×408

87

do you have enough money?

Bill and Ben are making a terrarium. Together they have $2.50.
Do they have enough to buy 3 bunches of baby tears?

You can estimate:	You can multiply the cost:
$ .80	$ .79
× 3	× 3
$2.40	$2.37

Yes, they have enough money.

Do Bill and Ben have enough money? Write YES or NO.

1. They have $2.50.
They want 3 packs.
of soil mixture.

2. They have $2.50.
They want 4 packs
of pebbles.

Glass container	$2.25
Pebbles	.59
Charcoal	.64
Soil mixture	.98
Fern	1.50
Moss	.69
Nerve Plant	.75
Baby Tears	.79

88

Do you have enough money? Write YES or NO.

3. You have $5.00.
   You want 7 packs of moss.

4. You have $3.25.
   You want 5 bunches of baby tears.

5. You have $1.75.
   You want 3 packs of pebbles.

6. You have $2.00.
   You want 2 bags of soil mixture.

7. You have $5.75.
   You want 4 ferns.

8. You have $1.50.
   You want 3 bags of charcoal.

9. You have $5.00.
   You want a glass container, a fern,
   and a pack of moss.

10. You have $3.00.
    You want a bag of charcoal, a bag of
    soil mixture, a bag of pebbles,
    and a bunch of baby tears.

Test

Write =, >, or <.

1. 3×6 ● 6×3 (p. 68)　2. 7×7 ● 9×7 (p. 68)　3. 5×8 ● 8×4 (p. 68)

Multiply.

4. $6 \times 2 = \underline{}$ (p. 66)　5. $9 \times 4 = \underline{}$ (p. 66)　6. $(2 \times 2) \times 8 = \underline{}$ (p. 68)

7. $\begin{array}{r} 7 \\ \times 7 \\ \hline \end{array}$ (p. 66)

8. $\begin{array}{r} 3 \\ \times 8 \\ \hline \end{array}$ (p. 66)

9. $\begin{array}{r} 90 \\ \times 4 \\ \hline \end{array}$ (p. 72)

10. $\begin{array}{r} 5000 \\ \times 3 \\ \hline \end{array}$ (p. 72)

11. $\begin{array}{r} 67 \\ \times 8 \\ \hline \end{array}$ (p. 74, 76)

12. $\begin{array}{r} 249 \\ \times 3 \\ \hline \end{array}$ (p. 74, 76)

13. $\begin{array}{r} 8079 \\ \times 4 \\ \hline \end{array}$ (p. 78)

14. $\begin{array}{r} 42,479 \\ \times 5 \\ \hline \end{array}$ (p. 78)

15. $\begin{array}{r} 16,753 \\ \times 7 \\ \hline \end{array}$ (p. 78)

16. $\begin{array}{r} 68 \\ \times 400 \\ \hline \end{array}$ (p. 80)

17. $\begin{array}{r} 30 \\ \times 70 \\ \hline \end{array}$ (p. 80)

18. $\begin{array}{r} 54 \\ \times 71 \\ \hline \end{array}$ (p. 82)

19. $\begin{array}{r} 86 \\ \times 43 \\ \hline \end{array}$ (p. 82)

20. $\begin{array}{r} 835 \\ \times 98 \\ \hline \end{array}$ (p. 82)

21. $\begin{array}{r} 752 \\ \times 64 \\ \hline \end{array}$ (p. 82)

22. $\begin{array}{r} 2468 \\ \times 79 \\ \hline \end{array}$ (p. 84)

23. $\begin{array}{r} 3596 \\ \times 16 \\ \hline \end{array}$ (p. 84)

24. $\begin{array}{r} 646 \\ \times 405 \\ \hline \end{array}$ (p. 86)

25. $\begin{array}{r} 543 \\ \times 378 \\ \hline \end{array}$ (p. 86)

bonus

Solve the problem.

26. A hamburger costs $.69.
How much do 3 hamburgers cost?

(p. 79)

27. A giant cheeseburger costs $1.08.
How much do 3 cheeseburgers cost?

(p. 79)

Temperature

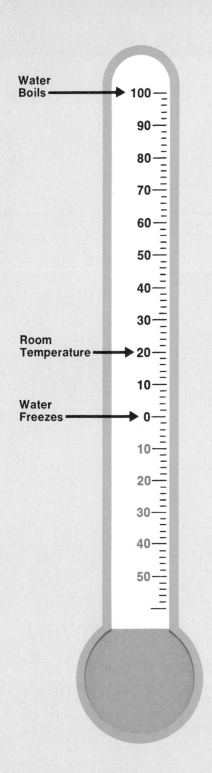

Water Boils
Room Temperature
Water Freezes

This thermometer has a **Celsius** scale.
It measures temperature in **degrees Celsius.**
To show 20 degrees Celsius,
you write 20°C.
At what temperature does
water freeze?
At what temperature does
water boil?

A temperature below zero
can be shown with a
negative sign before the numeral.
Then 10°C below zero is ⁻10°C.

Copy and complete the chart.

Temperature Before	Change	Temperature After
16°C	rise of 10°C	26°C
16°C	fall of 10°C	?
28°C	rise of 12°C	?
28°C	fall of 12°C	?
−10°C	rise of 6°C	?
−10°C	rise of 16°C	?
0°C	fall of 12°C	?
10°C	fall of 12°C	?

5 Graphing

Pictographs

This **pictograph** shows that in the United States fewer people live on farms every year.

FARM POPULATION
Each ♟ stands for one million people.

1920	♟♟♟♟♟♟♟♟♟♟♟♟♟♟♟♟♟♟♟♟♟♟♟♟♟♟♟♟♟♟♟
1930	♟♟♟♟♟♟♟♟♟♟♟♟♟♟♟♟♟♟♟♟♟♟♟♟♟♟♟♟♟♟♟
1940	♟♟♟♟♟♟♟♟♟♟♟♟♟♟♟♟♟♟♟♟♟♟♟♟♟♟♟♟♟♟♟
1950	♟♟♟♟♟♟♟♟♟♟♟♟♟♟♟♟♟♟♟♟♟♟♟♟
1960	♟♟♟♟♟♟♟♟♟♟♟♟♟♟♟♟
1970	♟♟♟♟♟♟♟♟♟♟♟
1975	♟♟♟♟♟♟♟♟♟

Graphs make it easier to compare numbers.

Look at the symbols for 1920.
Now look at the symbols for 1960.
There were about twice as many people
on farms in 1920 than in 1960.

Was the farm population in 1975 greater than or less than it was in 1960?
Was the farm population in 1975 greater than or less than it was in 1970?

Make a prediction about the farm population of the future.
Do you think it will be greater than or less than it is today?

92

NUMBER OF FARMS   Each 🏭 stands for one million farms.

1920	🏭 🏭 🏭 🏭 🏭 🏭 🏭 ▪
1930	🏭 🏭 🏭 🏭 🏭 🏭 🏭 ▪
1940	🏭 🏭 🏭 🏭 🏭 🏭 ▪
1950	🏭 🏭 🏭 🏭 🏭 🏭 ▪
1960	🏭 🏭 🏭 🏭 🏭
1970	🏭 🏭 🏭
1975	🏭 🏭 🏭

1. Compare 1920 with 1930. In 1930, were there more farms, fewer farms, or about the same number?
2. Compare 1960 with 1970. When were there fewer farms?
3. Use the graph to predict the future. Would you say the number of farms will increase, decrease, or stay about the same?

now do these

AVERAGE SIZE OF FARMS   Each ▪ stands for 10 hectares.

1920	▪ ▪ ▪ ▪ ▪ ▪
1930	▪ ▪ ▪ ▪ ▪ ▪
1940	▪ ▪ ▪ ▪ ▪ ▪ ▪
1950	▪ ▪ ▪ ▪ ▪ ▪ ▪ ▪
1960	▪ ▪ ▪ ▪ ▪ ▪ ▪ ▪ ▪ ▪
1970	▪ ▪ ▪ ▪ ▪ ▪ ▪ ▪ ▪ ▪ ▪ ▪
1975	▪ ▪ ▪ ▪ ▪ ▪ ▪ ▪ ▪ ▪ ▪ ▪ ▪ ▪ ▪

4. Is the average size of a farm increasing or decreasing?
5. The average size of a farm in the twenties was about 60 hectares. By what year did the average size double?
6. The number of farms is decreasing. The average size of a farm is increasing. Do you think farms today are producing more food, less food, or about the same amount as in 1920?

Bar Graphs

MAJOR APPLIANCES SOLD IN ONE YEAR IN THE U.S.A.

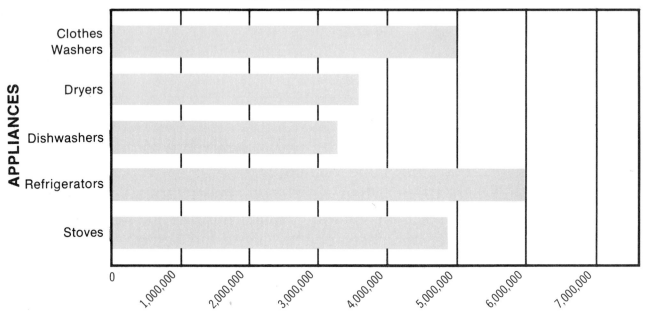

Suppose you sell major appliances.
This **bar graph** gives you useful information.

The shortest bar is for dishwashers.
You can expect to sell fewer dishwashers than other appliances.

Find the longest bar.
Why would you expect to sell more refrigerators than stoves?

Would you expect to sell more clothes washers or more dryers?
Why?

SMALL APPLIANCES SOLD IN ONE YEAR

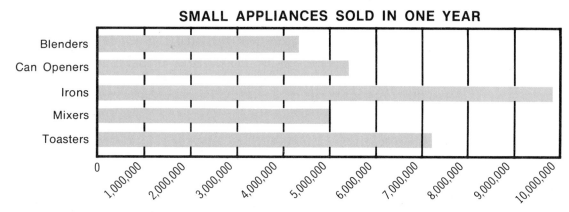

1. Which small appliance had the greatest number of sales?
2. Which appliance had the least number of sales?
3. Were more can openers or mixers sold?
4. Were more toasters or blenders sold?

now do these

ELECTRONIC APPLIANCES SOLD IN ONE YEAR

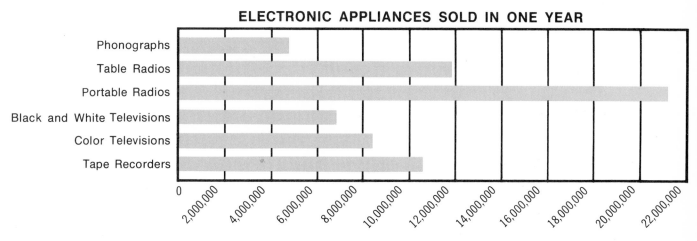

5. Which electronic appliance had the greatest number of sales?
6. Which appliance had the least number of sales?
7. Were more color or black and white televisions sold?
8. Were more phonographs or tape recorders sold?

Line Graphs

The Weather Bureau recorded the temperature every two hours for a twelve-hour period. The recordings are shown in the table.

Time	Midnight	2 A.M.	4 A.M.	6 A.M.	8 A.M.	10 A.M.	Noon
Temperature	10°C	12°C	8°C	6°C	6°C	12°C	14°C

The results were shown on a **line graph.**
A line graph is used to show changes.

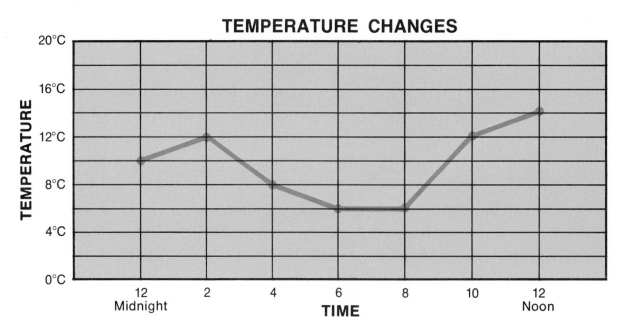

Between midnight and 2 A.M. the temperature increased.
During which other two-hour periods did the temperature increase?
Between 2 A.M. and 4 A.M. the temperature decreased.
During which other two-hour period did the temperature decrease?
The greatest increase was between 8 A.M. and 10 A.M.
During which two-hour period was the decrease the greatest?
During which period did the temperature remain the same?

Leroy's line graph shows his total sales of small appliances for one year.

1. During which months did the sales increase over the preceding month's sales?
2. During which months did the sales decrease from the preceding month's sales?
3. During which month did sales not change from the preceding month?

now do these

Maryanne's line graph shows her total sales of sporting goods for one year.

4. During which month did sales not change from the preceding month?
5. During which two different months did sales increase greatly?
6. During which month did sales decrease the most?
7. During which month did sales increase the most?

Finding Points

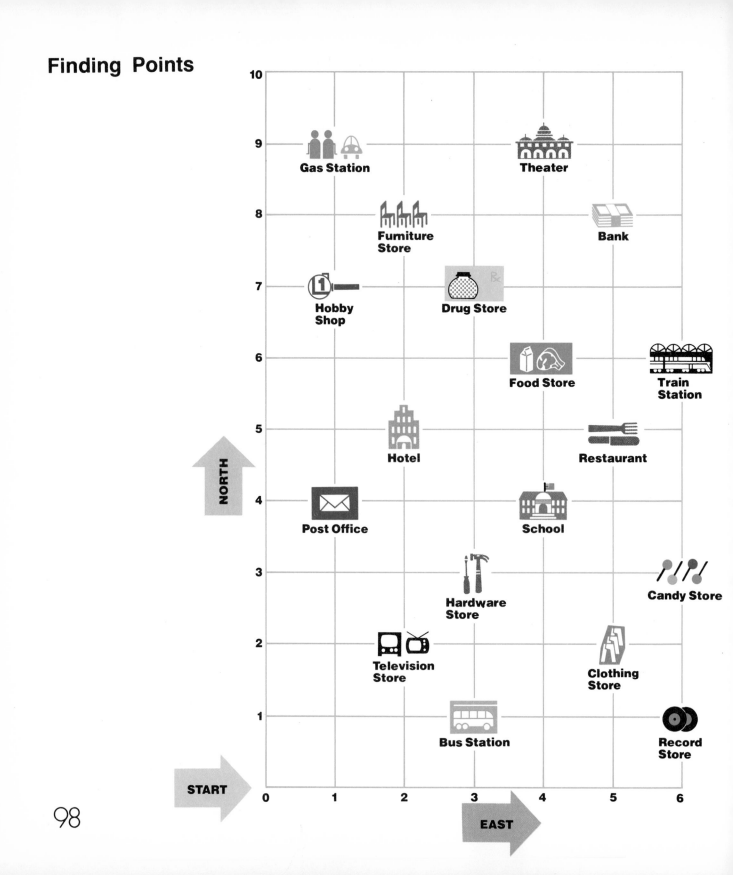

Start at 0. Go EAST 3. Then go NORTH 1.
You should be at the bus station.

Start at 0. Go EAST 5, NORTH 5.
What do you find?

Start at 0. Give directions for finding the school.
How many blocks EAST do you go? How many blocks NORTH?
Answer: EAST 4, NORTH 4.

try these

Start at 0. What do you find at the point?

1. EAST 5, NORTH 8   2. EAST 1, NORTH 4   3. EAST 3, NORTH 7

Give directions from 0 for:

4. Hotel   5. Theater   6. Television Store

now do these

Start at 0. What do you find at the point?

7. EAST 4, NORTH 9   8. EAST 3, NORTH 1   9. EAST 3, NORTH 3

10. EAST 5, NORTH 2   11. EAST 1, NORTH 9   12. EAST 6, NORTH 3

13. EAST 2, NORTH 2   14. EAST 2, NORTH 5   15. EAST 6, NORTH 1

Give directions from 0 for:

16. Food Store   17. Restaurant   18. Hobby Shop

19. School   20. Train Station   21. Drug Store

22. Furniture Store   23. Bank   24. Record Store

99

Graphing Points

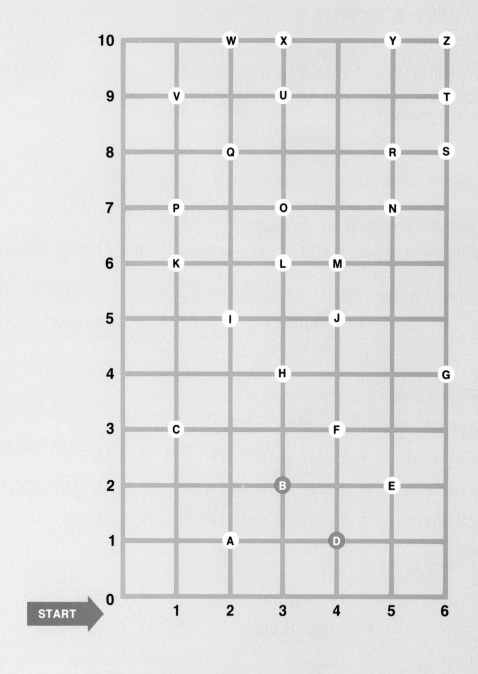

START

You can use an **ordered pair** of numbers to locate a point.
Always start at 0.
The first number tells how many spaces to the right.
The second number tells how many spaces up.
The ordered pair (3, 2) locates point B.

Point D is 4 spaces to the right and 1 space up.
The ordered pair for D is (4, 1).

try these

Which letter is at the point?

1. (2, 1)   2. (3, 2)   3. (3, 4)   4. (4, 3)   5. (6, 10)

What ordered pair tells the location of the point?

6. E   7. D   8. P   9. M   10. G

now do these

Which letter is at the point?

11. (3, 6)   12. (5, 2)   13. (5, 7)   14. (2, 8)   15. (6, 9)

16. (4, 5)   17. (1, 7)   18. (3, 10)   19. (3, 9)   20. (1, 6)

21. (5, 8)   22. (1, 9)   23. (2, 10)   24. (6, 8)   25. (5, 10)

What ordered pair tells the location of the point?

26. C   27. R   28. Z   29. U   30. K

31. I   32. F   33. X   34. J   35. S

36. A   37. O   38. Y   39. V   40. Q

Test

1. Which kind of book was read the most? (p. 94)

2. Which kind of book was read the least? (p. 94)

3. Were more biography books or more history books read? (p. 94)

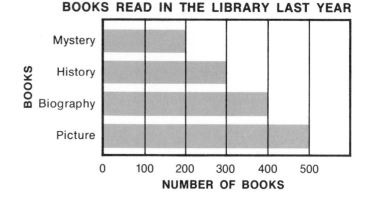

BOOKS READ IN THE LIBRARY LAST YEAR

4. On which day were the fewest number of students absent?
(p. 96)

5. On which two days were the same number of students absent?
(p. 96)

6. On which day did the absences increase the most from the day before?
(p. 96)

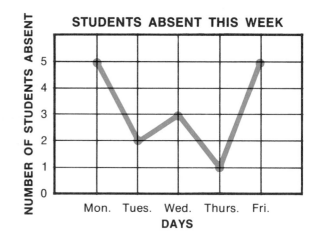

STUDENTS ABSENT THIS WEEK

What letter is at the point?

7. (2, 3) (p. 100)

8. (3, 2) (p. 100)

9. (4, 5) (p. 100)

10. (5, 1) (p. 100)

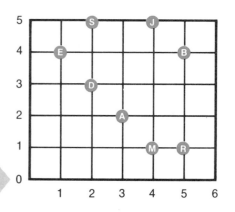

Longitude and Latitude

The earth is shaped
like a sphere.

Models of the earth often have
circles shown on them.

These are circles of
longitude and **latitude.**
They help to locate points
on the earth.

The **prime meridian** is part
of the circle of longitude
that passes through Greenwich, England.

Longitudes

Latitudes

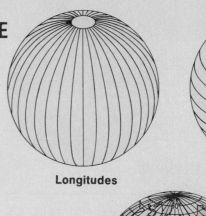

Longitudes and Latitudes

Longitude is the east-west measure from the prime meridian.
Latitude is the north-south measure from the equator.

Find New Orleans on the map.
New Orleans is about 90° west
of the prime meridian.
It is about 30° north of the equator.
New Orleans is at about 90°W, 30°N.

Which city is near the location?

1. 90°W, 39°N   **2.** 85°W, 35°N   **3.** 86°W, 40°N

Give the longitude and latitude for the city.

4. Birmingham, Alabama   **5.** Atlanta, Georgia
6. Nashville, Tennessee   **7.** Kansas City, Kansas

6 Dividing By Ones

Division

There are 24 students.
There are 4 tables.
The same number of students will sit at each table.
How many will sit at each table?

Separate 24 into 4 groups of the same size.
Use division to find how many are in each group?

$$24 \div 4 = 6$$

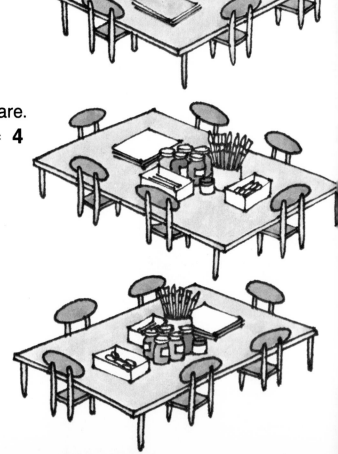

There are 24 students.
6 will sit at each table.
How many tables are needed?

Separate 24 into groups of 6 each.
Divide to find how many groups there are.

$$24 \div 6 = 4$$

Here are two ways to show division.

$$24 \div 6 = 4 \qquad 6\overline{)24}$$

quotient → 4

divisor

dividend

104

Find the quotient.

1. 64 ÷ 8 = __?__
2. 48 ÷ 6 = __?__
3. 24 ÷ 4 = __?__
4. 49 ÷ 7 = __?__
5. 27 ÷ 3 = __?__
6. 35 ÷ 5 = __?__

Divide.

7. 4)32
8. 2)18
9. 9)45
10. 7)56
11. 6)36
12. 8)72

now do these

Divide.

13. 9)63
14. 7)42
15. 4)36
16. 9)54
17. 3)15
18. 6)24

19. 7)35
20. 5)25
21. 2)14
22. 9)27
23. 4)28
24. 3)18

25. 5)40
26. 6)42
27. 9)36
28. 9)54
29. 5)15
30. 4)24

31. 8)40
32. 8)48
33. 7)28
34. 6)36
35. 5)30
36. 4)16

Solve the problem.

37. There are 28 students.
    There are 7 tables.
    The same number of students
    will sit at each table.
    How many will sit at each table?

38. There are 14 air-hockey players.
    There are 7 tables.
    The same number will play
    at each table.
    How many will play at each table?

39. There are 12 ping-pong players.
    4 play at each table.
    How many tables are needed?

40. There are 36 people.
    6 will sit at each picnic table.
    How many tables are needed?

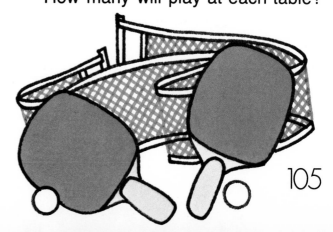

105

Division and Multiplication

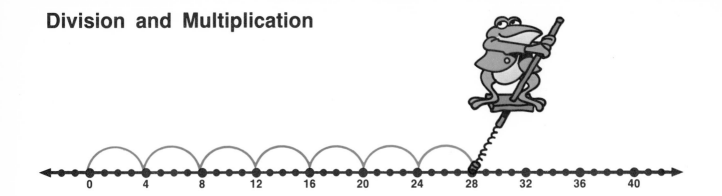

This frog covers 4 spaces in a single hop.
How many hops cover 28 spaces?   **? × 4 = 28**

Divide to find a missing factor.

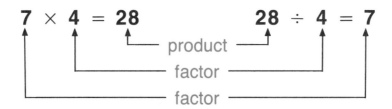

7 × 4 = 28   28 ÷ 4 = 7

product
factor
factor

7 hops will cover 28 spaces.

You can use multiplication to find quotients.

You want to find the quotient. ⟶ 42 ÷ 7 = **?**

You know the multiplication fact. ⟶ 6 × 7 = 42

So ⟶ 42 ÷ 7 = 6

Multiplication and division are related.
6, 7, and 42 belong to a **number family.**

    6 × 7 = 42   42 ÷ 7 = 6
    7 × 6 = 42   42 ÷ 6 = 7

106

Write the other related fact.

1. $4 \times 3 = 12$

   $3 \times 4 = 12$

   $12 \div 3 = 4$

2. $9 \times 2 = 18$

   $2 \times 9 = 18$

   $18 \div 9 = 2$

3. $5 \times 6 = 30$

   $30 \div 6 = 5$

   $30 \div 5 = 6$

Use the three numbers.
Write four related facts.

4. 3, 5, 15

5. 7, 4, 28

6. 9, 5, 45

Write four related facts.

7. 8, 5, 40

8. 9, 6, 54

9. 4, 5, 20

10. 8, 9, 72

11. 7, 8, 56

12. 3, 8, 24

13. 8, 6, 48

14. 7, 9, 63

15. 3, 6, 18

Find the missing factor.

16. $\underline{\ ?\ } \times 8 = 56$

17. $\underline{\ ?\ } \times 6 = 54$

18. $\underline{\ ?\ } \times 8 = 40$

19. $\underline{\ ?\ } \times 7 = 49$

20. $\underline{\ ?\ } \times 9 = 81$

21. $\underline{\ ?\ } \times 6 = 42$

22. $\underline{\ ?\ } \times 9 = 72$

23. $\underline{\ ?\ } \times 7 = 35$

24. $\underline{\ ?\ } \times 8 = 64$

Find the quotient.

25. $24 \div 6 = \underline{\ ?\ }$

26. $36 \div 4 = \underline{\ ?\ }$

27. $32 \div 8 = \underline{\ ?\ }$

28. $21 \div 7 = \underline{\ ?\ }$

29. $81 \div 9 = \underline{\ ?\ }$

30. $24 \div 3 = \underline{\ ?\ }$

31. $36 \div 9 = \underline{\ ?\ }$

32. $32 \div 4 = \underline{\ ?\ }$

33. $45 \div 9 = \underline{\ ?\ }$

quick check

To divide well, you must know your facts.
Study your facts. Then make the journey.
Can you make the whole trip without a mistake?

THE TRAIN RIDE

Drive engine number 2. (Divide each number by 2.)

THE SAFARI

Ride elephant number 3. (Divide each number by 3.)

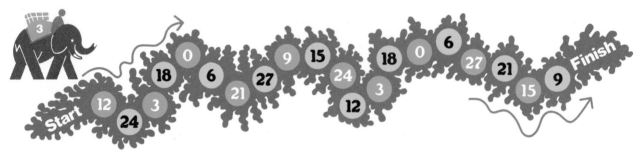

THE TAXI CAB RIDE

Drive cab number 4. (Divide each number by 4.)

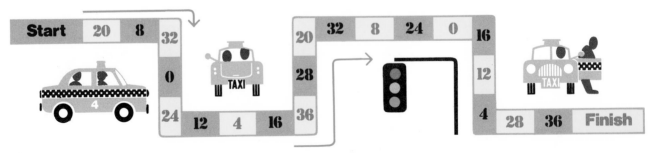

THE RACE

Ride horse number 5. (Divide each number by 5.)

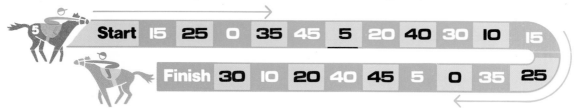

Start	15	25	0	35	45	5	20	40	30	10	15

Finish	30	10	20	40	45	5	0	35	25

THE DUNE BUGGY RIDE

Drive dune buggy number 6. (Divide each number by 6.)

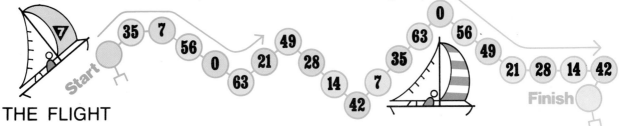

THE SAIL

Sail yacht number 7. (Divide each number by 7.)

THE FLIGHT

Fly plane number 8. (Divide each number by 8.)

THE SUBMARINE RIDE

Command submarine number 9. (Divide each number by 9.)

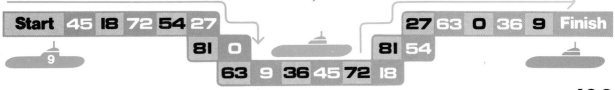

109

Division With Remainders

You have 22 peanuts.
You put 4 in each bag.
How many bags do you need?
How many peanuts will be left over?

$$4\overline{)22}$$

Find the quotient and the remainder.

Step 1

$$\begin{array}{r} 5 \\ 4\overline{)22} \end{array}$$

Find the quotient.
$5 \times 4 = 20$
$6 \times 4 = 24$
So, $4\overline{)22}$
is about 5.

Step 2

$$\begin{array}{r} 5 \\ 4\overline{)22} \\ 20 \end{array}$$

Multiply: $5 \times 4 = 20$.
Write the product
under 22.

Step 3

$$\begin{array}{r} 5 \text{ r2} \\ 4\overline{)22} \\ \underline{20} \\ 2 \end{array}$$

Subtract to find
the remainder.
Show the remainder
in the answer.

You need 5 bags. You will have 2 peanuts left over.

To check the answer:
Multiply the divisor by the quotient.
$5 \times 4 = 20$

Add the remainder.
$20 + 2 = 22$

$$\begin{array}{r} 5 \text{ r2} \\ 4\overline{)22} \\ \underline{20} \\ 2 \end{array}$$

The answer should equal the dividend.

110

Find the quotient and the remainder.
Check your answer.

1. 8)67   2. 6)45   3. 9)47   4. 7)50   5. 8)43   6. 6)38

now do these

Divide.

7. 4)34   8. 7)31   9. 3)20   10. 9)19   11. 5)48   12. 7)25

13. 5)23   14. 9)84   15. 4)27   16. 7)59   17. 3)29   18. 8)19

19. 8)60   20. 8)35   21. 5)44   22. 9)48   23. 5)19   24. 2)17

25. 6)33   26. 7)18   27. 3)26   28. 9)31   29. 8)50   30. 7)45

31. 5)22   32. 6)39   33. 5)38   34. 8)27   35. 9)57   36. 5)13

37. 6)58   38. 7)46   39. 9)64   40. 7)39   41. 5)34   42. 6)26

43. 8)30   44. 9)89   45. 4)30   46. 8)50   47. 9)75   48. 5)28

THINK ABOUT REMAINDERS

When you divide by 4, the remainder can be 0.
It can also be 1, 2, or 3.
It cannot be 4. Why?

What remainders can you get when you divide by

A. 2?   **B.** 3?   **C.** 5?   **D.** 6?   **E.** 7?   **F.** 8?   **G.** 9?

Dividing Tens

80 people are going to a concert.
4 buses will take them.
The same number will sit in each bus.
How many people will sit in each bus?

If you can divide ones, then you can divide tens.

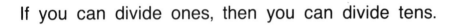

$$\frac{2}{4)8} \qquad \frac{2 \text{ tens}}{4)8 \text{ tens}} \qquad \frac{20}{4)80}$$

20 people will sit in each bus.

250 people attend the concert.
There are 6 sections in the concert hall.
The same number sit in each section.
About how many people sit in each section?

There are tens in the quotient.
Use facts to find how many.
$6)\overline{25}$ is about 4, so
$6)\overline{250}$ is about 40.

About 40 people sit in each section.

112

Divide.

1. 3)90   2. 7)210   3. 4)320   4. 5)350   5. 8)240

Below each problem are three estimates.
Which one shows the tens in the quotient?

6. 5)230   7. 2)190   8. 4)150   9. 3)200   10. 7)240
   30   70   30   50   20
   40   80   40   60   30
   50   90   50   70   40

now do these

Divide.

11. 2)60   12. 8)560   13. 7)280   14. 5)100   15. 7)420

16. 6)300   17. 9)810   18. 4)360   19. 3)60   20. 9)720

Estimate the quotient. (Show the tens.)

21. 9)580   22. 8)510   23. 5)180   24. 8)490   25. 8)360

26. 9)410   27. 4)300   28. 9)320   29. 8)280   30. 7)600

quick check

Divide.

1. 4)39   2. 8)65   3. 5)44   4. 7)52   5. 9)51

6. 2)80   7. 3)60   8. 7)630   9. 8)240   10. 9)360

Tens in the Quotient

Sometimes there are tens in the quotient.
There are more than 10 eights in 263.
There are fewer than 100 eights.

$$8\overline{)263}$$

$$1 \times 8 = 8$$
$$10 \times 8 = 80$$
$$100 \times 8 = 800$$

←——— 263

There are tens in the quotient.

Step 1	Step 2	Step 3
$$\begin{array}{r} 30 \\ 8\overline{)263} \\ \underline{240} \\ 23 \end{array}$$	$$\begin{array}{r} 2 \\ 30 \\ 8\overline{)263} \\ \underline{240} \\ 23 \\ \underline{16} \\ 7 \end{array}$$	$$\begin{array}{r} 32 \text{ r}7 \\ 2 \\ 30 \\ 8\overline{)263} \\ \underline{240} \\ 23 \\ \underline{16} \\ 7 \end{array}$$
Find the tens. $8\overline{)26}$ is about 3, so $8\overline{)263}$ is about 30. Multiply: $30 \times 8 = 240$. Subtract to find what is left to divide.	Find the ones. $8\overline{)23}$ is about 2. Multiply: $2 \times 8 = 16$. Subtract to find the remainder.	Add to find the quotient. Show the remainder in the answer.

Copy and complete.

```
        5              5             4
       80             60            20           30            20
1. 2)171      2. 7)458      3. 8)194      4. 7)253      5. 5)135
      160            420           160          210
       11             38            34
       10             35
        1
```

Divide.

6. 6)335   7. 9)851   8. 4)351   9. 9)763   10. 5)340

Divide.

11. 7)195   12. 8)608   13. 7)325   14. 5)294   15. 6)275

16. 4)384   17. 6)462   18. 8)653   19. 4)305   20. 9)657

21. 5)384   22. 3)254   23. 5)432   24. 4)273   25. 3)204

26. 9)198   27. 7)578   28. 9)493   29. 9)315   30. 8)285

31. 7)404   32. 8)510   33. 9)392   34. 5)240   35. 8)357

36. 5)473   37. 3)284   38. 5)193   39. 8)477   40. 9)567

115

A Shorter Way

Find the quotient and the remainder: $8\overline{)263}$.

<table>
<tr><td>

Step 1

$$
\begin{array}{r}
3 \\
8\overline{)263} \\
240 \\
\hline
23
\end{array}
$$

Find the tens.
$8\overline{)26}$ is about 3, so
$8\overline{)263}$ is about 30.
Write 3 in the tens
place in the quotient.
Multiply: $30 \times 8 = 240$.
Subtract.

</td><td>

Step 2

$$
\begin{array}{r}
32 \text{ r}7 \\
8\overline{)263} \\
240 \\
\hline
23 \\
16 \\
\hline
7
\end{array}
$$

Find the ones.
$8\overline{)23}$ is about 2.
Write 2 in the ones
place in the quotient.
Multiply: $2 \times 8 = 16$.
Subtract.   Show the
remainder in the answer.

</td></tr>
</table>

Copy and complete.

	6		68		7		3		6
1.	6)378	2.	4)275	3.	5)397	4.	8)265	5.	3)195
	360		240		350		240		
	18		35		47				

Divide.

6. 3)224   7. 8)113   8. 5)132   9. 4)195   10. 7)300

now do these

Divide.

11. 9)134   12. 6)111   13. 4)260   14. 9)297   15. 5)235

16. 4)332   17. 5)280   18. 8)279   19. 3)148   20. 3)280

21. 6)214   22. 6)444   23. 8)384   24. 9)400   25. 9)823

26. 3)171   27. 9)477   28. 7)441   29. 8)415   30. 4)397

31. 8)600   32. 5)319   33. 7)532   34. 6)500   35. 7)600

36. 7)665   37. 6)562   38. 9)666   39. 5)480   40. 6)443

The Mean

Althea threw 5 balls.
These are her scores.
    27, 31, 28, 30, 29
Find the **mean,** or
average, of the scores.

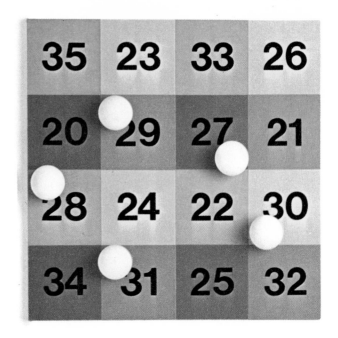

To find the mean:

1. Find the sum of the scores.
    27 + 31 + 28 + 30 + 29 = 145

2. Divide the sum by the number of scores.

$$
\begin{array}{r}
29 \leftarrow \text{mean} \\
\text{number of scores} \longrightarrow 5\overline{)145} \leftarrow \text{sum of scores} \\
\underline{100} \\
45 \\
\underline{45} \\
0
\end{array}
$$

The mean is 29.

Find the mean.

1. 20, 18, 16

2. 48, 39, 30, 55

3. 37, 19, 56, 30, 23

now do these

Find the mean.

4. 87, 11, 19

5. 84, 60, 74, 70

6. 13, 29, 45, 11, 47

7. 100, 67, 129, 96

8. 32, 25, 30, 28, 35

9. 17, 36, 46

10. 80, 105, 87, 94, 69

11. 34, 160, 85

12. 67, 29, 87, 49

13. 121, 87, 95, 121, 97, 85

14. 17, 8, 12, 5, 8, 4

15. 18, 6, 11, 15, 9, 13

16. 7, 8, 6, 3, 11, 9, 5

17. 52, 34, 62, 23, 71, 52

18. 80, 45, 60, 100, 37, 26, 30

Solve the problem.

19. Cindy and her family took a trip. What is the mean number of kilometers they traveled each day?

	Number of Kilometers
First day	330
Second day	281
Third day	310

SOMETHING TO THINK ABOUT

These are Arthur's scores: 27, 23, 25, 26, 24.
What is the mean?
Suppose these were Arthur's scores: 25, 25, 25, 25, 25.
What is the mean?
You can think of the mean this way.
It is the number that would be repeated if all the scores were the same.

35	23	33	26
20	29	27	21
28	24	22	30
34	31	25	32

Dividing Hundreds

The auditorium has 900 seats.
There are 3 sections.
Each section has the same number of seats.
How many seats are in each section?

If you can divide ones, then you can divide hundreds.

$$\begin{array}{r} 3 \\ 3\overline{)9} \end{array} \qquad \begin{array}{r} 3 \text{ hundreds} \\ 3\overline{)9 \text{ hundreds}} \end{array} \qquad \begin{array}{r} 300 \\ 3\overline{)900} \end{array}$$

Each section seats 300 people.

700 people are in the auditorium.
There are 3 sections.
The same number sit in each section.
About how many people sit in each section?

There are hundreds in the quotient.
Use facts to find how many.

$3\overline{)7}$ is about 2, so
$3\overline{)700}$ is about 200.

About 200 people sit in each section.

Divide.

1. 3)1200   2. 5)2000   3. 2)1600   4. 7)1400   5. 4)3200

Below each problem are three estimates.
Which one shows the hundreds in the quotient?

6. 4)1700   7. 2)900   8. 5)3700   9. 8)2500   10. 3)2600

   300   300   600   200   700

   400   400   700   300   800

   500   500   800   400   900

now do these

Divide.

11. 4)800   12. 2)1800   13. 7)2800   14. 8)5600   15. 7)4200

16. 9)8100   17. 2)400   18. 9)7200   19. 6)3000   20. 5)2500

Estimate the quotient.   (Show the hundreds.)

21. 9)5100   22. 5)1700   23. 3)800   24. 9)4100   25. 8)5000

26. 7)5900   27. 5)4800   28. 8)2800   29. 4)900   30. 3)2600

AMAZO

Copy and complete.

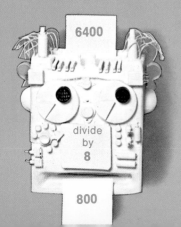

A.	DIVIDE BY 8		B.	DIVIDE BY 9	
	INPUT	OUTPUT		INPUT	OUTPUT
	6400	800		6300	700
	7200	?		1800	?
	1600	?		5400	?
	4000	?		2700	?
	3200	?		4500	?

121

Hundreds in the Quotient

Sometimes there are hundreds in the quotient.
There are more than 10 fours in 2338.
There are more than 100 fours in 2338.
There are fewer than 1000 fours in 2338.

$$4\overline{)2338}$$

$$1 \times 4 = 4$$
$$10 \times 4 = 40$$
$$100 \times 4 = 400 \quad \longleftarrow \quad 2338$$
$$1000 \times 4 = 4000$$

There are hundreds in the quotient.

Step 1	Step 2	Step 3
$$\begin{array}{r} 5 \\ 4\overline{)2338} \\ \underline{2000} \\ 338 \end{array}$$	$$\begin{array}{r} 58 \\ 4\overline{)2338} \\ \underline{2000} \\ 338 \\ \underline{320} \\ 18 \end{array}$$	$$\begin{array}{r} 584 \text{ r2} \\ 4\overline{)2338} \\ \underline{2000} \\ 338 \\ \underline{320} \\ 18 \\ \underline{16} \\ 2 \end{array}$$
Find the hundreds. $4\overline{)23}$ is about 5, so $4\overline{)2338}$ is about 500. Write 5 in the hundreds place in the quotient. Multiply: $500 \times 4 = 2000$. Subtract.	Find the tens. $4\overline{)33}$ is about 8, so $4\overline{)338}$ is about 80. Write 8 in the tens place in the quotient. Multiply: $80 \times 4 = 320$. Subtract.	Find the ones. $4\overline{)18}$ is about 4. Write 4 in the ones place in the quotient. Multiply: $4 \times 4 = 16$. Subtract. Show the remainder in the answer.

try these

Copy and complete.

	26		45		90		5		7
1.	7)1853	2.	8)3600	3.	4)3608	4.	6)3312	5.	8)6049
	1400		3200		3600		3000		
	453		400		8				
	420								
	33								

Divide.

6. 9)8424   7. 5)2345   8. 6)4575   9. 8)6723   10. 9)4029

now do these

Divide.

11. 7)3164   12. 9)7526   13. 5)2895   14. 8)5063   15. 4)3049

16. 9)6475   17. 7)3925   18. 5)3415   19. 6)2409   20. 5)1365

21. 8)2748   22. 9)5672   23. 8)1528   24. 5)3845   25. 7)4500

26. 8)4708   27. 9)3123   28. 3)2704   29. 5)4423   30. 9)4859

MONEY AND DIVIDING

Divide amounts of money as if you were dividing whole numbers. Write the dollar sign and the cents point in the answer.

```
      $ 2.47
5 )$12.35
      10 00
       2 35
       2 00
         35
         35
          0
```

Divide

A. 4)$24.48   **B.** 6)$37.26   **C.** 3)$17.58

123

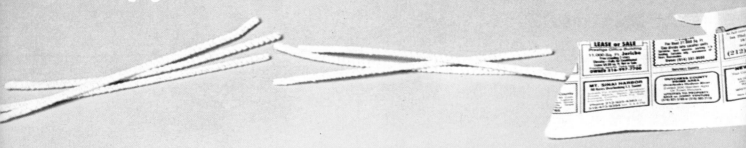

multiply or divide?

To solve the problem, do you multiply or do you divide?

Problem 1

8 art-club members are making papier-mâché cats.
They will use 32 sheets of newspaper.
How many sheets is this for each member?

Solution

You must divide.

$$8\overline{)32}\ \ \overset{4}{}$$

Each will use 4 sheets.

Problem 2

The members will put 120 sequins on each cat.
How many sequins are needed for 8 cats?

Solution

You must multiply.

$$\begin{array}{r} 120 \\ \times\ \ 8 \\ \hline 960 \end{array}$$

960 sequins are needed.

Write MULTIPLY or DIVIDE to tell how you would solve.

1. There are 4 packs of pipe cleaners.
   There are 140 pipe cleaners in each.
   How many pipe cleaners are there in all?

2. There are 112 pieces of felt.
   8 members will share them equally.
   How many pieces will each get?

3. There are 2 felt ears on each cat.
   How many felt ears must be made for 8 cats?

4. There are 8 members. Each 2 will share a pair of scissors.
   How many scissors are needed?

Solve the problem.

5. There are 672 strips of newspaper. 8 members will share them equally. How many strips will each get?

6. Each member makes 2 bowls of papier-mâché. There are 8 members. How many bowls of papier-mâché will be prepared?

7. It takes 25 minutes to put on a layer of papier-mâché. It takes 3 layers to make a cat. How many minutes will it take to put on the papier-mâché?

8. 40 cups are filled with paint. There are 5 different colors. How many cups of each color are there?

9. There are 16 paint brushes in a box. There are 4 boxes. How many paint brushes are there in all?

10. Each member needs 5 paint brushes. There are 8 members. How many paint brushes are needed in all?

Test

Find the missing factor.

1. _?_ × 7 = 35 (p. 106)   **2.** _?_ × 8 = 64 (p. 106)

Divide.

3. 56 ÷ 8 = _?_ (p. 104)   **4.** 63 ÷ 7 = _?_ (p. 104)

      (p. 104)   (p. 104)   (p. 110)   (p. 110)   (p. 112)

5. $4\overline{)16}$ **6.** $2\overline{)16}$ **7.** $6\overline{)43}$ **8.** $9\overline{)31}$ **9.** $8\overline{)640}$

      (p. 112)   (p. 114, 116)   (p. 114, 116)   (p. 120)   (p. 120)

10. $3\overline{)90}$ **11.** $8\overline{)665}$ **12.** $7\overline{)370}$ **13.** $5\overline{)2500}$ **14.** $4\overline{)2000}$

      (p. 122)   (p. 122)   (p. 122)   (p. 122)

15. $3\overline{)9042}$ **16.** $6\overline{)4458}$ **17.** $9\overline{)3891}$ **18.** $5\overline{)3579}$

Find the mean.

19. 87, 84, 72 (p. 118)   **20.** 60, 57, 83, 100 (p. 118)

bonus

Solve the problem.

21. You have $7.35.
You have 5 envelopes.
The same amount of money
will go into each envelope.
How much money will go
into each envelope? (p. 122)

22. 6 people share the cost of lunch.
Lunch costs $32.40.
How much should each pay?
(p. 122)

126

The Median

Here are Cindy's bowling scores for 9 games.
39, 90, 95, 90, 92, 95, 90, 94, 98
What is Cindy's mean score?

783 ÷ 9 = ?

Here are Cindy's scores arranged from least to greatest.
39, 90, 90, 90, 92, 94, 95, 95, 98
Which score is in the middle?
The middle score is the **median.**

All but one of Cindy's scores are in the nineties.
Find the mean of these 8 scores.
Compare it with the mean of the 9 scores.
How does one low score affect the mean score?
Did the one low score affect her median score?

Find the mean and the median.

1. 82, 43, 131, 94, 85

2. 69, 23, 129, 83, 81

3. 82, 72, 69, 92, 95, 109, 55

4. 39, 51, 22, 68, 40, 35, 60

5. 60, 32, 96, 44, 84, 108, 24

6. 43, 63, 85, 72, 55, 88, 77

7. 37, 13, 65, 21, 57, 52, 26, 32, 48

8. 46, 23, 65, 27, 80, 13, 38, 52, 70

Under the Cards

Try to tell which digits are hidden.

■ What number is 4 x 7?
Then the digit under ■ is 8.

■ Could the digit under ■ be 2? Why not?
Why must the digit be 1?

```
  ■ 3 7
×     4
  5 4 ■
```

Now think about this.
Take one step at a time.

■ First find the digit under ■.
Why must it be 1, 3, 5, 7, or 9?
Which of those numbers
gives you the 45 in 645?

■ Since 3 is the digit under ■,
and since only 3 × 2 = 6, the
digit under ■ is 2.

Now it will be easy to finish.
What is under ☐ ? What is under ■?

```
    ■ 1 5
×     2 ■
    6 4 5
  4 ☐ 0 0
  4 9 ■ 5
```

Which digits are hidden?

1.
```
    ■ 1 3
×     3 4
    8 5 2
  ■ 3 ☐ 0
  7 2 ■ 2
```

2.
```
    ■ 0 5
×     4 ■
  2 8 3 5
1 ☐ 2 0 0
1 ■ 0 3 5
```

3.
```
    ■ 2 3
×   ■ 5
  6 1 5
☐ 9 2 0
■ 5 3 5
```

4.
```
  8 0 ■
×   ■ 3
2 4 0 6
1 ☐ 0 4 0
1 ■ 4 4 6
```

5.
```
    7 ■ 3
×     4 ■
  2 1 3 9
2 8 ☐ 2 0
3 0 ■ 5 9
```

7 Dividing By Tens And Ones

How Many Tens?

60 oranges.
10 in a box.
_?_ boxes.

How many tens in 60?
Think of 60 as 6 tens.
The answer is 6.

$$10\overline{)60} = 6$$

320 peaches.
10 in a box.
_?_ boxes.

How many tens in 320?
Think of 320 as 32 tens.
The answer is 32.

$$10\overline{)320} = 32$$

Divide.

1. $10\overline{)20}$

2. $10\overline{)40}$

3. $10\overline{)60}$

4. $10\overline{)50}$

5. $10\overline{)70}$

6. $10\overline{)200}$

7. $10\overline{)400}$

8. $10\overline{)700}$

9. $10\overline{)900}$

10. $10\overline{)600}$

11. $10\overline{)250}$

12. $10\overline{)620}$

13. $10\overline{)630}$

14. $10\overline{)850}$

15. $10\overline{)970}$

16. $10\overline{)740}$

17. $10\overline{)370}$

18. $10\overline{)450}$

19. $10\overline{)770}$

20. $10\overline{)590}$

Using Facts to Divide

80 people are on floats.
20 are on each float.
How many floats are there?

$$20\overline{)80}$$

Think: $2\overline{)8}^{\,4}$ $20\overline{)80}^{\,4}$

There are 4 floats.

There are 210 musicians.
There are 30 in each band.
How many bands are there?

$$30\overline{)210}$$

Think: $3\overline{)21}^{\,7}$ $30\overline{)210}^{\,7}$

There are 7 bands.

130

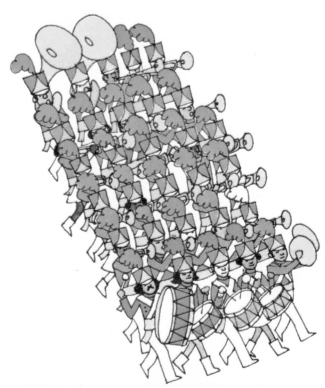

Divide.

1. $40\overline{)80}$ 2. $70\overline{)210}$ 3. $50\overline{)300}$ 4. $30\overline{)90}$ 5. $80\overline{)240}$

now do these

Divide.

6. $20\overline{)40}$ 7. $60\overline{)360}$ 8. $70\overline{)490}$ 9. $50\overline{)450}$ 10. $30\overline{)60}$

11. $70\overline{)630}$ 12. $40\overline{)280}$ 13. $80\overline{)720}$ 14. $60\overline{)180}$ 15. $90\overline{)720}$

16. $60\overline{)480}$ 17. $90\overline{)630}$ 18. $70\overline{)560}$ 19. $80\overline{)320}$ 20. $40\overline{)240}$

21. $80\overline{)640}$ 22. $70\overline{)420}$ 23. $90\overline{)540}$ 24. $50\overline{)400}$ 25. $60\overline{)540}$

26. $70\overline{)350}$ 27. $90\overline{)360}$ 28. $60\overline{)240}$ 29. $40\overline{)320}$ 30. $80\overline{)560}$

31. $60\overline{)120}$ 32. $70\overline{)280}$ 33. $40\overline{)360}$ 34. $80\overline{)160}$ 35. $90\overline{)270}$

36. $90\overline{)450}$ 37. $80\overline{)480}$ 38. $70\overline{)140}$ 39. $60\overline{)420}$ 40. $40\overline{)200}$

PATTERNS

Each number is 4 times greater than the number named before it. What are the next two numbers?

7	28	112	?	?

What are the next two numbers in the pattern?

A.
4	32	256	?	?

B.
3	21	147	?	?

C.
5	30	180	?	?

D.
8	24	72	?	?

131

Dividing by Tens

Lois has collected 234 stamps.
She can paste 40 on each page.
How many pages does she need?

$$40\overline{)234}$$

Step 1	Step 2	Step 3
$$40\overline{)234}^{5}$$	$$40\overline{)234}^{5}$$ 200	$$40\overline{)234}^{5\;r34}$$ 200 34
Estimate the quotient. $4\overline{)23}$ is about 5, so $40\overline{)234}$ is about 5. Try 5.	Multiply: $5 \times 40 = 200$. Write the product under 234.	Subtract. Show the remainder in the answer.

She needs 6 pages.
Why 6 and not 5?

Copy and complete.

$$\begin{array}{r} 3 \\ 70)\overline{235} \\ \underline{210} \\ 25 \end{array}$$	$$\begin{array}{r} 4 \\ 30)\overline{147} \\ \underline{120} \\ 27 \end{array}$$	$$\begin{array}{r} 7 \\ 50)\overline{374} \\ \underline{350} \end{array}$$	$$\begin{array}{r} 3 \\ 90)\overline{312} \\ \underline{270} \end{array}$$	$$\begin{array}{r} 6 \\ 40)\overline{256} \end{array}$$

1. $70)\overline{235}$ 2. $30)\overline{147}$ 3. $50)\overline{374}$ 4. $90)\overline{312}$ 5. $40)\overline{256}$

Divide.

6. $50)\overline{474}$ 7. $30)\overline{283}$ 8. $50)\overline{194}$ 9. $80)\overline{475}$ 10. $90)\overline{564}$

now do these

Divide.

11. $70)\overline{406}$ 12. $80)\overline{511}$ 13. $90)\overline{393}$ 14. $50)\overline{247}$ 15. $80)\overline{358}$

16. $90)\overline{197}$ 17. $70)\overline{586}$ 18. $90)\overline{494}$ 19. $80)\overline{286}$ 20. $90)\overline{321}$

21. $30)\overline{204}$ 22. $40)\overline{273}$ 23. $50)\overline{433}$ 24. $30)\overline{254}$ 25. $50)\overline{384}$

26. $40)\overline{385}$ 27. $60)\overline{462}$ 28. $80)\overline{654}$ 29. $40)\overline{307}$ 30. $90)\overline{658}$

Solve the problem.

31. There are 150 stamps.
There are 50 in each envelope.
How many envelopes are there?

32. There are 600 stamps.
There are 20 envelopes.
How many are in each envelope?

33. There are 490 stamps.
There are 70 pages.
How many are on each page?

34. There are 210 stamps.
30 fit on a page.
How many pages are needed?

Dividing by Tens and Ones

Each day a dispatcher sends
336 buses out on their routes.
There are 42 different routes.
The same number of buses serve
each route.
How many buses serve each route?

$$42\overline{)336}$$

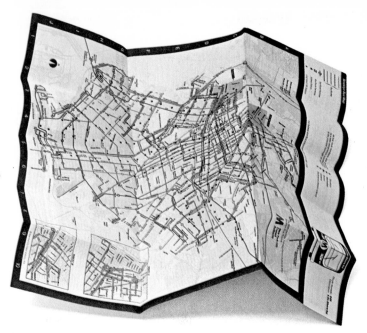

Step 1	Step 2	Step 3
$$\begin{array}{r} 8 \\ 42\overline{)336} \end{array}$$	$$\begin{array}{r} 8 \\ 42\overline{)336} \\ 336 \end{array}$$	$$\begin{array}{r} 8 \\ 42\overline{)336} \\ \underline{336} \\ 0 \end{array}$$
Estimate the quotient. 42 is near 40. $4\overline{)33}$ is about 8, so $40\overline{)336}$ is about 8. Try 8.	Multiply: $8 \times 42 = 336$.	Subtract. When the remainder is 0, do not show it in the answer.

8 buses serve each route.

134

Copy and complete.

7	5	2	8	3

1. 31)227   2. 72)364   3. 93)197   4. 64)512   5. 42)138
   217   360   186
   ___   ___   ___
    10

Divide.

6. 53)283   7. 42)132   8. 53)172   9. 22)176   10. 31)190

now do these

Divide.

11. 63)189   12. 82)358   13. 41)215   14. 42)215   15. 43)217

16. 91)642   17. 62)372   18. 44)352   19. 92)739   20. 53)374

21. 72)195   22. 81)597   23. 73)302   24. 51)295   25. 62)265

26. 42)388   27. 61)453   28. 82)656   29. 43)307   30. 91)675

31. 32)207   32. 41)264   33. 52)443   34. 33)265   35. 51)357

36. 92)179   37. 72)607   38. 91)484   39. 82)276   40. 71)504

41. 84)695   42. 72)224   43. 31)265   44. 43)394   45. 54)243

Too Much

Sometimes your first estimate
is too much.

Estimate the quotient.

Think: $60\overline{)495}$

Since $6\overline{)49}$ is about 8,
you should try 8.

But 8 is too much.
So, try 7.

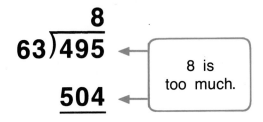

8 is
too much.

$$\begin{array}{r} 8 \\ 63\overline{)495} \\ 504 \end{array}$$

Step 1

$$\begin{array}{r} 7 \\ 63\overline{)495} \\ 441 \end{array}$$

Find the quotient.
Multiply.

Step 2

$$\begin{array}{r} 7 \\ 63\overline{)495} \\ \underline{441} \\ 54 \end{array}$$

Subtract.

Step 3

$$\begin{array}{r} 7 \ \text{r}54 \\ 63\overline{)495} \\ \underline{441} \\ 54 \end{array}$$

Show the remainder.

Is the first estimate too much?
Write YES or NO.

1. $\overset{8}{63\overline{)488}}$ 2. $\overset{9}{74\overline{)648}}$ 3. $\overset{7}{53\overline{)384}}$ 4. $\overset{8}{34\overline{)255}}$ 5. $\overset{7}{41\overline{)290}}$

Divide.

6. $34\overline{)256}$ 7. $43\overline{)342}$ 8. $63\overline{)427}$ 9. $23\overline{)193}$ 10. $54\overline{)369}$

now do these

Divide.

11. $83\overline{)589}$ 12. $44\overline{)378}$ 13. $94\overline{)843}$ 14. $42\overline{)409}$ 15. $73\overline{)507}$

16. $82\overline{)405}$ 17. $63\overline{)380}$ 18. $32\overline{)227}$ 19. $64\overline{)355}$ 20. $62\overline{)427}$

21. $74\overline{)449}$ 22. $62\overline{)552}$ 23. $82\overline{)339}$ 24. $71\overline{)619}$ 25. $92\overline{)637}$

26. $72\overline{)284}$ 27. $53\overline{)421}$ 28. $93\overline{)546}$ 29. $52\overline{)482}$ 30. $41\overline{)249}$

31. $73\overline{)375}$ 32. $34\overline{)267}$ 33. $54\overline{)476}$ 34. $62\overline{)276}$ 35. $24\overline{)174}$

BUTTON, BUTTON, WHO HAS THE BUTTON?

These are four buttons on your calculator.
Decide which one you would push
to solve the problem.

Then solve.

A. There are 60 people on the ferris wheel.
   15 stay on.
   How many people get off?

B. There are 15 cars.
   There are 4 people in each car.
   How many people are there in all?

C. 33 people wait on line.
   8 more join them.
   How many people are there altogether?

D. There are 24 students.
   4 fit in each car.
   How many cars are needed?

137

Dividing by Tens and Ones

The florist has cut 250 roses.
She will put 36 in each box
to ship them to the dealers.
How many boxes does she need?

$$36\overline{)250}$$

Step 1	Step 2	Step 3
6 $36\overline{)250}$	6 $36\overline{)250}$ 216	$6\ r34$ $36\overline{)250}$ $\underline{216}$ 34
Estimate the quotient. 36 is near 40. $4\overline{)25}$ is about 6, so $40\overline{)250}$ is about 6. Try 6.	Multiply.	Subtract. Show the remainder.

The florist can fill 6 boxes.
How many more roses must be cut to fill 7 boxes?

138

Copy and complete.

1. $\begin{array}{r} 5 \\ 35\overline{)204} \\ \underline{175} \\ 29 \end{array}$
2. $\begin{array}{r} 6 \\ 58\overline{)369} \\ \underline{348} \end{array}$
3. $\begin{array}{r} 8 \\ 66\overline{)567} \\ \underline{528} \end{array}$
4. $\begin{array}{r} 6 \\ 47\overline{)307} \end{array}$
5. $\begin{array}{r} 9 \\ 89\overline{)821} \end{array}$

Divide.

6. $46\overline{)213}$
7. $77\overline{)659}$
8. $59\overline{)449}$
9. $45\overline{)403}$
10. $68\overline{)374}$

now do these

Divide.

11. $38\overline{)335}$
12. $56\overline{)557}$
13. $75\overline{)492}$
14. $67\overline{)649}$
15. $49\overline{)423}$

16. $57\overline{)257}$
17. $48\overline{)359}$
18. $36\overline{)247}$
19. $69\overline{)439}$
20. $55\overline{)490}$

21. $65\overline{)507}$
22. $87\overline{)649}$
23. $76\overline{)579}$
24. $78\overline{)744}$
25. $79\overline{)268}$

26. $37\overline{)282}$
27. $56\overline{)194}$
28. $48\overline{)176}$
29. $79\overline{)427}$
30. $65\overline{)227}$

Solve the problem.

31. There are 182 carnations.
28 go in each spray.
How many sprays can be made?

32. There are 312 chrysanthemums.
48 go in each wreath.
How many wreaths can be made?

139

Not Enough

Sometimes your first estimate is not enough.

Estimate the quotient.

Think: $50\overline{)249}$

Since $5\overline{)24}$ is about 4, you should try 4.

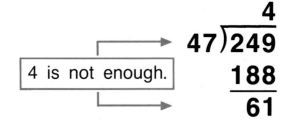

But when you multiply and subtract, you have more than 47 left over.

So, try 5.

Step 1

$$47\overline{)249} \quad 5$$
$$235$$

Find the quotient. Multiply.

Step 2

$$47\overline{)249} \quad 5$$
$$\underline{235}$$
$$14$$

Subtract.

Step 3

$$47\overline{)249} \quad 5\ r14$$
$$\underline{235}$$
$$14$$

Show the remainder.

Is the first estimate enough? Write YES or NO.

1. $\overset{3}{57\overline{)231}}$ 2. $\overset{6}{65\overline{)455}}$ 3. $\overset{6}{86\overline{)579}}$ 4. $\overset{6}{38\overline{)279}}$ 5. $\overset{7}{47\overline{)354}}$

Divide.

6. $55\overline{)495}$ 7. $69\overline{)485}$ 8. $77\overline{)475}$ 9. $26\overline{)193}$ 10. $57\overline{)470}$

now do these

Divide.

11. $85\overline{)342}$ 12. $88\overline{)704}$ 13. $39\overline{)368}$ 14. $69\overline{)419}$ 15. $86\overline{)556}$

16. $48\overline{)348}$ 17. $76\overline{)532}$ 18. $77\overline{)619}$ 19. $38\overline{)304}$ 20. $46\overline{)203}$

21. $56\overline{)547}$ 22. $68\overline{)343}$ 23. $55\overline{)447}$ 24. $79\overline{)239}$ 25. $45\overline{)368}$

26. $49\overline{)392}$ 27. $79\overline{)428}$ 28. $67\overline{)224}$ 29. $66\overline{)473}$ 30. $65\overline{)229}$

31. $48\overline{)169}$ 32. $59\overline{)413}$ 33. $78\overline{)712}$ 34. $56\overline{)195}$ 35. $48\overline{)428}$

quick check

Divide.

1. $90\overline{)540}$ 2. $80\overline{)640}$ 3. $30\overline{)175}$ 4. $52\overline{)468}$ 5. $74\overline{)293}$

6. $63\overline{)421}$ 7. $47\overline{)362}$ 8. $38\overline{)285}$ 9. $25\overline{)182}$ 10. $58\overline{)237}$

Tens in the Quotient

A baker makes 722 cookies.
He puts them in bags to sell.
He puts 20 in each bag.
How many bags can he fill?

$$20\overline{)722}$$

Step 1

$$
\begin{array}{r}
3 \\
20\overline{)722} \\
600 \\
\hline
122
\end{array}
$$

Find the tens.
$2\overline{)7}$ is about 3, so
$20\overline{)72}$ is about 3, and
$20\overline{)722}$ is about 30.
Write 3 in the tens
place in the quotient.
Multiply: $30 \times 20 = 600$.
Subtract.

Step 2

$$
\begin{array}{r}
36 \\
20\overline{)722} \\
600 \\
\hline
122 \\
120 \\
\hline
2
\end{array}
$$

Find the ones.
$2\overline{)12}$ is 6, so
$20\overline{)122}$ is about 6.
Write 6 in the ones
place in the quotient.
Multiply: $6 \times 20 = 120$.
Subtract.

Step 3

$$
\begin{array}{r}
36 \text{ r2} \\
20\overline{)722} \\
600 \\
\hline
122 \\
120 \\
\hline
2
\end{array}
$$

Show the remainder
in the answer.

The baker can fill 36 bags.
His pet dog will eat the two left over.

142

Copy and complete.

```
        31                 26                  3                   4
1. 30)958         2. 70)1825         3. 40)1447          4. 60)2437
   900              1400               1200
    58               425
    30               420
    28
```

Divide.

5. 20)948   6. 40)967   7. 60)4375   8. 80)2569

now do these

Divide.

9. 30)938   10. 50)2317   11. 20)835   12. 40)2360

13. 40)2140   14. 70)3928   15. 50)3361   16. 30)985

17. 80)6156   18. 70)3159   19. 90)5048   20. 60)3545

21. 50)4358   22. 30)972   23. 40)2925   24. 80)5440

25. 70)2738   26. 50)2970   27. 20)972   28. 40)873

29. 30)2619   30. 90)7745   31. 70)5469   32. 30)2869

33. 60)4080   34. 20)649   35. 50)4669   36. 60)5541

More About Tens in the Quotient

Find the quotient and the remainder: 34)821.

Step 1

```
      2
34)821
   680
   141
```

Find the tens.
34 is near 30.
3)8 is about 2, so
30)821 is about 20.
Try 20.

Step 2

```
     24
34)821
   680
   141
   136
     5
```

Find the ones.
3)14 is about 4, so
30)141 is about 4.
Try 4.

Step 3

```
     24 r5
34)821
   680
   141
   136
     5
```

Show the remainder
in the answer.

Sometimes your first estimate is too much.
Find the quotient and the remainder: 73)2816.

Step 1

```
       4
73)2816
   2920
```

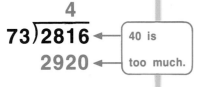

Find the tens.
73 is near 70,
7)28 is 4, so
70)2816 is about 40.
Try 40.
But 2920 > 2816.

Step 2

```
       3
73)2816
   2190
    626
```

Since 40 is too much,
try 30.

Step 3

```
      38 r42
73)2816
   2190
    626
    584
     42
```

Find the ones.
7)62 is about 8, so
70)626 is about 8.
Try 8.
Show the remainder.

144

Is the first estimate too much?
Write YES or NO.

1. $\overset{90}{24\overline{)1968}}$　　　2. $\overset{60}{21\overline{)1323}}$　　　3. $\overset{90}{62\overline{)5420}}$　　　4. $\overset{60}{44\overline{)2688}}$

Divide.

5. $22\overline{)1628}$　　　6. $53\overline{)3657}$　　　7. $63\overline{)3664}$　　　8. $43\overline{)3375}$

now do these

Divide.

9. $73\overline{)4246}$　　　10. $41\overline{)2665}$　　　11. $23\overline{)1869}$　　　12. $51\overline{)3428}$

13. $52\overline{)2236}$　　　14. $83\overline{)5644}$　　　15. $31\overline{)1994}$　　　16. $93\overline{)7254}$

17. $81\overline{)1869}$　　　18. $52\overline{)1674}$　　　19. $44\overline{)3443}$　　　20. $32\overline{)2304}$

21. $61\overline{)4758}$　　　22. $33\overline{)2683}$　　　23. $52\overline{)4108}$　　　24. $43\overline{)2452}$

25. $92\overline{)6348}$　　　26. $44\overline{)939}$　　　27. $44\overline{)3036}$　　　28. $43\overline{)989}$

PATTERNS

Each number is 5 times the number named before it. What are the next two numbers?

9	45	225	?	?

What are the next two numbers in the pattern?

A.

4	16	64	?	?

B.

9	36	144	?	?

C.

6	36	216	?	?

D.

5	35	245	?	?

145

More About Tens in the Quotient

Find the quotient and the remainder: 66)5763.

Step 1

```
      8
66)5763
   5280
    483
```

Find the tens.
66 is near 70.
7)57 is about 8, so
70)5763 is about 80.
Try 80.

Step 2

6 is not enough.

```
     86
66)5763
   5280
    483
    396
     87
```

Find the ones.
7)48 is about 6, so
70)483 is about 6.
Try 6.
But 87 > 66.

Step 3

```
     87 r21
66)5763
   5280
    483
    462
     21
```

Since 6 is not
enough, try 7.
Show the remainder.

Find the quotient and the remainder: 46)3444.

Step 1

60 is not enough.

```
      6
46)3444
   2760
    684
```

Find the tens.
46 is near 50.
5)34 is about 6, so
50)3444 is about 60.
Try 60.
But 68 > 46.

Step 2

```
      7
46)3444
   3220
    224
```

Since 60 is not
enough, try 70.

Step 3

```
     74 r40
46)3444
   3220
    224
    184
     40
```

Find the ones.
5)22 is about 4, so
50)224 is about 4.
Try 4.
Show the remainder.

146

try these

Is the first estimate enough?
Write YES or NO.

1. $36\overline{)1479}$ estimate 30

2. $58\overline{)4128}$ estimate 60

3. $67\overline{)1619}$ estimate 20

4. $46\overline{)4193}$ estimate 80

Divide.

5. $25\overline{)1535}$

6. $35\overline{)2488}$

7. $26\overline{)1872}$

8. $48\overline{)3499}$

now do these

Divide.

9. $55\overline{)3960}$

10. $38\overline{)2553}$

11. $55\overline{)4899}$

12. $37\overline{)2294}$

13. $39\overline{)1883}$

14. $76\overline{)2214}$

15. $87\overline{)3916}$

16. $27\overline{)2226}$

17. $57\overline{)3534}$

18. $39\overline{)3159}$

19. $77\overline{)4465}$

20. $48\overline{)3312}$

21. $78\overline{)5238}$

22. $29\overline{)898}$

23. $75\overline{)5925}$

24. $48\overline{)2457}$

25. $47\overline{)3884}$

26. $65\overline{)2415}$

27. $27\overline{)1335}$

28. $89\overline{)2587}$

PATTERNS

Each number is 6 times the number named before it. What are the next two numbers?

8	48	288	?	?

What are the next two numbers in the pattern?

A.
10	90	810	?	?

B.
12	96	768	?	?

C.
15	105	735	?	?

D.
27	135	675	?	?

147

Hundreds in the Quotient

A company paid $3784 to have
new tires put on its 22 cars.
How much did it cost for each car?

$$22\overline{)3784}$$

Step 1

$$
\begin{array}{r}
1 \\
22\overline{)3784} \\
2200 \\
\hline
1584
\end{array}
$$

Find the hundreds.
22 is near 20.
$2\overline{)3}$ is about 1, so
$20\overline{)3784}$ is about 100.
Try 100.
Write 1 in the hundreds
place in the quotient.
$100 \times 22 = 2200$
Subtract.

Step 2

$$
\begin{array}{r}
17 \\
22\overline{)3784} \\
2200 \\
\hline
1584 \\
1540 \\
\hline
44
\end{array}
$$

Find the tens.
$2\overline{)15}$ is about 7, so
$20\overline{)1584}$ is about 70.
Try 70.
Write 7 in the tens
place in the quotient.
$70 \times 22 = 1540$
Subtract.

Step 3

$$
\begin{array}{r}
172 \\
22\overline{)3784} \\
2200 \\
\hline
1584 \\
1540 \\
\hline
44 \\
44 \\
\hline
0
\end{array}
$$

Find the ones.
$2\overline{)4}$ is 2, so
$20\overline{)44}$ is about 2.
Try 2.
Write 2 in the ones
place in the quotient.
$2 \times 22 = 44$
Subtract.

It cost $172 to put new tires on each car.

148

try these

Copy and complete.

11	13	21	2
1. 25)2975	2. 46)6079	3. 31)6609	4. 23)4780
2500	4600	6200	
475	1479		
250	1380		

Divide.

5. 56)6279   6. 49)5488   7. 26)6275   8. 52)5930

now do these

Divide.

9. 83)9296   10. 72)8219   11. 48)5718   12. 27)8829

13. 75)9075   14. 65)7345   15. 54)6114   16. 47)5681

17. 66)9288   18. 73)8979   19. 63)8812   20. 55)6765

21. 38)8094   22. 82)9278   23. 74)8369   24. 56)6279

BUTTON, BUTTON, WHO HAS THE BUTTON?

These are four buttons on your calculator. Decide which one you would push to solve the problem. Then solve.

A. Mary saves $3.75 a week.
   How much does she save in 6 weeks?

B. 3 tee shirts cost $9.15.
   How much does one cost?

C. Carlos has $15.98.
   He earns $4.30.
   How much does he have now?

D. Brad has $10.35.
   He spends $3.98 for a record.
   How much does he have left?

149

thinking about the remainder

Often when you divide, there is a remainder in your answer.
However, the answer to the problem might be a whole number.
Sometimes the answer to the problem will be the quotient.
Other times the answer will be the next greater whole number.

Problem 1

Fran is a travel agent. Her company offers a special *See America Trip.*
96 people will see America by bus.
Each bus can carry 53 people.
How many buses are needed?

Solution

$$\begin{array}{r} 1 \text{ r}43 \\ 53\overline{)96} \\ 53 \\ \hline 43 \end{array}$$

2 buses are needed.

Problem 2

Fran can earn a bonus. For every 50 persons who take the trip, she earns a one-week vacation.
96 people take the tour. How many weeks of vacation does Fran earn?

Solution

$$\begin{array}{r} 1 \text{ r}46 \\ 50\overline{)96} \\ 50 \\ \hline 46 \end{array}$$

She earns 1 week of vacation.

Is the answer 3 or is it 4?

1. 55 people will go on a special tour. Fran must arrange for tour guides. There will be one guide for each 15 people. How many guides must Fran get?

2. Fran can travel at special rates. She has 25 days she can use for vacations. Each trip that she wants to take lasts 7 days. How many of these trips can she take?

Solve the problem.

3. 24 people are on a tour. They plan to take a side trip by car. Each car can carry 5 people. How many cars are needed?

4. Fran must change some reservations. She will use the telephone. Each call will take 3 minutes. She has only 50 minutes. How many calls can she make?

5. 35 tourists are waiting to take a plane trip over a canyon. The plane can carry 12 people each trip. How many trips must the plane make?

6. Fran wants to earn a bonus. She must sign up 24 people to take a tour. She has 5 days in which to do this. How many must she sign up each day?

7. 66 people on one tour stop at a restaurant. 10 people can sit at a table. How many tables do they need?

8. Fran works 5 days every week. She has worked 148 days so far this year. How many full weeks is this?

Test

Divide.

1. (p. 129) $10\overline{)370}$

2. (p. 130) $70\overline{)210}$

3. (p. 132) $60\overline{)357}$

4. (p. 134) $73\overline{)295}$

5. (p. 140) $58\overline{)473}$

6. (p. 134) $32\overline{)264}$

7. (p. 136) $82\overline{)653}$

8. (p. 138) $29\overline{)108}$

9. (p. 136) $91\overline{)816}$

10. (p. 140) $45\overline{)331}$

11. (p. 138) $68\overline{)679}$

12. (p. 140) $76\overline{)474}$

13. (p. 140) $16\overline{)136}$

14. (p. 146) $67\overline{)5362}$

15. (p. 146) $88\overline{)4735}$

16. (p. 146) $39\overline{)1604}$

17. (p. 144) $54\overline{)2204}$

18. (p. 144) $94\overline{)7635}$

19. (p. 146) $77\overline{)1001}$

20. (p. 148) $23\overline{)3760}$

21. (p. 148) $66\overline{)8134}$

22. (p. 148) $42\overline{)6931}$

23. (p. 148) $85\overline{)8509}$

24. (p. 148) $54\overline{)8392}$

25. (p. 148) $79\overline{)9962}$

bonus

Solve the problem.

26. You have 650 pennies.
You can put 50 pennies into each roll.
How many rolls do you need?

(p. 132)

27. You have 225 concert tickets.
You have 15 days to sell them.
How many tickets must
you sell each day?

(p. 146)

Keeping up

Name 1000 more.

1. 482, 963, 402 (p. 10)   2. 23, 319, 865 (p. 10)   3. 83, 701, 609, 000 (p. 10)

Name 1,000,000 more.

4. 643, 813, 002 (p. 10)   5. 29, 430, 016 (p. 10)   6. 603, 400, 785, 020 (p. 10)

Name 1,000,000,000 more.

7. 43, 685, 400, 231 (p. 10)   8. 409, 600, 301, 400 (p. 10)   9. 869, 400, 000, 000 (p. 10)

Add.

10.	11.	12.	13.	14.
$3.75	$7.09	$50.59	$ .29	$ .79
4.86	9.07	3.87	7.89	.86
+ 5.79	+ 3.06	+ 46.48	+ 31.96	+ 10.37
(p. 58)	(p. 58)	(p. 58)	(p. 58)	(p. 58)

Subtract.

15.	16.	17.	18.	19.
$24.00	$37.06	$30.74	$67.23	$80.00
− 16.79	− 12.97	− 12.69	− 6.79	− 29.45
(p. 58)	(p. 58)	(p. 58)	(p. 58)	(p. 58)

Multiply.

20.	21.	22.	23.	24.
6750	6709	7609	6987	7089
× 7	× 9	× 8	× 9	× 7
(p. 78)	(p. 78)	(p. 78)	(p. 78)	(p. 78)

25.	26.	27.	28.	29.
786	960	456	465	879
× 67	× 80	×789	×780	×604
(p. 82)	(p. 80)	(p. 86)	(p. 86)	(p. 86)

Divide.

(p. 122)   (p. 122)   (p. 114, 116)   (p. 114, 116)   (p. 122)

30. 4)2927   31. 9)8127   32. 6)473   33. 7)627   34. 9)4233

153

Codes

SECRET CODE CHART

A B C D E F G H I J K L M N O P Q R S T U V W X Y Z

00 01 02 03 04 05 06 07 08 09 10 11 12 13 14 15 16 17 18 19 20 21 22 23 24 25

You can use numbers to send secret messages to a friend.
Each numeral can stand for a letter. Look at the secret code chart.
00 stands for A. 03 stands for D. 11 stands for L, and so forth.
Now here is a secret message. It gives you the state song of North Carolina.

19-07-04   14-11-03   13-14-17-19-07   18-19-00-19-04

Substitute the right letter for each number.
Here is the song.

19-07-04   14-11-03   13-14-17-19-07   18-19-00-19-04

T H E   O L D   N O R T H   S T A T E

Use the code. Find the state song.

1. 08   11-14-21-04   24-14-20,   02-00-11-08-05-14-17-13-08-00

2. 19-04-23-00-18,   14-20-17   19-04-23-00-18

3. 12-24   14-11-03   10-04-13-19-20-02-10-24   07-14-12-04

4. 01-04-00-20-19-08-05-20-11   14-07-08-14

5. 02-00-17-17-24   12-04   01-00-02-10   19-14   14-11-03   21-08-17-06-08-13-08-00

A cryptographer is someone who works with codes.
The code you just used is not a difficult one.
A cryptographer could crack the code quite easily.
So, let's make it a little more difficult.

Make an agreement with your friend. The first number in
each secret message will tell how much to add to the numbers
in the message. Then use the secret code chart.
This code gives you the nickname of Pennsylvania.

05 14-02-25 5-25-19-13-14-9-8-25 13-14-21-14-25

The 05 at the beginning tells your friend to add 5 to each
number in the message. Then use the code chart. (When you
get near the end of the alphabet, you start over. For example,
24 would mean count ahead 5, or 24, 25, 00, 01, 02, 03. It is 03.)

05 14-02-25   5 -25-19-13-14- 9 - 8 -25   13-14-21-14-25

19-07-04   10-04-24-18-19-14-13-04   18-19-00-19-04

T H E K E Y S T O N E S T A T E

Use the code. Find the state nickname.

6. Alabama-05   **14-02-25   02-25-21-12-14   09-00   24-03-18-03-25**

7. Georgia-03 **16-04-01 01-09-12-05-14-01 15-16-23-16-01 11-02 16-04-01 15-11-17-16-04**

8. Illinois-01   **18-06-03   10-25-12-02   13-04   10-07-12-01-13-10-12**

9. New York-04   **15-03-00   00-08-11-04-13-00   14-15-22-15-00**

10. Florida-02   **17-05-02   16-18-11-16-05-06-11-02   16-17-24-17-02**

8 Number Theory

Divisibility

Divide one number by another.
If the remainder is 0, then the first number
is divisible by the second.

14 is divisible by 2.   15 is not divisible by 2.

$$
\begin{array}{r} 7 \\ 2\overline{)14} \\ 14 \\ \hline 0 \end{array}
\qquad\qquad
\begin{array}{r} 7 \\ 2\overline{)15} \\ 14 \\ \hline 1 \end{array}
$$

Here are five even numbers. $\longrightarrow$ **2, 4, 6, 8, 10**
Divide each by 2.
What is the remainder?

Here are five odd numbers. $\longrightarrow$ **3, 5, 7, 9, 11**
Divide each by 2.
What is the remainder?

Even numbers are divisible by 2.   Odd numbers are not.

If a numeral has a 0 or a 5 in the ones place,
then the number is divisible by 5.

These numbers are divisible by 5. $\longrightarrow$ **0, 5, 10, 15, 20, 25, 30**

Which of these numbers are divisible by 10?
How can you tell when a numeral names
a number that is divisible by 10?

156

Is the first number divisible by the second? Write YES or NO.

1. 8, 2   2. 36, 4   3. 53, 9   4. 17, 3   5. 95, 5

Is the first number divisible by the second? Write YES or NO.

6. 64, 9   7. 81, 8   8. 19, 3   9. 14, 2   10. 24, 5

11. 57, 7   12. 40, 4   13. 80, 10   14. 21, 6   15. 56, 9

16. 35, 4   17. 13, 2   18. 72, 8   19. 80, 6   20. 49, 7

21. 15, 5   22. 54, 6   23. 33, 3   24. 81, 9   25. 96, 6

Is the number divisible by 2? Write YES or NO.

26. 25   27. 24   28. 35   29. 60   30. 16

31. 20   32. 19   33. 40   34. 85   35. 23

Is the number divisible by 5? Write YES or NO.

36. 25   37. 24   38. 35   39. 60   40. 16

41. 20   42. 19   43. 40   44. 85   45. 23

Is the number divisible by 10? Write YES or NO.

46. 25   47. 24   48. 35   49. 60   50. 16

51. 20   52. 19   53. 40   54. 85   55. 23

157

Factors

Two factors of 12 are 3 and 4. $3 \times 4 = 12$

A number is divisible
by its **factors**.

$$3\overline{)12} \quad\quad 4\overline{)12}$$

$$\begin{array}{r} 4 \\ 3\overline{)12} \\ \underline{12} \\ 0 \end{array} \quad\quad \begin{array}{r} 3 \\ 4\overline{)12} \\ \underline{12} \\ 0 \end{array}$$

Find all the factors of 12.   List them in order.

Step 1   Write 12 as the product of two whole numbers
in as many ways as possible.

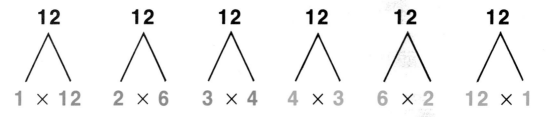

Step 2   List the whole numbers in order.   Show each only once.

1, 2, 3, 4, 6, 12

try these

Find the missing factor.

1. $\underline{\ ?\ } \times 6 = 6$ 2. $\underline{\ ?\ } \times 3 = 6$

3. $\underline{\ ?\ } \times 10 = 10$ 4. $\underline{\ ?\ } \times 5 = 10$

Find all the factors.   List them in order.

5. 6   6. 10   7. 3   8. 16

now do these

Find the missing factor.

9. $\underline{\ ?\ } \times 4 = 20$ 10. $\underline{\ ?\ } \times 3 = 21$

11. $\underline{\ ?\ } \times 12 = 36$ 12. $\underline{\ ?\ } \times 5 = 30$

13. $\underline{\ ?\ } \times 10 = 50$ 14. $\underline{\ ?\ } \times 6 = 60$

15. $\underline{\ ?\ } \times 3 = 33$ 16. $\underline{\ ?\ } \times 5 = 25$

Find all the factors.   List them in order.

17. 9   18. 20   19. 21   20. 15

21. 25   22. 18   23. 32   24. 27

25. 33   26. 36   27. 35   28. 40

29. 30   30. 42   31. 48   32. 50

33. 54   34. 60   35. 72   36. 75

PRIME NUMBERS

A **prime number** has exactly two factors: itself and 1.

The number 1 is not a prime number.

Which of these are prime numbers?

Number	Factors
2	1, 2
3	1, 3
4	1, 2, 4
5	1, 5
6	1, 2, 3, 6

The numbers 2, 3, and 5 are prime numbers.

List all the prime numbers between 1 and 50.

Compare your list with that of a friend.

Did both of you find all of the prime numbers?

Greatest Common Factor

Sometimes two numbers have the same factor.

factors of 8 ⟶ **1, 2, 4, 8**

Sometimes they share more than one factor.

factors of 12 ⟶ **1, 2, 3, 4, 6, 12**

These factors are **common factors.**

common factors ⟶ **1, 2, 4**

Find the **greatest common factor** of 16 and 24.

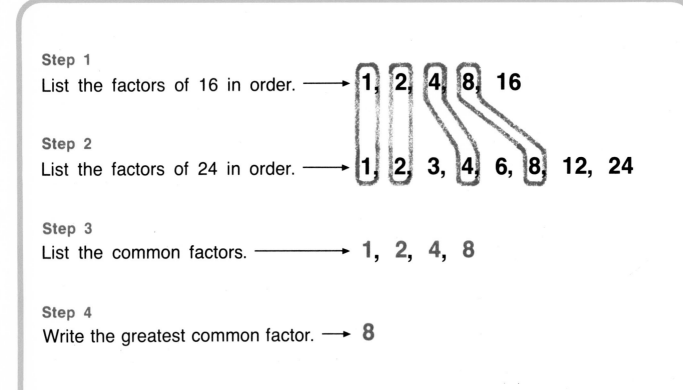

Step 1

List the factors of 16 in order. ⟶ **1, 2, 4, 8, 16**

Step 2

List the factors of 24 in order. ⟶ **1, 2, 3, 4, 6, 8, 12, 24**

Step 3

List the common factors. ⟶ **1, 2, 4, 8**

Step 4

Write the greatest common factor. ⟶ **8**

List all the factors in order.

1. 36   2. 24   3. 18

List the common factors in order.

4. 36, 24   5. 24, 18   6. 18, 12

Find the greatest common factor.

7. 36, 24   8. 24, 18   9. 18, 12

now do these

List the common factors in order.

10. 4, 16   11. 10, 25   12. 8, 32

13. 54, 27   14. 48, 32   15. 72, 18

Find the greatest common factor.

16. 4, 16   17. 10, 25   18. 8, 32

19. 54, 27   20. 48, 32   21. 72, 18

22. 10, 40   23. 36, 54   24. 32, 8

25. 32, 72   26. 18, 48   27. 54, 12

28. 5, 25   29. 10, 75   30. 25, 50

31. 25, 75   32. 40, 80   33. 40, 60

PRIME FACTORS

To find the **prime factors** of 24, make a factor tree.

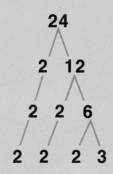

2 and 3 are prime factors of 24.

Complete this factor tree to find the prime factors of 30.

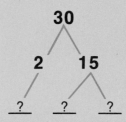

Find the prime factors of the number.

A. 42   **B.** 60   **C.** 98

Least Common Multiple

Multiply a number by 1, 2, 3, and so on.
Each product is a **multiple** of that number.

$$1 \times \mathbf{3} \quad 2 \times \mathbf{3} \quad 3 \times \mathbf{3} \quad 4 \times \mathbf{3}$$

Here are four multiples of 3. → 3,   6,   9,   12
Name the next two multiples of 3.

List five multiples of 2 in order.   Start with 2.
            2, 4, 6, 8, 10

Find the **least common multiple** of 2 and 3.

Step 1   List multiples of 3. → **3, 6, 9, 12, 15, 18, ···**

Step 2   List multiples of 2. → **2, 4, 6, 8, 10, 12, 14, 16, 18, ···**

Step 3   List the common
         multiples. ──────→ **6, 12, 18, ···**

Step 4   Write the least
         common multiple. → **6**

List five multiples in order. Start with the number.

1. 4   2. 5   3. 7   4. 9   5. 18

Find the least common multiple.

6. 4, 5   7. 5, 7   8. 9, 18   9. 4, 7   10. 4, 18

now do these

List five multiples in order. Start with the number.

11. 6   12. 8   13. 10   14. 11   15. 12

16. 15   17. 20   18. 25   19. 50   20. 100

List the first three common multiples.

21. 6, 8   22. 10, 25   23. 12, 20   24. 10, 15   25. 6, 11

26. 6, 10   27. 8, 12   28. 20, 25   29. 20, 50   30. 50, 100

Find the least common multiple.

31. 6, 8   32. 10, 25   33. 12, 20   34. 10, 15   35. 6, 11

36. 6, 10   37. 8, 12   38. 20, 25   39. 20, 50   40. 50, 100

GIVE IT A TRY

Find the least common multiple of the numbers in the group.

A. 3, 4, 6   B. 4, 5, 8   C. 2, 4, 8, 16   D. 2, 5, 8, 10

163

Test

Find the missing factor.

1. _?_ × 6 = 42 (p. 158)   **2.** _?_ × 8 = 56 (p. 158)   **3.** _?_ × 3 = 18 (p. 158)

4. _?_ × 10 = 70 (p. 158)   **5.** _?_ × 9 = 81 (p. 158)

Find all the factors. List them in order.

6. 9 (p. 158)   **7.** 13 (p. 158)   **8.** 35 (p. 158)   **9.** 22 (p. 158)   **10.** 27 (p. 158)

Find the greatest common factor.

11. 5, 25 (p. 160) **12.** 30, 9 (p. 160)   **13.** 8, 20 (p. 160) **14.** 24, 36 (p. 160) **15.** 16, 44 (p. 160)

Find the least common multiple.

16. 2, 7 (p. 162)   **17.** 10, 15 (p. 162) **18.** 6, 13 (p. 162) **19.** 20, 60 (p. 162) **20.** 5, 9 (p. 162)

Is the first number divisible by the second?
Write YES or NO.

21. 14, 6 (p. 156) **22.** 81, 9 (p. 156) **23.** 74, 7 (p. 156) **24.** 42, 3 (p. 156) **25.** 95, 5 (p. 156)

Keeping up

What number does the red digit name?

1. 837 (p. 6)   **2.** 903 (p. 6)   **3.** 6431 (p. 6)   **4.** 8324 (p. 6)

5. 65,831 (p. 6)   **6.** 92,307 (p. 6)   **7.** 532,764 (p. 6)   **8.** 806,543 (p. 6)

Write > or <.

9. 437,852 ⬤ 623,582 (p. 12)   **10.** 631,425 ⬤ 630,425 (p. 12)

11. 5,648,270 ⬤ 5,628,270 (p. 12)   **12.** 8,037,400 ⬤ 8,037,402 (p. 12)

Add.

13.
$$\begin{array}{r} 37 \\ 698 \\ +4289 \\ \hline \end{array}$$
(p. 34)

14.
$$\begin{array}{r} 98 \\ 57 \\ +2047 \\ \hline \end{array}$$
(p. 34)

15.
$$\begin{array}{r} 807 \\ 706 \\ 509 \\ +278 \\ \hline \end{array}$$
(p. 34)

16.
$$\begin{array}{r} 9028 \\ 497 \\ 2568 \\ +4321 \\ \hline \end{array}$$
(p. 34)

Subtract.

17.
$$\begin{array}{r} 7000 \\ -4597 \\ \hline \end{array}$$
(p. 56)

18.
$$\begin{array}{r} 5964 \\ -879 \\ \hline \end{array}$$
(p. 54)

19.
$$\begin{array}{r} 2900 \\ -1784 \\ \hline \end{array}$$
(p. 56)

20.
$$\begin{array}{r} 4085 \\ -279 \\ \hline \end{array}$$
(p. 54)

Multiply.

21.
$$\begin{array}{r} 6808 \\ \times\ 37 \\ \hline \end{array}$$
(p. 84)

22.
$$\begin{array}{r} 1890 \\ \times\ 70 \\ \hline \end{array}$$
(p. 84)

23.
$$\begin{array}{r} 654 \\ \times 897 \\ \hline \end{array}$$
(p. 86)

24.
$$\begin{array}{r} 357 \\ \times 690 \\ \hline \end{array}$$
(p. 86)

Divide.

25. $7\overline{)589}$ (p. 114, 116)   **26.** $8\overline{)487}$ (p. 114, 116)   **27.** $6\overline{)5718}$ (p. 122)   **28.** $9\overline{)7026}$ (p. 122)

29. $67\overline{)344}$ (p. 140)   **30.** $94\overline{)644}$ (p. 136)   **31.** $49\overline{)2992}$ (p. 146)   **32.** $84\overline{)5906}$ (p. 144)

Divisibility

Here is a way to find whether a number is divisible by 3.

Number	Find the sum of the digits.	If the sum is divisible by 3, then the number is divisible by 3.
27	$2 + 7 = 9$	Yes
81	$8 + 1 = 9$	Yes
92	$9 + 2 = 11$	No
150	$1 + 5 + 0 = 6$	Yes
216	$2 + 1 + 6 = 9$	Yes
351	$3 + 5 + 1 = 9$	Yes
472	$4 + 7 + 2 = 13$	No

Is the number divisible by 3?   Write YES or NO.

1. 18   2. 51   3. 75   4. 82   5. 43

6. 230   7. 249   8. 275   9. 146   10. 552

Here is a way to find whether a number is divisible by 9.

Number	Find the sum of the digits.	If the sum is divisible by 9, then the number is divisible by 9.
72	$7 + 2 = 9$	Yes
91	$9 + 1 = 10$	No
162	$1 + 6 + 2 = 9$	Yes
201	$2 + 0 + 1 = 3$	No
324	$3 + 2 + 4 = 9$	Yes
576	$5 + 7 + 6 = 18$	Yes

Is the number divisible by 9? Write YES or NO.

11. 54   **12.** 87   **13.** 102   **14.** 153   **15.** 243

16. 324   **17.** 391   **18.** 516   **19.** 648   **20.** 602

9 Fractions

Fractions

Five friends bought a pizza.
They cut it into 5 fair shares.
Each will get one fair share.
Each gets one fifth of the pizza.

A **fraction** tells what part each friend will get.

one share → $\underline{1}$ ← numerator

shares in all → 5 ← denominator

Each pizza is cut into fair shares.
The fraction tells what part is still on the plate.

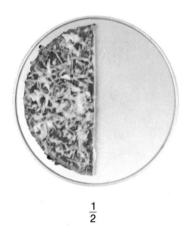

$\frac{1}{2}$

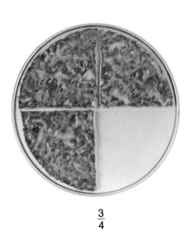

$\frac{3}{4}$

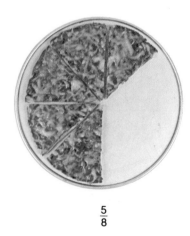

$\frac{5}{8}$

What does the denominator tell you?
What does the numerator tell you?

168

What part is still on the plate? Write the fraction.

1.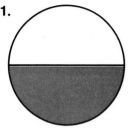

2.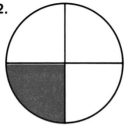

3.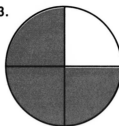

4.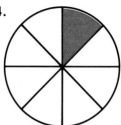

now do these

What part is still on the plate? Write the fraction.

5.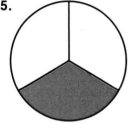

6.

7.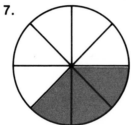

8.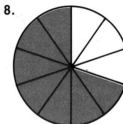

9.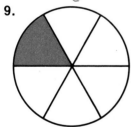

10.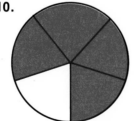

11.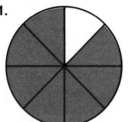

12.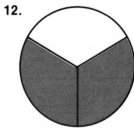

13.

14.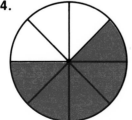

15.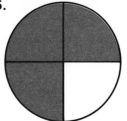

16.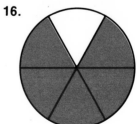

169

Fractions and Groups

Some glasses have orange juice. Some have grape juice.

$\dfrac{4}{10}$ ← glasses with orange juice
← glasses in all

Four tenths of the glasses have orange juice.

The glasses are put on trays.

$\dfrac{2}{5}$ ← trays with orange juice
← trays in all

Two fifths of the trays have orange juice.

170

What part has orange juice?   Write the fraction.

1.

2.

3.

now do these

What part has orange juice?   Write the fraction.

4.

5.

6.

What part has grape juice?   Write the fraction.

7.

8.

9.

What part has grape juice?   Write the fraction.

10.

11.

12.

Finding Parts of a Group

There are 12 tropical fish.
$\frac{1}{3}$ of them are mine.
How many are mine?

$\frac{1}{3}$ of 12 = ?

Think:

Separate them into 3 groups. ⟶ **12 ÷ 3 = 4**
There are 4 in each group.

4 tropical fish are mine.

There are 20 tropical fish.
$\frac{3}{4}$ of them are yours.
How many are yours?

$\frac{3}{4}$ of 20 = ?

Think:

Separate them into 4 groups. ⟶ **20 ÷ 4 = 5**
You get 3 of the groups. ⟶ **3 × 5 = 15**

15 tropical fish are yours.

Complete the sentence.

1.

$\frac{1}{6}$ of 12 = ___?___

Think:
Divide by 6.

2.

$\frac{5}{6}$ of 12 = ___?___

Think:
Divide by 6.
Multiply by 5.

now do these

Complete the sentence.

3. $\frac{1}{8}$ of 24 = ___?___

4. $\frac{1}{5}$ of 15 = ___?___

5. $\frac{1}{8}$ of 16 = ___?___

6. $\frac{1}{6}$ of 18 = ___?___

7. $\frac{1}{10}$ of 40 = ___?___

8. $\frac{1}{4}$ of 12 = ___?___

9. $\frac{3}{6}$ of 24 = ___?___

10. $\frac{3}{10}$ of 30 = ___?___

11. $\frac{2}{3}$ of 18 = ___?___

12. $\frac{4}{6}$ of 36 = ___?___

13. $\frac{5}{10}$ of 40 = ___?___

14. $\frac{1}{4}$ of 28 = ___?___

15. $\frac{5}{6}$ of 30 = ___?___

16. $\frac{7}{10}$ of 50 = ___?___

17. $\frac{3}{4}$ of 32 = ___?___

18. $\frac{3}{5}$ of 45 = ___?___

19. $\frac{3}{8}$ of 32 = ___?___

20. $\frac{4}{5}$ of 30 = ___?___

A FISH STORY

Pat and Marty have
24 tropical fish. $\frac{3}{4}$ of them
are guppies. How many
of the fish are guppies?

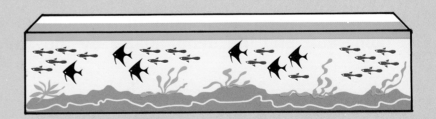

173

Equivalent Fractions

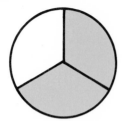

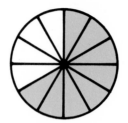

Cut a pie into thirds.
$\frac{2}{3}$ of it is yours.

Cut a pie into twelfths.
$\frac{8}{12}$ of it is yours.

In both cases, you get the same amount of pie.
$\frac{2}{3}$ and $\frac{8}{12}$ are equivalent fractions. $\frac{2}{3} = \frac{8}{12}$
Equivalent fractions name the same number.

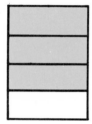

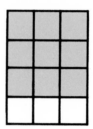

Cut a cake into fourths.
$\frac{3}{4}$ of it is yours.

Cut a cake into twelfths.
$\frac{9}{12}$ of it is yours.

In both cases, you get the same amount of cake.
$\frac{3}{4}$ and $\frac{9}{12}$ are equivalent fractions. $\frac{3}{4} = \frac{9}{12}$

**To find an equivalent fraction, you can multiply the
numerator and the denominator by the same number.**

$$\frac{2}{3} = \frac{4 \times 2}{4 \times 3} = \frac{8}{12} \qquad \frac{3}{4} = \frac{3 \times 3}{3 \times 4} = \frac{9}{12}$$

174

Multiply the numerator and the denominator by 2 to find an equivalent fraction.

1. $\frac{1}{3} = \frac{2 \times 1}{2 \times 3} = \underline{\ ?\ }$

2. $\frac{1}{5}$

3. $\frac{2}{3}$

4. $\frac{3}{4}$

5. $\frac{5}{8}$

Multiply the numerator and the denominator by 5 to find an equivalent fraction.

6. $\frac{3}{4} = \frac{5 \times 3}{5 \times 4} = \underline{\ ?\ }$

7. $\frac{2}{4}$

8. $\frac{5}{6}$

9. $\frac{3}{8}$

10. $\frac{4}{10}$

Multiply the numerator and the denominator by 3 to find an equivalent fraction.

11. $\frac{1}{4}$

12. $\frac{2}{3}$

13. $\frac{3}{6}$

14. $\frac{2}{5}$

15. $\frac{1}{2}$

16. $\frac{7}{8}$

Multiply the numerator and the denominator by 4 to find an equivalent fraction.

17. $\frac{2}{3}$

18. $\frac{3}{4}$

19. $\frac{7}{10}$

20. $\frac{3}{8}$

21. $\frac{2}{5}$

22. $\frac{3}{6}$

Multiply the numerator and the denominator by 10 to find an equivalent fraction.

23. $\frac{2}{8}$

24. $\frac{1}{2}$

25. $\frac{4}{5}$

26. $\frac{4}{6}$

27. $\frac{2}{3}$

28. $\frac{3}{4}$

A PIECE OF CAKE

Abe and Andrew went to a party.
Cake was served.
Abe ate $\frac{1}{8}$ of the cake.
Andrew had 2 smaller pieces.
He ate $\frac{2}{16}$ of the cake.
Who ate more cake?

175

Finding Equivalent Fractions

David and Denise are baking a cake.
Each will get $\frac{1}{2}$.

When it is baked, they will cut it
into 8 pieces of the same size.
How many eighths should each get?

$$\frac{1}{2} = \frac{?}{8}$$

Think: What times 2 is 8?
Since 4 times 2 = 8,
multiply the numerator by 4.
Each should get $\frac{4}{8}$ of the cake.

$$\frac{1}{2} = \frac{4 \times 1}{4 \times 2} = \frac{4}{8}$$

Make the fractions equivalent.

$$\frac{2}{3} = \frac{?}{15} \qquad\qquad \frac{3}{4} = \frac{?}{12}$$

Think:

$? \times 3 = 15$

$$\frac{2}{3} = \frac{5 \times 2}{5 \times 3} = \frac{10}{15}$$

Think:

$? \times 4 = 12$

$$\frac{3}{4} = \frac{3 \times 3}{3 \times 4} = \frac{9}{12}$$

176

Copy and complete to make the fractions equivalent.

1. $\frac{1}{2} = \frac{?}{4}$ 2. $\frac{1}{3} = \frac{?}{6}$ 3. $\frac{2}{4} = \frac{?}{8}$ 4. $\frac{3}{5} = \frac{?}{10}$

— now do these

Make the fractions equivalent.

5. $\frac{2}{3} = \frac{?}{6}$ 6. $\frac{1}{5} = \frac{?}{10}$ 7. $\frac{4}{6} = \frac{?}{12}$ 8. $\frac{4}{8} = \frac{?}{16}$

9. $\frac{3}{4} = \frac{?}{8}$ 10. $\frac{1}{3} = \frac{?}{12}$ 11. $\frac{5}{8} = \frac{?}{16}$ 12. $\frac{2}{5} = \frac{?}{15}$

13. $\frac{2}{5} = \frac{?}{10}$ 14. $\frac{2}{3} = \frac{?}{9}$ 15. $\frac{1}{4} = \frac{?}{12}$ 16. $\frac{7}{8} = \frac{?}{16}$

17. $\frac{1}{2} = \frac{?}{10}$ 18. $\frac{4}{5} = \frac{?}{15}$ 19. $\frac{2}{4} = \frac{?}{16}$ 20. $\frac{4}{5} = \frac{?}{10}$

21. $\frac{1}{4} = \frac{?}{8}$ 22. $\frac{3}{5} = \frac{?}{15}$ 23. $\frac{1}{3} = \frac{?}{15}$ 24. $\frac{5}{6} = \frac{?}{12}$

25. $\frac{3}{8} = \frac{?}{16}$ 26. $\frac{2}{6} = \frac{?}{12}$ 27. $\frac{1}{2} = \frac{?}{6}$ 28. $\frac{2}{3} = \frac{?}{12}$

FROM HERE TO THERE

Amy rides her bicycle to school.
The distance is 2500 meters.
She is $\frac{3}{5}$ of the way there.
How many meters is this?

$$\frac{3}{5} = \frac{?}{2500}$$

177

Simplest Name

$\frac{1}{2}$, $\frac{2}{4}$, and $\frac{4}{8}$ are equivalent fractions.

To find an equivalent fraction, you can divide the numerator and the denominator by the same number.

$$\frac{2}{4} = \frac{2 \div 2}{4 \div 2} = \frac{1}{2} \qquad \frac{4}{8} = \frac{4 \div 4}{8 \div 4} = \frac{1}{2}$$

$\frac{1}{2}$ is the **simplest name** for $\frac{1}{2}$, $\frac{2}{4}$, and $\frac{4}{8}$.

A fraction is the simplest name when the numerator and the denominator have no common factor greater than 1.

Find the simplest name for $\frac{12}{16}$.

Step 1 Find the greatest common factor of 12 and 16.

$$12 \longrightarrow 1, 2, 3, 4, 6, 12$$
$$16 \longrightarrow 1, 2, 4, 8, 16$$

Step 2 Divide the numerator and the denominator by 4.
$$\frac{12}{16} = \frac{12 \div 4}{16 \div 4} = \frac{3}{4}$$

The simplest name for $\frac{12}{16}$ is $\frac{3}{4}$.

178

Divide the numerator and the denominator by 2
to find the simplest name.

1. $\frac{4}{8}$
2. $\frac{6}{16}$
3. $\frac{2}{8}$
4. $\frac{6}{10}$
5. $\frac{10}{32}$
6. $\frac{18}{32}$

Find the greatest common factor.

7. 4 and 16
8. 6 and 8
9. 12 and 16

Write the simplest name.

10. $\frac{4}{16}$
11. $\frac{4}{8}$
12. $\frac{12}{16}$
13. $\frac{10}{12}$
14. $\frac{12}{15}$
15. $\frac{8}{10}$

now do these

Find the greatest common factor.

16. 18 and 24
17. 16 and 36
18. 27 and 24
19. 12 and 21
20. 36 and 28
21. 16 and 24
22. 36 and 27
23. 12 and 32
24. 28 and 12
25. 29 and 42
26. 18 and 42
27. 12 and 27

Write the simplest name.

28. $\frac{8}{12}$
29. $\frac{14}{16}$
30. $\frac{4}{10}$
31. $\frac{9}{12}$
32. $\frac{10}{15}$
33. $\frac{10}{20}$

34. $\frac{16}{32}$
35. $\frac{6}{9}$
36. $\frac{24}{36}$
37. $\frac{21}{28}$
38. $\frac{15}{25}$
39. $\frac{8}{16}$

40. $\frac{6}{8}$
41. $\frac{24}{27}$
42. $\frac{18}{32}$
43. $\frac{14}{20}$
44. $\frac{14}{28}$
45. $\frac{15}{30}$

Least Common Denominator

 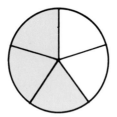

Which is greater?

$\frac{2}{5}$ or $\frac{3}{5}$

Which is greater?

$\frac{3}{5}$ or $\frac{2}{3}$

It is easier to compare fractions when
both have the same denominator.

You can rename fractions to have the same denominator.
You can use the **least common denominator** for $\frac{3}{5}$ and $\frac{2}{3}$.

Step 1 Find the least common multiple of the denominators.
This multiple is the least common denominator.

3 ⟶ 3, 6, 9, 12, 15

5 ⟶ 5, 10, 15

Step 2 Rename the fractions. Use 15 as the denominator.

$$\frac{3}{5} = \frac{?}{15}$$

Think: $\underline{\ ?\ } \times 5 = 15$

$$\frac{3}{5} = \frac{3 \times 3}{3 \times 5} = \frac{9}{15}$$

$$\frac{2}{3} = \frac{?}{15}$$

Think: $\underline{\ ?\ } \times 3 = 15$

$$\frac{2}{3} = \frac{5 \times 2}{5 \times 3} = \frac{10}{15}$$

Since $\frac{10}{15} > \frac{9}{15}$, then $\frac{2}{3} > \frac{3}{5}$.

Find the least common multiple.

1. 4, 8   **2.** 5, 10   **3.** 6, 9   **4.** 10, 15

Find the least common denominator. Rename the fractions.

5. $\frac{3}{4}, \frac{5}{8}$ **6.** $\frac{2}{5}, \frac{3}{10}$ **7.** $\frac{5}{6}, \frac{1}{9}$ **8.** $\frac{7}{10}, \frac{8}{15}$

now do these

Find the least common denominator. Rename the fractions.

9. $\frac{2}{5}, \frac{7}{8}$ **10.** $\frac{1}{2}, \frac{3}{4}$ **11.** $\frac{5}{6}, \frac{3}{4}$ **12.** $\frac{2}{3}, \frac{5}{9}$

13. $\frac{2}{3}, \frac{5}{6}$ **14.** $\frac{1}{5}, \frac{1}{3}$ **15.** $\frac{1}{4}, \frac{2}{7}$ **16.** $\frac{3}{4}, \frac{2}{3}$

17. $\frac{2}{3}, \frac{1}{7}$ **18.** $\frac{3}{4}, \frac{4}{5}$ **19.** $\frac{1}{3}, \frac{5}{8}$ **20.** $\frac{3}{5}, \frac{4}{6}$

Write > or <.

21. $\frac{3}{4} \bigcirc \frac{5}{8}$ **22.** $\frac{3}{5} \bigcirc \frac{3}{4}$ **23.** $\frac{5}{6} \bigcirc \frac{5}{8}$ **24.** $\frac{2}{7} \bigcirc \frac{2}{3}$

25. $\frac{2}{3} \bigcirc \frac{9}{15}$ **26.** $\frac{8}{12} \bigcirc \frac{5}{8}$ **27.** $\frac{1}{2} \bigcirc \frac{9}{16}$ **28.** $\frac{3}{4} \bigcirc \frac{7}{10}$

quick check

Complete the sentence.

1. $\frac{1}{5}$ of 25 = $\underline{\ ?\ }$

2. $\frac{3}{8}$ of 48 = $\underline{\ ?\ }$

3. $\frac{9}{10}$ of 80 = $\underline{\ ?\ }$

Make the fractions equivalent.

4. $\frac{3}{4} = \frac{?}{16}$

5. $\frac{1}{5} = \frac{?}{15}$

6. $\frac{5}{8} = \frac{?}{24}$

Write the simplest name.

7. $\frac{4}{12}$

8. $\frac{18}{20}$

9. $\frac{35}{45}$

10. $\frac{32}{48}$

Addition and Subtraction

Juan ate $\frac{3}{8}$ of the pie.
Bruce ate $\frac{1}{8}$.

How much did they eat in all?

$$\frac{3}{8} + \frac{1}{8} = \ ?$$

When the denominators are the same, add the numerators.

$$\frac{3}{8} + \frac{1}{8} = \frac{4}{8}$$

What is the simplest name for $\frac{4}{8}$?
So, the boys ate $\frac{1}{2}$ of the pie altogether.

$\frac{4}{8}$ of a pie is on a plate.
Anita ate $\frac{2}{8}$.

How much is left?

$$\frac{4}{8} - \frac{2}{8} = \ ?$$

When the denominators are the same, subtract the numerators.

$$\frac{4}{8} - \frac{2}{8} = \frac{2}{8}$$

What is the simplest name for $\frac{2}{8}$?
So, $\frac{1}{4}$ of the pie is left.

try these

Add. Write the simplest name for the answer.

1. $\frac{5}{8} + \frac{2}{8} = \underline{}$

2. $\frac{1}{6} + \frac{3}{6} = \underline{}$

3. $\frac{1}{4} + \frac{1}{4} = \underline{}$

Subtract. Write the simplest name for the answer.

4. $\frac{7}{8} - \frac{3}{8} = \underline{}$

5. $\frac{5}{6} - \frac{2}{6} = \underline{}$

6. $\frac{7}{10} - \frac{2}{10} = \underline{}$

now do these

Add. Write the simplest name for the answer.

7. $\frac{3}{6} + \frac{2}{6} = \underline{}$

8. $\frac{1}{4} + \frac{2}{4} = \underline{}$

9. $\frac{2}{5} + \frac{2}{5} = \underline{}$

10. $\frac{5}{10} + \frac{3}{10} = \underline{}$

11. $\frac{3}{8} + \frac{3}{8} = \underline{}$

12. $\frac{4}{9} + \frac{2}{9} = \underline{}$

Subtract. Write the simplest name for the answer.

13. $\frac{4}{5} - \frac{3}{5} = \underline{}$

14. $\frac{5}{6} - \frac{1}{6} = \underline{}$

15. $\frac{3}{4} - \frac{2}{4} = \underline{}$

16. $\frac{8}{9} - \frac{5}{9} = \underline{}$

17. $\frac{9}{10} - \frac{7}{10} = \underline{}$

18. $\frac{7}{8} - \frac{5}{8} = \underline{}$

SEE YOU LATER

The time is 3:00.
One-half hour later it will be 3:30.

Look at the clock.
What time will it be one-half hour later?

A.

B.

C.

D.

183

Addition with Unlike Denominators

Charles ate $\frac{1}{4}$ of the pie.

Pablo ate $\frac{1}{6}$ of the pie.

How much did they eat in all?

$$\frac{1}{4} + \frac{1}{6} = ?$$

When the denominators are not the same,
rename the fractions to have the same denominator.
Use the least common denominator.

You want to add. ⟶ $\frac{1}{4} + \frac{1}{6}$

Step 1 Find the least common denominator. ⟶ $\frac{}{12} + \frac{}{12}$

$$4 \longrightarrow 4, 8, 12$$
$$6 \longrightarrow 6, 12$$

Step 2 Rename the fractions. ⟶ $\frac{3}{12} + \frac{2}{12}$

$$\frac{1}{4} = \frac{?}{12} \qquad \frac{1}{6} = \frac{?}{12}$$

Step 3 Add the numerators. ⟶ $\frac{3}{12} + \frac{2}{12} = \frac{5}{12}$
The denominator is 12.

Charles and Pablo ate $\frac{5}{12}$ of the pie.

184

Find the least common denominator.

1. $\frac{3}{4}, \frac{1}{8}$ **2.** $\frac{1}{3}, \frac{2}{5}$ **3.** $\frac{1}{6}, \frac{3}{8}$

Add.

4. $\frac{3}{4} + \frac{1}{8} = \underline{\ ?\ }$ **5.** $\frac{1}{3} + \frac{2}{5} = \underline{\ ?\ }$ **6.** $\frac{1}{6} + \frac{3}{8} = \underline{\ ?\ }$

now do these

Add.

7. $\frac{3}{4} + \frac{2}{12} = \underline{\ ?\ }$ **8.** $\frac{3}{10} + \frac{2}{5} = \underline{\ ?\ }$ **9.** $\frac{3}{8} + \frac{1}{6} = \underline{\ ?\ }$

10. $\frac{3}{6} + \frac{4}{9} = \underline{\ ?\ }$ **11.** $\frac{1}{4} + \frac{3}{16} = \underline{\ ?\ }$ **12.** $\frac{3}{8} + \frac{5}{16} = \underline{\ ?\ }$

13. $\frac{3}{4} + \frac{1}{6} = \underline{\ ?\ }$ **14.** $\frac{3}{8} + \frac{1}{4} = \underline{\ ?\ }$ **15.** $\frac{5}{9} + \frac{1}{3} = \underline{\ ?\ }$

16. $\frac{1}{2} + \frac{1}{3} = \underline{\ ?\ }$ **17.** $\frac{1}{4} + \frac{1}{3} = \underline{\ ?\ }$ **18.** $\frac{2}{5} + \frac{1}{2} = \underline{\ ?\ }$

19. $\frac{3}{5} + \frac{3}{10} = \underline{\ ?\ }$ **20.** $\frac{2}{3} + \frac{1}{6} = \underline{\ ?\ }$ **21.** $\frac{3}{5} + \frac{2}{15} = \underline{\ ?\ }$

SEE YOU LATER

The time is 3:00.
One-quarter hour later it will be 3:15.

Look at the clock.
What time will it be one-quarter hour later?

A.    **B.**    **C.**    **D.**

Subtraction With Unlike Denominators

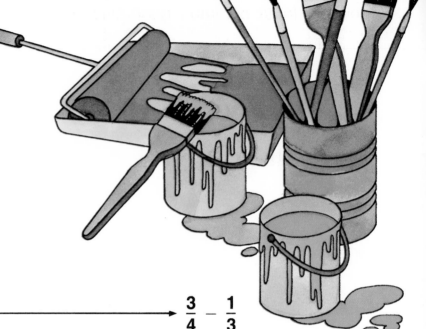

Dan is painting a mural on $\frac{3}{4}$ of the wall. So far, he has painted $\frac{1}{3}$ of the wall. What part of the wall does he still have to paint?

$$\frac{3}{4} - \frac{1}{3} = \ ?$$

You want to subtract. ⟶ $\frac{3}{4} - \frac{1}{3}$

Step 1 Find the least common denominator. ⟶ $\overline{12} - \overline{12}$

$$4 \longrightarrow 4, 8, 12$$
$$3 \longrightarrow 3, 6, 9, 12$$

Step 2 Rename the fractions. ⟶ $\frac{9}{12} - \frac{4}{12}$

$$\frac{3}{4} = \frac{?}{12} \qquad \frac{1}{3} = \frac{?}{12}$$

Step 3 Subtract the numerators. ⟶ $\frac{9}{12} - \frac{4}{12} = \frac{5}{12}$
The denominator is 12.

Dan still has $\frac{5}{12}$ of the wall to paint.

Find the least common denominator.

1. $\frac{3}{4}, \frac{3}{8}$

2. $\frac{3}{4}, \frac{5}{16}$

3. $\frac{7}{8}, \frac{1}{12}$

Subtract.

4. $\frac{3}{4} - \frac{3}{8} = \underline{\ ?\ }$

5. $\frac{3}{4} - \frac{5}{16} = \underline{\ ?\ }$

6. $\frac{7}{8} - \frac{1}{12} = \underline{\ ?\ }$

now do these

Subtract.

7. $\frac{3}{4} - \frac{1}{6} = \underline{\ ?\ }$

8. $\frac{7}{10} - \frac{2}{5} = \underline{\ ?\ }$

9. $\frac{7}{8} - \frac{3}{4} = \underline{\ ?\ }$

10. $\frac{5}{6} - \frac{5}{12} = \underline{\ ?\ }$

11. $\frac{3}{5} - \frac{3}{10} = \underline{\ ?\ }$

12. $\frac{2}{3} - \frac{3}{5} = \underline{\ ?\ }$

13. $\frac{11}{12} - \frac{5}{6} = \underline{\ ?\ }$

14. $\frac{3}{4} - \frac{1}{3} = \underline{\ ?\ }$

15. $\frac{5}{8} - \frac{2}{6} = \underline{\ ?\ }$

16. $\frac{13}{16} - \frac{3}{4} = \underline{\ ?\ }$

17. $\frac{9}{10} - \frac{3}{5} = \underline{\ ?\ }$

18. $\frac{7}{12} - \frac{1}{3} = \underline{\ ?\ }$

19. $\frac{5}{9} - \frac{1}{3} = \underline{\ ?\ }$

20. $\frac{5}{6} - \frac{1}{4} = \underline{\ ?\ }$

21. $\frac{4}{5} - \frac{1}{3} = \underline{\ ?\ }$

SEE YOU LATER

The time is 3:00.
Three-quarters of an hour later it will be 3:45.

Look at the clock.
What time will it be three-quarters of an hour later?

A.

B.

C.

D.

Another Way

Ron ate $\frac{1}{4}$ of a pie on Tuesday.
He ate $\frac{2}{5}$ of a pie on Wednesday.
How much did he eat on both days?

$$\frac{1}{4} + \frac{2}{5} = \ ?$$

Addition can be shown another way.

Step 1

$$\frac{1}{4}$$

$$+\frac{2}{5}$$

Write the fractions.

Step 2

$$\frac{1}{4} = \frac{5}{20}$$

$$+\frac{2}{5} = \frac{8}{20}$$

Find the least common denominator. Rename the fractions.

Step 3

$$\frac{1}{4} = \frac{5}{20}$$

$$+\frac{2}{5} = \frac{8}{20}$$

$$\frac{13}{20}$$

Add the numerators.

Subtract $\frac{2}{5}$ from $\frac{7}{10}$.

Step 1

$$\frac{7}{10}$$

$$-\frac{2}{5}$$

Write the fractions.

Step 2

$$\frac{7}{10} = \frac{7}{10}$$

$$-\frac{2}{5} = \frac{4}{10}$$

Find the least common denominator. Rename the fractions.

Step 3

$$\frac{7}{10} = \frac{7}{10}$$

$$-\frac{2}{5} = \frac{4}{10}$$

$$\frac{3}{10}$$

Subtract the numerators.

Add.

1. $\dfrac{1}{4}$
$+\dfrac{3}{8}$

2. $\dfrac{1}{3}$
$+\dfrac{2}{6}$

3. $\dfrac{2}{5}$
$+\dfrac{4}{10}$

4. $\dfrac{1}{2}$
$+\dfrac{2}{5}$

5. $\dfrac{1}{4}$
$+\dfrac{4}{6}$

6. $\dfrac{2}{3}$
$+\dfrac{1}{4}$

Subtract.

7. $\dfrac{15}{16}$
$-\dfrac{7}{8}$

8. $\dfrac{11}{12}$
$-\dfrac{2}{3}$

9. $\dfrac{13}{15}$
$-\dfrac{4}{5}$

10. $\dfrac{5}{6}$
$-\dfrac{3}{8}$

11. $\dfrac{3}{4}$
$-\dfrac{2}{3}$

12. $\dfrac{2}{3}$
$-\dfrac{3}{5}$

Add.

13. $\dfrac{2}{3}$
$+\dfrac{2}{9}$

14. $\dfrac{3}{5}$
$+\dfrac{2}{10}$

15. $\dfrac{3}{4}$
$+\dfrac{2}{12}$

16. $\dfrac{5}{8}$
$+\dfrac{3}{16}$

17. $\dfrac{2}{3}$
$+\dfrac{3}{12}$

18. $\dfrac{7}{15}$
$+\dfrac{2}{5}$

19. $\dfrac{1}{4}$
$+\dfrac{5}{10}$

20. $\dfrac{2}{3}$
$+\dfrac{1}{5}$

21. $\dfrac{1}{2}$
$+\dfrac{2}{9}$

22. $\dfrac{2}{6}$
$+\dfrac{1}{4}$

23. $\dfrac{1}{6}$
$+\dfrac{5}{8}$

24. $\dfrac{5}{6}$
$+\dfrac{1}{9}$

Subtract.

25. $\dfrac{5}{6}$
$-\dfrac{5}{8}$

26. $\dfrac{3}{4}$
$-\dfrac{1}{6}$

27. $\dfrac{5}{8}$
$-\dfrac{1}{3}$

28. $\dfrac{2}{3}$
$-\dfrac{1}{4}$

29. $\dfrac{5}{6}$
$-\dfrac{1}{4}$

30. $\dfrac{4}{5}$
$-\dfrac{2}{3}$

31. $\dfrac{11}{12}$
$-\dfrac{3}{4}$

32. $\dfrac{13}{16}$
$-\dfrac{5}{8}$

33. $\dfrac{13}{15}$
$-\dfrac{2}{3}$

34. $\dfrac{15}{16}$
$-\dfrac{3}{4}$

35. $\dfrac{11}{15}$
$-\dfrac{3}{5}$

36. $\dfrac{11}{12}$
$-\dfrac{2}{3}$

Test

What part is red? Write the fraction.

1. 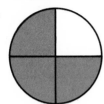 (p. 168)

2.
(p. 170)

3.
(p. 170)

Complete the sentence.

4. $\frac{1}{3}$ of 21 = ___?___ (p. 172)   **5.** $\frac{3}{5}$ of 45 = ___?___ (p. 172)   **6.** $\frac{7}{8}$ of 16 = ___?___ (p. 172)

Make the fractions equivalent.

7. $\frac{2}{3} = \frac{?}{6}$ (p. 176)   **8.** $\frac{3}{5} = \frac{?}{10}$ (p. 176)   **9.** $\frac{6}{8} = \frac{?}{16}$ (p. 176)

Write the simplest name.

10. $\frac{9}{15}$ (p. 178)   **11.** $\frac{6}{8}$ (p. 178)   **12.** $\frac{4}{32}$ (p. 178)

Write > or <.

13. $\frac{3}{5}$ ● $\frac{2}{4}$ (p. 180)   **14.** $\frac{7}{15}$ ● $\frac{2}{3}$ (p. 180)   **15.** $\frac{5}{8}$ ● $\frac{7}{16}$ (p. 180)

Add. Write the simplest name for the answer.

16. $\frac{8}{12} + \frac{2}{12}$ = ___?___ (p. 182)   **17.** $\frac{4}{15} + \frac{1}{15}$ = ___?___ (p. 182)   **18.** $\frac{1}{4} + \frac{2}{3}$ = ___?___ (p. 184)

19. $\frac{5}{6} + \frac{1}{9}$ = ___?___ (p. 184)   **20.** $\frac{1}{10} + \frac{8}{15}$ = ___?___ (p. 184)

Subtract. Write the simplest name for the answer.

21. $\frac{10}{12} - \frac{3}{12}$ = ___?___ (p. 182)   **22.** $\frac{7}{8} - \frac{3}{8}$ = ___?___ (p. 182)   **23.** $\frac{7}{8} - \frac{3}{4}$ = ___?___ (p. 186)

24. $\frac{8}{15} - \frac{5}{10}$ = ___?___ (p. 186)   **25.** $\frac{5}{6} - \frac{5}{9}$ = ___?___ (p. 186)

Keeping up

Find the greatest common factor.

1. 16, 12 (p. 160) **2.** 15, 9 (p. 160) **3.** 18, 24 (p. 160) **4.** 27, 36 (p. 160)

Find the least common multiple.

5. 6, 4 (p. 162) **6.** 3, 9 (p. 162) **7.** 8, 6 (p. 162) **8.** 15, 25 (p. 162)

Add.

9.
```
  689
  247
  965
+ 907
```
(p. 34)

10.
```
 8335
 2719
  827
+3419
```
(p. 34)

11.
```
 1087
 3082
+5917
```
(p. 34)

12.
```
   56
  387
+8498
```
(p. 34)

Subtract.

13.
```
 3705
-3647
```
(p. 54)

14.
```
 6077
- 369
```
(p. 54)

15.
```
 9000
-7896
```
(p. 56)

16.
```
 1800
- 739
```
(p. 56)

Multiply.

17.
```
 8767
×   8
```
(p. 78)

18.
```
 7609
×  78
```
(p. 84)

19.
```
  790
×480
```
(p. 86)

20.
```
  789
×705
```
(p. 86)

Divide.

(p. 122) (p. 122) (p. 122) (p. 122)

21. 7)2702 **22.** 9)3681 **23.** 6)3954 **24.** 8)3760

(p. 146) (p. 144) (p. 144) (p. 146)

25. 65)4169 **26.** 82)7268 **27.** 74)6587 **28.** 26)1698

191

Flow Charts

The steps for doing something can be shown in a **flow chart.**
The flow chart below is for adding fractions.

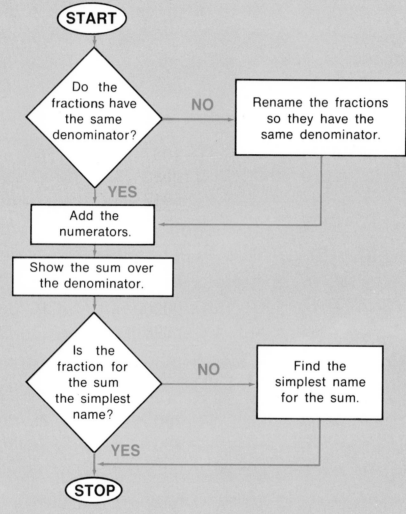

What shape are the boxes with questions?
What shape are the boxes with directions?

If your answer for the first question
in the flow chart is NO, what do you do?
If your answer is YES, what do you do?

If your answer for the second question is NO, what do you do?
If your answer is YES, what do you do?

192 *Enrichment*

10 Mixed Numerals

Fractions and One

There are 2 halves in 1.

$$\frac{2}{2} = 1$$

There are 4 fourths in 1.

$$\frac{4}{4} = 1$$

There are 3 thirds in 1.

$$\frac{3}{3} = 1$$

There are 5 fifths in 1.

$$\frac{5}{5} = 1$$

A fraction names 1 when the numerator and the denominator are the same.

Write the fraction.

1. $\frac{?}{2} = 1$

2. $\frac{?}{4} = 1$

3. $\frac{?}{8} = 1$

4. $\frac{?}{16} = 1$

5. $\frac{?}{3} = 1$

6. $\frac{?}{5} = 1$

7. $\frac{?}{10} = 1$

8. $\frac{?}{6} = 1$

9. $\frac{?}{7} = 1$

10. $\frac{?}{20} = 1$

11. $\frac{?}{25} = 1$

12. $\frac{?}{50} = 1$

Fractions and Whole Numbers

 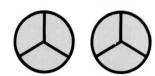

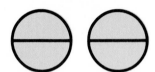 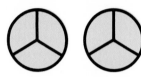

There are 6 halves in 3.

$$\frac{6}{2} = 3$$

There are 12 thirds in 4.

$$\frac{12}{3} = 4$$

There are 8 fourths in 2.

$$\frac{8}{4} = 2$$

A fraction names a whole number when the numerator is a multiple of the denominator.

What whole number is named by $\frac{15}{5}$?

$$\frac{15}{5} = ?$$

To find the whole number, think:
15 divided by 5 is what number?

$15 \div 5 = 3$, so

$$\frac{15}{5} = 3$$

How many fourths are there in 6?

$$\frac{?}{4} = 6$$

To find the numerator, think:
what number divided by 4 is 6?

$24 \div 4 = 6$, so

$$\frac{24}{4} = 6$$

194

Write the numeral for a whole number.

1. $\frac{12}{4} = \underline{\ ?\ }$ 2. $\frac{24}{6} = \underline{\ ?\ }$ 3. $\frac{14}{2} = \underline{\ ?\ }$ 4. $\frac{28}{7} = \underline{\ ?\ }$

Write the fraction.

5. $\frac{?}{3} = 4$ 6. $\frac{?}{8} = 7$ 7. $\frac{?}{6} = 3$ 8. $\frac{?}{5} = 4$

now do these

Write the numeral for a whole number.

9. $\frac{6}{2} = \underline{\ ?\ }$ 10. $\frac{12}{4} = \underline{\ ?\ }$ 11. $\frac{24}{8} = \underline{\ ?\ }$ 12. $\frac{48}{16} = \underline{\ ?\ }$

13. $\frac{10}{2} = \underline{\ ?\ }$ 14. $\frac{16}{4} = \underline{\ ?\ }$ 15. $\frac{40}{8} = \underline{\ ?\ }$ 16. $\frac{32}{16} = \underline{\ ?\ }$

17. $\frac{10}{5} = \underline{\ ?\ }$ 18. $\frac{45}{5} = \underline{\ ?\ }$ 19. $\frac{30}{10} = \underline{\ ?\ }$ 20. $\frac{50}{10} = \underline{\ ?\ }$

Write the fraction.

21. $\frac{?}{2} = 4$ 22. $\frac{?}{4} = 4$ 23. $\frac{?}{8} = 4$ 24. $\frac{?}{16} = 4$

25. $\frac{?}{2} = 6$ 26. $\frac{?}{4} = 6$ 27. $\frac{?}{8} = 6$ 28. $\frac{?}{16} = 6$

29. $\frac{?}{5} = 3$ 30. $\frac{?}{5} = 7$ 31. $\frac{?}{10} = 4$ 32. $\frac{?}{10} = 9$

JUST FOR A CHANGE

A. Janice has 41¢ in her pocket. She has 4 coins. What are the coins?

B. Marco has 62¢ in his pocket. He has 6 coins. What are the coins?

C. Louise has 67¢ in her pocket. She has 9 coins. What are the coins?

195

Mixed Numerals

Some numbers can be named with a **mixed numeral.**

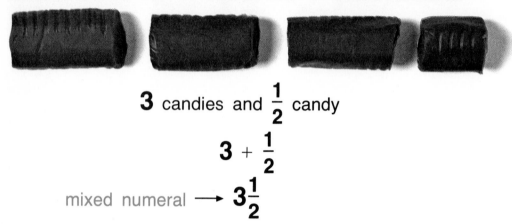

3 candies and $\dfrac{1}{2}$ candy

$3 + \dfrac{1}{2}$

mixed numeral $\longrightarrow$ $3\dfrac{1}{2}$

Each unit is marked in fourths. How long is the pencil?

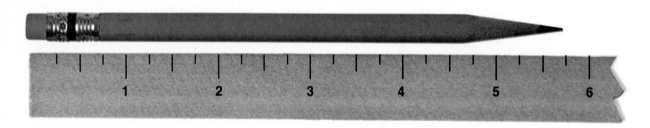

5 units and $\dfrac{3}{4}$ unit

$5 + \dfrac{3}{4}$

$5\dfrac{3}{4}$

196

Write a mixed numeral.

1. 7 and $\frac{5}{6}$ 2. 4 and $\frac{1}{2}$ 3. 7 and $\frac{3}{4}$ 4. 5 and $\frac{7}{8}$

5. $3 + \frac{9}{10}$ 6. $6 + \frac{2}{3}$ 7. $2 + \frac{5}{16}$ 8. $12 + \frac{1}{4}$

now do these

Write a mixed numeral.

9. 8 and $\frac{1}{16}$ 10. 2 and $\frac{5}{8}$ 11. 9 and $\frac{2}{3}$ 12. 5 and $\frac{1}{2}$

13. 9 and $\frac{7}{8}$ 14. 10 and $\frac{4}{9}$ 15. 4 and $\frac{3}{10}$ 16. 3 and $\frac{4}{5}$

17. $3 + \frac{9}{10}$ 18. $4 + \frac{3}{5}$ 19. $2 + \frac{1}{3}$ 20. $5 + \frac{7}{8}$

21. $8 + \frac{4}{5}$ 22. $7 + \frac{1}{2}$ 23. $6 + \frac{15}{16}$ 24. $1 + \frac{1}{4}$

25. What number is three-fourths of the way from 1 to 2?

26. What number is five-eighths of the way from 2 to 3?

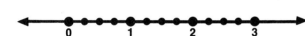

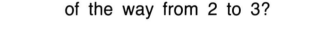

 TIME OUT

The time is 3:00.
In $1\frac{1}{2}$ hours, the time will be 4:30.

Look at the clock.
What time will it be in $1\frac{1}{2}$ hours?

A.   B.   C.   D.

197

Mixed Numerals and Fractions

How many pies?

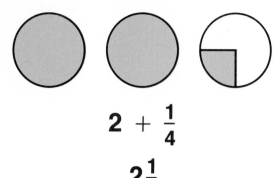

$$2 + \frac{1}{4}$$

$$2\frac{1}{4}$$

How many fourths?

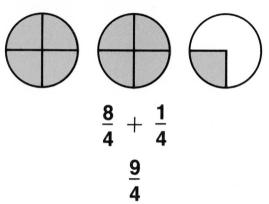

$$\frac{8}{4} + \frac{1}{4}$$

$$\frac{9}{4}$$

Write a fraction for $2\frac{1}{4}$.

Step 1 Think of addition. ⟶	$2 + \frac{1}{4}$
Step 2 Name 2 using fourths. ⟶	$\frac{8}{4} + \frac{1}{4}$
Step 3 Add. ⟶	$\frac{9}{4}$

Write a fraction for $3\frac{1}{5}$.

Step 1 Think of addition. ⟶	$3 + \frac{1}{5}$
Step 2 Name 3 using fifths. ⟶	$\frac{15}{5} + \frac{1}{5}$
Step 3 Add. ⟶	$\frac{16}{5}$

Write the fraction.

1. $3 + \frac{1}{2}$

   $\frac{6}{2} + \frac{1}{2}$

   $\underline{\quad ? \quad}$

2. $4 + \frac{1}{3}$

   $\frac{12}{3} + \frac{1}{3}$

   $\underline{\quad ? \quad}$

3. $1 + \frac{4}{5}$

   $\frac{5}{5} + \frac{4}{5}$

   $\underline{\quad ? \quad}$

4. $2 + \frac{3}{8}$

   $\frac{16}{8} + \frac{3}{8}$

   $\underline{\quad ? \quad}$

5. $1\frac{2}{3}$

6. $4\frac{3}{4}$

7. $2\frac{5}{8}$

8. $3\frac{2}{3}$

9. $1\frac{1}{3}$

10. $2\frac{2}{5}$

now do these

Write the fraction.

11. $1\frac{5}{8}$
12. $3\frac{5}{6}$
13. $6\frac{3}{4}$
14. $3\frac{3}{4}$
15. $4\frac{2}{3}$
16. $6\frac{3}{5}$

17. $5\frac{2}{3}$
18. $7\frac{1}{2}$
19. $1\frac{3}{4}$
20. $4\frac{4}{5}$
21. $2\frac{2}{3}$
22. $6\frac{2}{3}$

23. $2\frac{1}{5}$
24. $4\frac{1}{2}$
25. $1\frac{1}{2}$
26. $8\frac{1}{3}$
27. $1\frac{5}{6}$
28. $3\frac{1}{2}$

29. $2\frac{1}{2}$
30. $9\frac{1}{2}$
31. $6\frac{1}{3}$
32. $5\frac{1}{4}$
33. $3\frac{2}{5}$
34. $4\frac{4}{7}$

DO YOU HAVE THE TIME?

Each day has 24 hours.

   1 day (d) = 24 hours (h)

   2 days (d) = 48 hours (h)

   $\frac{1}{2}$ day (d) = 12 hours (h)

   $\frac{1}{4}$ day (d) = 6 hours (h)

Stone carved sundial.
Time about 1:30.

Complete.

A. 5 d = _?_ h   B. 7 d = _?_ h

C. $\frac{1}{4}$ d = _?_ h   D. $\frac{3}{4}$ d = _?_ h

E. 4 d = _?_ h   F. $2\frac{1}{2}$ d = _?_ h

G. $1\frac{1}{2}$ d = _?_ h   H. $2\frac{1}{4}$ d = _?_ h

199

Fractions and Mixed Numerals

How many fourths?

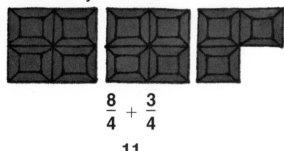

$$\frac{8}{4} + \frac{3}{4}$$

$$\frac{11}{4}$$

How many candy bars?

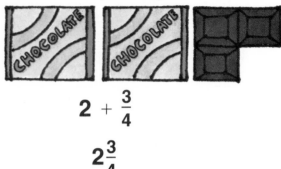

$$2 + \frac{3}{4}$$

$$2\frac{3}{4}$$

Write a mixed numeral for $\frac{11}{4}$.

Step 1 Find the number of wholes. ⟶ $\frac{11}{4}$
  Think: $\frac{4}{4}, \frac{8}{4}, \frac{12}{4}, \cdots$

Step 2 Rename the fraction. ⟶ $\frac{8}{4} + \frac{3}{4}$
  Think: $\frac{8}{4} + \frac{3}{4} = \frac{11}{4}$

Step 3 Rename the whole number. ⟶ $2 + \frac{3}{4}$

Step 4 Add. ⟶ $2\frac{3}{4}$

Write a mixed numeral for $\frac{14}{3}$.

Step 1 Find the number of wholes. ⟶ $\frac{14}{3}$
  Think: $\frac{3}{3}, \frac{6}{3}, \frac{9}{3}, \frac{12}{3}, \frac{15}{3}, \cdots$

Step 2 Rename the fraction. ⟶ $\frac{12}{3} + \frac{2}{3}$

Step 3 Rename the whole number. ⟶ $4 + \frac{2}{3}$

Step 4 Add. ⟶ $4\frac{2}{3}$

Write the mixed numeral.

1. $\frac{9}{8}$
   $\frac{8}{8} + \frac{1}{8}$
   $1 + \frac{1}{8}$
   $\underline{\quad?\quad}$

2. $\frac{7}{2}$
   $\frac{6}{2} + \frac{1}{2}$
   $3 + \frac{1}{2}$
   $\underline{\quad?\quad}$

3. $\frac{8}{3}$
   $\frac{6}{3} + \frac{2}{3}$
   $2 + \frac{2}{3}$
   $\underline{\quad?\quad}$

4. $\frac{19}{8}$
   $\frac{16}{8} + \frac{3}{8}$
   $2 + \frac{3}{8}$
   $\underline{\quad?\quad}$

5. $\frac{7}{3}$
6. $\frac{13}{3}$
7. $\frac{9}{5}$
8. $\frac{19}{4}$
9. $\frac{13}{4}$
10. $\frac{17}{5}$

Write the mixed numeral.

11. $\frac{16}{3}$
12. $\frac{11}{8}$
13. $\frac{3}{2}$
14. $\frac{15}{2}$
15. $\frac{15}{4}$
16. $\frac{19}{2}$

17. $\frac{11}{6}$
18. $\frac{5}{3}$
19. $\frac{12}{5}$
20. $\frac{17}{6}$
21. $\frac{22}{7}$
22. $\frac{21}{10}$

23. $\frac{24}{5}$
24. $\frac{13}{2}$
25. $\frac{10}{3}$
26. $\frac{9}{4}$
27. $\frac{17}{8}$
28. $\frac{14}{3}$

29. $\frac{15}{8}$
30. $\frac{11}{2}$
31. $\frac{8}{3}$
32. $\frac{9}{2}$
33. $\frac{5}{2}$
34. $\frac{28}{5}$

YEAR IN, YEAR OUT

Each year has 12 months.

1 year (yr) = 12 months (mo)

2 years (yr) = 24 months (mo)

$\frac{1}{2}$ year (yr) = 6 months (mo)

$\frac{1}{4}$ year (yr) = 3 months (mo)

Complete.

A. 4 yr = $\underline{\quad?\quad}$ mo
B. 10 yr = $\underline{\quad?\quad}$ mo
C. $\frac{1}{4}$ yr = $\underline{\quad?\quad}$ mo
D. $\frac{3}{4}$ yr = $\underline{\quad?\quad}$ mo
E. 5 yr = $\underline{\quad?\quad}$ mo
F. $1\frac{1}{4}$ yr = $\underline{\quad?\quad}$ mo
G. $1\frac{1}{2}$ yr = $\underline{\quad?\quad}$ mo
H. $2\frac{1}{2}$ yr = $\underline{\quad?\quad}$ mo

Dividing to Find Mixed Numerals

You know one way to find mixed numerals for fractions.

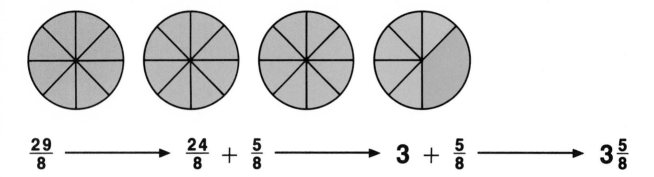

$$\frac{29}{8} \longrightarrow \frac{24}{8} + \frac{5}{8} \longrightarrow 3 + \frac{5}{8} \longrightarrow 3\frac{5}{8}$$

You can also divide to find the mixed numeral for $\frac{29}{8}$.

Step 1

$$\begin{array}{r} 3 \\ 8\overline{)29} \\ 24 \\ \hline 5 \end{array}$$

Divide the numerator
by the denominator.

Step 2

$$\begin{array}{r} 3\frac{5}{8} \\ 8\overline{)29} \\ 24 \\ \hline 5 \end{array}$$

Show the remainder in a fraction.
The remainder is the numerator.
The divisor is the denominator.

202

Divide. Show the remainder in a fraction.

1. $3\overline{)7}$ 2. $5\overline{)18}$ 3. $2\overline{)15}$ 4. $8\overline{)43}$ 5. $6\overline{)37}$ 6. $9\overline{)85}$

Write the mixed numeral. Use division.

7. $\frac{11}{2}$ 8. $\frac{27}{4}$ 9. $\frac{35}{8}$ 10. $\frac{17}{3}$ 11. $\frac{19}{2}$ 12. $\frac{25}{4}$

Divide to find the mixed numeral.

13. $\frac{11}{8}$ 14. $\frac{5}{2}$ 15. $\frac{11}{3}$ 16. $\frac{13}{5}$ 17. $\frac{7}{6}$ 18. $\frac{22}{7}$

19. $\frac{13}{2}$ 20. $\frac{20}{3}$ 21. $\frac{17}{4}$ 22. $\frac{33}{8}$ 23. $\frac{9}{2}$ 24. $\frac{10}{9}$

25. $\frac{7}{2}$ 26. $\frac{13}{2}$ 27. $\frac{13}{8}$ 28. $\frac{14}{3}$ 29. $\frac{25}{3}$ 30. $\frac{15}{2}$

31. $\frac{23}{5}$ 32. $\frac{9}{8}$ 33. $\frac{31}{5}$ 34. $\frac{25}{6}$ 35. $\frac{16}{5}$ 36. $\frac{21}{10}$

quick check

Write the fraction.

1. $4\frac{1}{2}$ 2. $6\frac{3}{4}$ 3. $5\frac{1}{6}$ 4. $8\frac{7}{10}$

Write the mixed numeral.

5. 3 and $\frac{5}{6}$ 6. $9 + \frac{7}{8}$ 7. $\frac{11}{2}$ 8. $\frac{35}{8}$

9. $\frac{24}{7}$ 10. $\frac{57}{10}$

203

Addition and Subtraction

Add: $3\frac{1}{8} + 2\frac{3}{8}$.

Step 1

$$3\frac{1}{8}$$
$$+2\frac{3}{8}$$
$$\overline{\frac{4}{8}}$$

Add $\frac{1}{8}$ and $\frac{3}{8}$.

Step 2

$$3\frac{1}{8}$$
$$+2\frac{3}{8}$$
$$\overline{5\frac{4}{8}}$$

Add 3 and 2.

Step 3

$$3\frac{1}{8}$$
$$+2\frac{3}{8}$$
$$\overline{5\frac{4}{8}} = 5\frac{1}{2}$$

Write the simplest name.

Subtract: $7\frac{3}{8} - 2\frac{1}{8}$.

Step 1

$$7\frac{3}{8}$$
$$-2\frac{1}{8}$$
$$\overline{\frac{2}{8}}$$

Subtract $\frac{1}{8}$ from $\frac{3}{8}$.

Step 2

$$7\frac{3}{8}$$
$$-2\frac{1}{8}$$
$$\overline{5\frac{2}{8}}$$

Subtract 2 from 7.

Step 3

$$7\frac{3}{8}$$
$$-2\frac{1}{8}$$
$$\overline{5\frac{2}{8}} = 5\frac{1}{4}$$

Write the simplest name.

Add. Write the simplest name for the answer.

1. $3\frac{1}{5}$ **2.** $6\frac{1}{4}$ **3.** $8\frac{3}{10}$ **4.** $4\frac{3}{8}$ **5.** $7\frac{1}{3}$

$+6\frac{2}{5}$ $+2\frac{1}{4}$ $+9\frac{1}{10}$ $+5$ $+6\frac{1}{3}$

Subtract. Write the simplest name for the answer.

6. $10\frac{3}{4}$ **7.** $7\frac{3}{5}$ **8.** $9\frac{5}{8}$ **9.** $2\frac{9}{10}$ **10.** $8\frac{2}{3}$

$-\ 2\frac{1}{4}$ $-4\frac{2}{5}$ -3 $-1\frac{7}{10}$ $-3\frac{1}{3}$

Add. Write the simplest name for the answer.

11. $9\frac{3}{5}$ **12.** $4\frac{1}{4}$ **13.** $8\frac{3}{10}$ **14.** $1\frac{9}{16}$ **15.** $7\frac{7}{8}$

$+4\frac{1}{5}$ $+5\frac{2}{4}$ $+2\frac{3}{10}$ $+5\frac{3}{16}$ $+11$

16. $8\frac{7}{10}$ **17.** $5\frac{5}{16}$ **18.** $5\frac{1}{4}$ **19.** $9\frac{2}{5}$ **20.** $2\frac{1}{8}$

$+1\frac{1}{10}$ $+6\frac{7}{16}$ $+5\frac{1}{4}$ $+7\frac{2}{5}$ $+9\frac{5}{8}$

Subtract. Write the simplest name for the answer.

21. $10\frac{3}{4}$ **22.** $11\frac{9}{10}$ **23.** $9\frac{3}{5}$ **24.** $4\frac{7}{8}$ **25.** $6\frac{11}{16}$

$-\ 4\frac{1}{4}$ $-\ 6\frac{4}{10}$ $-8\frac{2}{5}$ -4 $-3\frac{3}{16}$

26. $4\frac{4}{5}$ **27.** $9\frac{9}{16}$ **28.** $11\frac{3}{8}$ **29.** $15\frac{17}{20}$ **30.** $19\frac{7}{10}$

$-2\frac{1}{5}$ -7 $-\ 4\frac{2}{8}$ $-\ 8\frac{11}{20}$ $-\ 4\frac{3}{10}$

Addition and Renaming

Jack and Jill went up the hill
To fetch some pails of water.
Jack got $3\frac{6}{8}$ pails, Jill $4\frac{5}{8}$,
All for their thirsty daughter.

How many pails did they get in all?

Step 1

$$3\frac{6}{8}$$
$$+4\frac{5}{8}$$
$$\overline{\quad\frac{11}{8}}$$

Add $\frac{6}{8}$ and $\frac{5}{8}$.

Step 2

$$3\frac{6}{8}$$
$$+4\frac{5}{8}$$
$$\overline{7\frac{11}{8}}$$

Add 3 and 4.

Step 3

$$3\frac{6}{8}$$
$$+4\frac{5}{8}$$
$$\overline{7\frac{11}{8}} = 8\frac{3}{8}$$

$\frac{11}{8}$ is greater than 1.
So, you must rename.
Think: $7\frac{11}{8} = 7 + 1\frac{3}{8}$.
Add the 7 and 1.

They got $8\frac{3}{8}$ pails.

206

Copy and complete.

1. $3\frac{4}{5}$
$+5\frac{3}{5}$
$\overline{}$
$8\frac{7}{5} = \underline{\ ?\ }$

2. $5\frac{1}{8}$
$+6\frac{7}{8}$
$\overline{}$
$11\frac{8}{8} = \underline{\ ?\ }$

3. $7\frac{2}{3}$
$+8\frac{2}{3}$
$\overline{}$
$15\frac{4}{3} = \underline{\ ?\ }$

Add. Write the simplest name for the answer.

4. $6\frac{1}{2}$
$+8\frac{1}{2}$
$\overline{}$

5. $9\frac{7}{10}$
$+4\frac{5}{10}$
$\overline{}$

6. $3\frac{5}{8}$
$+2\frac{5}{8}$
$\overline{}$

7. $6\frac{3}{4}$
$+2\frac{2}{4}$
$\overline{}$

8. $8\frac{2}{5}$
$+13\frac{4}{5}$
$\overline{}$

Add. Write the simplest name for the answer.

9. $8\frac{3}{4}$
$+6\frac{2}{4}$
$\overline{}$

10. $14\frac{2}{3}$
$+\ 3\frac{1}{3}$
$\overline{}$

11. $7\frac{4}{5}$
$+2\frac{3}{5}$
$\overline{}$

12. $8\frac{1}{2}$
$+5\frac{1}{2}$
$\overline{}$

13. $9\frac{7}{12}$
$+7\frac{7}{12}$
$\overline{}$

14. $31\frac{5}{8}$
$+\ 9\frac{7}{8}$
$\overline{}$

15. $10\frac{11}{16}$
$+\ 9\frac{9}{16}$
$\overline{}$

16. $6\frac{9}{10}$
$+7\frac{7}{10}$
$\overline{}$

17. $4\frac{4}{9}$
$+7\frac{5}{9}$
$\overline{}$

18. $12\frac{9}{15}$
$+\ 8\frac{7}{15}$
$\overline{}$

19. $3\frac{1}{3}$
6
$+7\frac{2}{3}$
$\overline{}$

20. $2\frac{3}{5}$
$6\frac{1}{5}$
$+7\frac{4}{5}$
$\overline{}$

21. $4\frac{1}{4}$
$5\frac{3}{4}$
$+6\frac{1}{4}$
$\overline{}$

22. $8\frac{1}{6}$
$7\frac{5}{6}$
$+3$
$\overline{}$

23. $6\frac{4}{7}$
$4\frac{5}{7}$
$+3\frac{2}{7}$
$\overline{}$

Renaming the Addends

Peter, Peter, pumpkin eater,
Ate $4\frac{1}{3}$ pumpkin cakes.
He went to the store.
Ate $2\frac{4}{5}$ more.
Now Peter's stomach aches.

How many cakes did Peter eat?

Step 1

$$4\frac{1}{3} = 4\frac{5}{15}$$
$$+2\frac{4}{5} = 2\frac{12}{15}$$

Find the least common denominator. Rename the mixed numerals.

Step 2

$$4\frac{1}{3} = 4\frac{5}{15}$$
$$+2\frac{4}{5} = 2\frac{12}{15}$$
$$\frac{17}{15}$$

Add $\frac{5}{15}$ and $\frac{12}{15}$.

Step 3

$$4\frac{1}{3} = 4\frac{5}{15}$$
$$+2\frac{4}{5} = 2\frac{12}{15}$$
$$6\frac{17}{15} = 7\frac{2}{15}$$

Add 4 and 2. Rename the answer.

Peter ate $7\frac{2}{15}$ cakes.

208

Copy and complete.

1. $6\frac{3}{4} = 6\frac{9}{12}$

$+8\frac{1}{3} = 8\frac{4}{12}$

2. $12\frac{3}{4} = 12\frac{9}{12}$

$+ 5\frac{5}{6} = 5\frac{10}{12}$

3. $7\frac{2}{5} = 7\frac{?}{10}$

$+4\frac{3}{10} = 4\frac{3}{10}$

Add. Write the simplest name for the answer.

4. $5\frac{2}{3}$
$+6\frac{1}{4}$

5. $8\frac{3}{5}$
$+9\frac{7}{10}$

6. $16\frac{2}{7}$
$+ 3\frac{1}{2}$

7. $7\frac{1}{2}$
$+6\frac{5}{8}$

8. $14\frac{1}{4}$
$+ 8\frac{3}{8}$

Add. Write the simplest name for the answer.

9. $4\frac{9}{12}$
$+7\frac{1}{6}$

10. $9\frac{1}{3}$
$+7\frac{7}{9}$

11. $4\frac{1}{5}$
$+6\frac{1}{4}$

12. $3\frac{1}{2}$
$+5\frac{2}{3}$

13. $2\frac{1}{2}$
$+4\frac{2}{5}$

14. $4\frac{1}{4}$
$+8\frac{3}{8}$

15. $2\frac{3}{4}$
$+6\frac{11}{16}$

16. $6\frac{2}{3}$
$+5\frac{5}{6}$

17. $8\frac{3}{4}$
$+3\frac{2}{3}$

18. $1\frac{4}{5}$
$+2\frac{1}{2}$

19. $6\frac{3}{4}$
$8\frac{1}{3}$
$+1\frac{1}{4}$

20. $8\frac{1}{2}$
$9\frac{2}{3}$
$+5\frac{1}{4}$

21. $6\frac{3}{5}$
$2\frac{1}{3}$
$+5\frac{1}{5}$

22. $8\frac{1}{8}$
$4\frac{5}{12}$
$+3\frac{1}{2}$

23. $7\frac{1}{6}$
$9\frac{1}{3}$
$+7\frac{1}{2}$

Renaming to Subtract

This is the house that Jack built.
He can clean it in $4\frac{1}{2}$ hours.
Dusting and sweeping,
Doing housekeeping,
Right up to the top of the towers.

He has been cleaning for $2\frac{1}{3}$ hours.
How much longer must he clean?

Step 1

$$4\frac{1}{2} = 4\frac{3}{6}$$
$$-2\frac{1}{3} = 2\frac{2}{6}$$

Find the least common denominator. Rename the mixed numerals.

Step 2

$$4\frac{1}{2} = 4\frac{3}{6}$$
$$-2\frac{1}{3} = 2\frac{2}{6}$$
$$\frac{1}{6}$$

Subtract $\frac{2}{6}$ from $\frac{3}{6}$.

Step 3

$$4\frac{1}{2} = 4\frac{3}{6}$$
$$-2\frac{1}{3} = 2\frac{2}{6}$$
$$2\frac{1}{6}$$

Subtract 2 from 4.

He must clean $2\frac{1}{6}$ more hours.

210

Copy and complete.

1. $7\frac{2}{3} = 7\frac{4}{6}$

   $-5\frac{1}{2} = 5\frac{3}{6}$

2. $14\frac{5}{8} = 14\frac{5}{8}$

   $-9\frac{1}{4} = 9\frac{2}{8}$

3. $6\frac{4}{5} = 6\frac{?}{15}$

   $-1\frac{2}{3} = 1\frac{?}{15}$

Subtract.

4. $4\frac{7}{10}$
   $-3\frac{2}{5}$

5. $9\frac{3}{4}$
   $-5\frac{1}{3}$

6. $11\frac{7}{8}$
   $-6\frac{5}{6}$

7. $7\frac{3}{4}$
   $-2\frac{2}{5}$

8. $10\frac{11}{16}$
   $-3\frac{3}{8}$

Subtract.   Write the simplest name for the answer.

9. $15\frac{4}{5}$
   $-11\frac{3}{10}$

10. $9\frac{3}{4}$
   $-5\frac{1}{8}$

11. $8\frac{11}{16}$
   $-2\frac{1}{4}$

12. $14\frac{1}{2}$
   $-6\frac{1}{3}$

13. $20\frac{3}{4}$
   $-13\frac{2}{3}$

14. $13\frac{3}{4}$
   $-9\frac{1}{2}$

15. $21\frac{4}{5}$
   $-7\frac{3}{4}$

16. $11\frac{7}{8}$
   $-6\frac{5}{16}$

17. $18\frac{5}{6}$
   $-9\frac{3}{8}$

18. $16\frac{3}{5}$
   $-7\frac{1}{3}$

19. $17\frac{1}{2}$
   $-8\frac{2}{5}$

20. $19\frac{3}{5}$
   $-13\frac{1}{10}$

21. $9\frac{7}{9}$
   $-6\frac{2}{3}$

22. $8\frac{7}{8}$
   $-7\frac{1}{4}$

23. $10\frac{5}{6}$
   $-5\frac{2}{3}$

24. $15\frac{7}{10}$
   $-7\frac{2}{5}$

25. $12\frac{9}{16}$
   $-6\frac{3}{8}$

26. $14\frac{3}{4}$
   $-6\frac{2}{3}$

27. $17\frac{3}{5}$
   $-9\frac{1}{4}$

28. $24\frac{3}{6}$
   $-6\frac{1}{3}$

Subtraction and Renaming

Subtract: $6\frac{1}{4} - 2\frac{3}{4}$.

Step 1

$$6\frac{1}{4} = 5\frac{5}{4}$$
$$-2\frac{3}{4} = 2\frac{3}{4}$$

$\frac{3}{4}$ is greater than $\frac{1}{4}$.
So, rename $6\frac{1}{4}$.
Think: $6\frac{1}{4} = 5 + 1\frac{1}{4}$,
or $5 + \frac{5}{4}$, or $5\frac{5}{4}$.

Step 2

$$6\frac{1}{4} = 5\frac{5}{4}$$
$$-2\frac{3}{4} = 2\frac{3}{4}$$
$$3\frac{2}{4}$$

Subtract $\frac{3}{4}$ from $\frac{5}{4}$.
Subtract 2 from 5.

Step 3

$$6\frac{1}{4} = 5\frac{5}{4}$$
$$-2\frac{3}{4} = 2\frac{3}{4}$$
$$3\frac{2}{4} = 3\frac{1}{2}$$

Write the simplest name.

Subtract: $5 - 3\frac{2}{3}$.

Step 1

$$5 = 4\frac{3}{3}$$
$$-3\frac{2}{3} = 3\frac{2}{3}$$

Rename 5.
Think: $5 = 4 + \frac{3}{3}$, or $4\frac{3}{3}$.

Step 2

$$5 = 4\frac{3}{3}$$
$$-3\frac{2}{3} = 3\frac{2}{3}$$
$$\frac{1}{3}$$

Subtract $\frac{2}{3}$ from $\frac{3}{3}$.

Step 3

$$5 = 4\frac{3}{3}$$
$$-3\frac{2}{3} = 3\frac{2}{3}$$
$$1\frac{1}{3}$$

Subtract 3 from 4.

212

Copy and complete.

1. $5\frac{3}{8} = 4\frac{11}{8}$
   $-1\frac{7}{8} = 1\frac{7}{8}$

2. $8 = 7\frac{8}{8}$
   $-5\frac{7}{8} = 5\frac{7}{8}$

3. $6\frac{1}{3} = 5\frac{?}{3}$
   $-2\frac{2}{3} = 2\frac{2}{3}$

Subtract. Write the simplest name for the answer.

4. $7\frac{1}{8}$
   $-2\frac{5}{8}$

5. $5\frac{1}{5}$
   $-\frac{3}{5}$

6. 10
   $-5\frac{3}{4}$

7. 15
   $-7\frac{1}{3}$

8. $6\frac{1}{4}$
   $-4\frac{3}{4}$

Subtract. Write the simplest name for the answer.

9. $16\frac{2}{7}$
   $-9\frac{3}{7}$

10. 16
    $-9\frac{3}{4}$

11. 7
    $-6\frac{1}{4}$

12. $13\frac{7}{12}$
    $-\frac{11}{12}$

13. 9
    $-4\frac{3}{7}$

14. $15\frac{3}{10}$
    $-6\frac{9}{10}$

15. 17
    $-6\frac{9}{10}$

16. $12\frac{3}{5}$
    $-3\frac{4}{5}$

17. 12
    $-8\frac{5}{6}$

18. 5
    $-3\frac{2}{5}$

19. $16\frac{2}{5}$
    $-4\frac{3}{5}$

20. 15
    $-9\frac{1}{2}$

21. 9
    $-7\frac{2}{3}$

22. $14\frac{5}{8}$
    $-4\frac{7}{8}$

23. $17\frac{1}{10}$
    $-8\frac{7}{10}$

24. 8
    $-6\frac{7}{10}$

25. $20\frac{1}{4}$
    $-16\frac{3}{4}$

26. 14
    $-9\frac{1}{3}$

27. $8\frac{1}{8}$
    $-7\frac{7}{8}$

28. 17
    $-6\frac{3}{8}$

Renaming Twice

Little Jack Horner
Sitting in a corner.
Having eaten $2\frac{2}{3}$ pies.
He started with $3\frac{1}{5}$.
But now you can see
His stomach is bigger than his eyes.

How much pie is left?

Step 1

$$3\frac{1}{5} = 3\frac{3}{15}$$
$$-2\frac{2}{3} = 2\frac{10}{15}$$

Find the least
common denominator.
Rename the
mixed numerals.

Step 2

$$3\frac{1}{5} = 3\frac{3}{15} = 2\frac{18}{15}$$
$$-2\frac{2}{3} = 2\frac{10}{15} = 2\frac{10}{15}$$

$\frac{10}{15}$ is greater than $\frac{3}{15}$.
Rename $3\frac{3}{15}$.
Think: $3\frac{3}{15} = 2 + 1\frac{3}{15}$,
or $2 + \frac{18}{15}$, or $2\frac{18}{15}$.

Step 3

$$3\frac{1}{5} = 3\frac{3}{15} = 2\frac{18}{15}$$
$$-2\frac{2}{3} = 2\frac{10}{15} = 2\frac{10}{15}$$
$$\frac{8}{15}$$

Subtract $\frac{10}{15}$ from $\frac{18}{15}$.
Subtract 2 from 2.

There is $\frac{8}{15}$ left.

214

Copy and complete.

1. $9\frac{1}{4} = 9\frac{1}{4} = 8\frac{5}{4}$

   $-2\frac{1}{2} = 2\frac{2}{4} = 2\frac{2}{4}$

2. $3\frac{1}{3} = 3\frac{4}{12} = 2\frac{?}{12}$

   $-1\frac{3}{4} = 1\frac{9}{12} = 1\frac{9}{12}$

Subtract. Write the simplest name for the answer.

3. $8\frac{1}{5}$
   $-4\frac{1}{2}$

4. $10\frac{1}{4}$
   $-\ 3\frac{5}{8}$

5. $14\frac{1}{4}$
   $-\ 8\frac{2}{3}$

6. $7\frac{2}{5}$
   $-4\frac{2}{3}$

7. $8\frac{1}{2}$
   $-2\frac{5}{8}$

Subtract. Write the simplest name for the answer.

8. $4\frac{2}{7}$
   $-3\frac{1}{2}$

9. $9\frac{1}{6}$
   $-8\frac{2}{3}$

10. $10\frac{2}{9}$
    $-\ 3\frac{2}{3}$

11. $13\frac{3}{5}$
    $-\ 7\frac{7}{10}$

12. $6\frac{1}{4}$
    $-4\frac{1}{2}$

13. $21\frac{1}{2}$
    $-\ 7\frac{7}{8}$

14. $9\frac{1}{5}$
    $-6\frac{3}{4}$

15. $5\frac{3}{10}$
    $-4\frac{3}{5}$

16. $16\frac{1}{4}$
    $-\ 7\frac{7}{8}$

17. $11\frac{1}{3}$
    $-\ 2\frac{4}{5}$

18. $13\frac{3}{10}$
    $-\ 8\frac{4}{5}$

19. $11\frac{1}{5}$
    $-\ 4\frac{2}{3}$

20. $9\frac{3}{4}$
    $-7\frac{7}{8}$

21. $20\frac{1}{4}$
    $-14\frac{2}{3}$

22. $6\frac{3}{7}$
    $-3\frac{2}{3}$

23. $18\frac{7}{20}$
    $-\ 9\frac{9}{10}$

24. $9\frac{4}{5}$
    $-5\frac{9}{10}$

25. $15\frac{1}{3}$
    $-\ 6\frac{3}{4}$

26. $11\frac{3}{8}$
    $-\ 3\frac{3}{4}$

27. $13\frac{1}{3}$
    $-\ 9\frac{5}{7}$

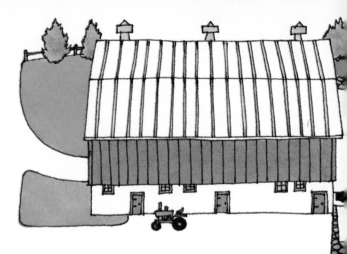

missing information

Some problems give you enough information
to solve them. Others may not.
In which problem below is information missing?

Problem

The Bellaire Dairy Farm has 25 cows.
$\frac{4}{5}$ of them are Holsteins.
How many are Holsteins?

Solution

Part that are Holsteins	Number of cows	Number of Holsteins
↓	↓	↓
$\frac{4}{5}$ ×	25 =	?

You have enough information.
20 cows are Holsteins.

Problem

A large cow eats $6\frac{8}{10}$ kilograms
of grain each day. She also
eats many kilograms of silage and hay.
How much does she eat in all?

Solution

Kg of grain	Kg of silage and hay	Total
↓	↓	↓
$6\frac{8}{10}$ +	? =	?

Information is missing. You do
not know how much silage and hay
is eaten.

Do you have enough information? Write YES or NO.

1. A cow is milked for $2\frac{1}{2}$ minutes
in the morning. She is milked
for $2\frac{1}{4}$ minutes in the evening.
How many minutes is that in all?

2. $\frac{3}{4}$ of all milk sold is Grade A.
One store sells many cases.
How many cases of Grade A
does the store sell?

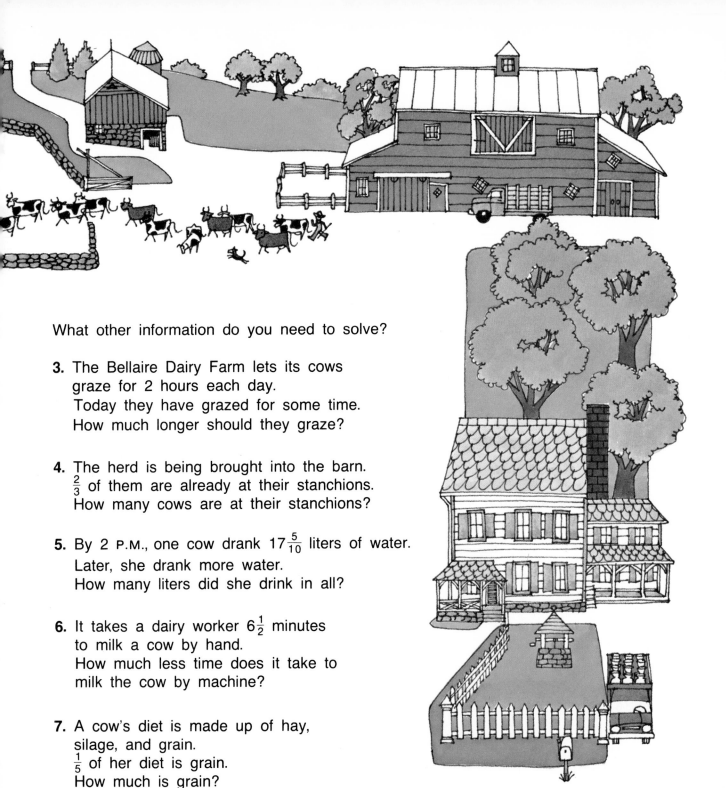

What other information do you need to solve?

3. The Bellaire Dairy Farm lets its cows
   graze for 2 hours each day.
   Today they have grazed for some time.
   How much longer should they graze?

4. The herd is being brought into the barn.
   $\frac{2}{3}$ of them are already at their stanchions.
   How many cows are at their stanchions?

5. By 2 P.M., one cow drank $17\frac{5}{10}$ liters of water.
   Later, she drank more water.
   How many liters did she drink in all?

6. It takes a dairy worker $6\frac{1}{2}$ minutes
   to milk a cow by hand.
   How much less time does it take to
   milk the cow by machine?

7. A cow's diet is made up of hay,
   silage, and grain.
   $\frac{1}{5}$ of her diet is grain.
   How much is grain?

Problem-solving Help 217

Test

Write the numeral for a whole number.

1. $\frac{8}{2} = \underline{\;?\;}$ (p. 194)

2. $\frac{40}{5} = \underline{\;?\;}$ (p. 194)

3. $\frac{18}{3} = \underline{\;?\;}$ (p. 194)

Write the fraction.

4. $\frac{?}{4} = 7$ (p. 194)

5. $\frac{?}{6} = 9$ (p. 194)

6. $\frac{?}{8} = 2$ (p. 194)

7. $3\frac{5}{8}$ (p. 198)

8. $4\frac{1}{2}$ (p. 198)

9. $6\frac{2}{3}$ (p. 198)

Write the mixed numeral.

10. $\frac{14}{5}$ (p. 200, 202)

11. $\frac{9}{7}$ (p. 200, 202)

12. $\frac{41}{9}$ (p. 200, 202)

13. $\frac{8}{7}$ (p. 200, 202)

14. $\frac{23}{4}$ (p. 200, 202)

15. $\frac{71}{8}$ (p. 200, 202)

Add.   Write the simplest name for the answer.

16. $4\frac{3}{10}$ $+9\frac{5}{10}$ (p. 204)

17. $9\frac{2}{5}$ $+9\frac{4}{5}$ (p. 206)

18. $13\frac{3}{4}$ $+ 7\frac{1}{4}$ (p. 206)

19. $7\frac{4}{7}$ $+8\frac{1}{2}$ (p. 208)

20. $7\frac{2}{10}$ $9\frac{4}{5}$ $+5\frac{1}{2}$ (p. 208)

Subtract.   Write the simplest name for the answer.

21. $12\frac{13}{16}$ $- 9\frac{1}{16}$ (p. 204)

22. $7\frac{2}{5}$ $-2\frac{1}{10}$ (p. 210)

23. $14\frac{1}{3}$ $- 5\frac{2}{3}$ (p. 212)

24. $6\frac{1}{4}$ $-2\frac{7}{8}$ (p. 214)

25. $8\frac{1}{5}$ $-4\frac{4}{15}$ (p. 214)

218

Keeping up

Find the greatest common factor.

1. 24, 18 (p. 160) **2.** 28, 35 (p. 160) **3.** 21, 24 (p. 160) **4.** 12, 27 (p. 160)

Write the simplest name.

5. $\frac{6}{9}$ (p. 178) **6.** $\frac{18}{32}$ (p. 178) **7.** $\frac{10}{15}$ (p. 178) **8.** $\frac{18}{36}$ (p. 178)

Find the least common multiple.

9. 3, 4 (p. 162) **10.** 5, 3 (p. 162) **11.** 3, 6 (p. 162) **12.** 6, 9 (p. 162)

Add. Write the simplest name for the answer.

13. $\frac{1}{4}$ $+\frac{5}{12}$ (p. 184)

14. $\frac{2}{3}$ $+\frac{3}{12}$ (p. 184)

15. $\frac{7}{15}$ $+\frac{2}{5}$ (p. 184)

16. $\frac{2}{3}$ $+\frac{1}{5}$ (p. 184)

Subtract. Write the simplest name for the answer.

17. $\frac{3}{4}$ $-\frac{1}{6}$ (p. 186)

18. $\frac{2}{3}$ $-\frac{1}{4}$ (p. 186)

19. $\frac{11}{12}$ $-\frac{3}{4}$ (p. 186)

20. $\frac{11}{15}$ $-\frac{3}{5}$ (p. 186)

Multiply.

21. 4689 $\times$ 6 (p. 78)

22. 3970 $\times$ 80 (p. 84)

23. 687 $\times 609$ (p. 86)

24. 476 $\times 236$ (p. 86)

Divide.

25. (p. 122) $8\overline{)3400}$

26. (p. 122) $7\overline{)4252}$

27. (p. 122) $9\overline{)6847}$

28. (p. 122) $8\overline{)7898}$

29. (p. 144) $83\overline{)7406}$

30. (p. 146) $78\overline{)4760}$

31. (p. 144) $64\overline{)4997}$

32. (p. 146) $38\overline{)2059}$

Probability and Predictions

Make a spinner. Use a card and a pencil.
Color the card as shown.

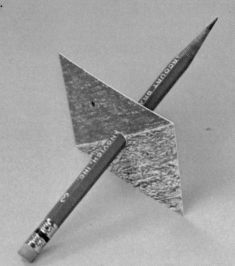

MAKE A PREDICTION
Suppose you spin it 20 times.
What do you think will happen?

   A It will land on a green edge
       more often.

   B It will land on a red edge
       more often.

   C It will land on red and green
       about the same number of times.

INVESTIGATE
1. Spin the spinner 20 times. Record the color each time.

Color	Tally	Total
Red		
Green		

   How do your results compare with your prediction?

2. Write a fraction for the part of the spins that was red.
   Example: If it landed on red 13 times, the fraction would be $\frac{13}{20}$.

3. Write a fraction for the part of the spins that was green.

MAKE A PREDICTION

Make a spinner like this one.
Suppose you spin it 20 times.
What part of the spins will
be red? (Write a fraction.)

INVESTIGATE

4. Spin it 20 times. Record the results.

Color	Prediction	Tally	Fraction
Red			
Yellow			
Blue			
Green			

5. What part of the spins was red?
Compare your results with your prediction.

MAKE A PREDICTION

Make a spinner like this one.
Suppose you spin it 18 times.
What part of the spins will
be red? (Write a fraction.)

INVESTIGATE

6. Spin it 18 times. Record the results.

Color	Prediction	Tally	Fraction
Red			
Yellow			
Blue			
Orange			
Green			
White			

7. What part of the spins was red?
Compare your results with your prediction.

Enrichment 221

11 Measurement

Centimeter

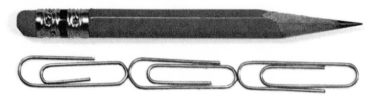

Measurement is comparing an object with a unit.
Many things can be used as units.
We could say the length of this pencil is 3 paper clips.

Most people use standard units of measurement.
A **centimeter (cm)** is a standard unit of length.
The length of the pencil is 9 cm.

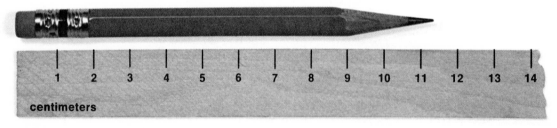

The length of this pencil is between 11 cm and 12 cm.
It is nearer to 11 cm.
The length is 11 cm to the nearest centimeter.

Measure to the nearest centimeter.

1.

2.

3.

Measure to the nearest centimeter.

4.

5.

6.

7.

8.

9.

10.

11.

12.

Millimeter

Each centimeter unit is separated into 10 smaller units.
Each smaller unit is a **millimeter (mm).**

10 millimeters = 1 centimeter

The length of this pencil is 12 cm.
To find the length in millimeters, multiply by 10.
The length is 120 mm.

The length of this pencil is 150 mm.
To find the length in centimeters, divide by 10.
The length is 15 cm.

Measure to the nearest millimeter.

1.

2.

Measure to the nearest millimeter.

3.

4.

5.

6.

7.

8.

Complete.

9. 2 cm = _?_ mm   10. 7 cm = _?_ mm   11. 10 cm = _?_ mm

12. 34 cm = _?_ mm   13. 56 cm = _?_ mm   14. 85 cm = _?_ mm

15. _?_ cm = 10 mm   16. _?_ cm = 30 mm   17. _?_ cm = 60 mm

18. _?_ cm = 120 mm 19. _?_ cm = 240 mm 20. _?_ cm = 470 mm

225

Meter and Kilometer

The length of this strip is 10 centimeters.
Make 10 of these strips. Tape them together.
The length of your new strip is one **meter (m).**

100 centimeters = 1 meter

Use your meter strip to measure to the nearest meter.
About how high is your desk? About how high is a door?

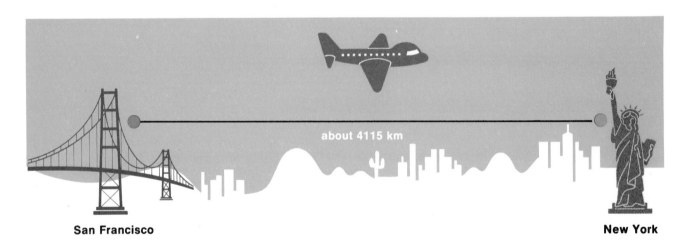

about 4115 km

San Francisco

New York

Suppose you made 1000 meter strips and taped them together.
The length of your new strip would be one **kilometer (km).**

1000 meters = 1 kilometer

You can walk a distance of 1 km in about 12 minutes.
The distance between San Francisco and New York City is about 4115 km.

try these

Which unit would you use to measure?
Write CENTIMETER, METER, or KILOMETER.

1. Your height.
2. Height of an apartment building.
3. Distance between Miami and Dallas.
4. Length of your desk.
5. Length of an office building.
6. Length of the Mississippi River.

now do these

Complete.   100 cm = 1 m

7. 200 cm = ? m
8. 400 cm = ? m
9. 1600 cm = ? m
10. 5600 cm = ? m
11. ? cm = 5 m
12. ? cm = 10 m
13. ? cm = 14 m
14. ? cm = 36 m

Complete.   1000 mm = 1 m

15. 2000 mm = ? m
16. 12,000 mm = ? m
17. ? mm = 5 m
18. ? mm = 25 m

Complete.   1000 m = 1 km

19. 8000 m = ? km
20. 18,000 m = ? km
21. ? m = 10 km
22. ? m = 48 km

LITTLE UNITS, BIG NUMBERS

There are 100,000 centimeters in a kilometer.
What is the distance in centimeters?

A. From Atlanta, Georgia, to
Houston, Texas: 1128 km

B. From Phoenix, Arizona, to
Cleveland, Ohio: 2815 km

There are 1,000,000 millimeters in a kilometer.
What is the distance in millimeters?

C. From Portland, Oregon, to
Washington, D.C.: 3788 km

D. From Chicago, Illinois, to
Miami, Florida: 1912 km

227

Perimeter

The distance around a figure is its **perimeter.**

Find the perimeter of the triangle.
1. Measure each side.

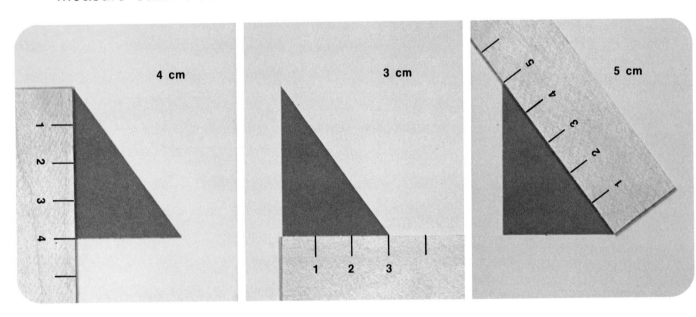

2. Find the sum of the measures.

$$
\begin{array}{r}
3 \\
4 \\
+5 \\
\hline
12
\end{array}
$$

The perimeter is 12 cm.

1. Find the perimeter in centimeters.

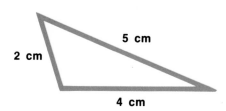

2. Find the perimeter in millimeters.

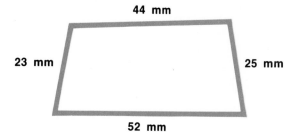

Find the perimeter in centimeters.

3.

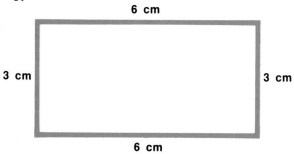

4.

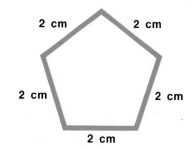

Find the perimeter in millimeters.

5.

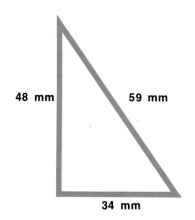

6.

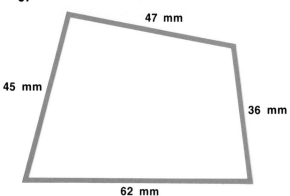

Area

The red figure is
1 **square centimeter.**

How many are needed
to cover the yellow figure?

The **area** of the yellow figure
is 15 square centimeters.

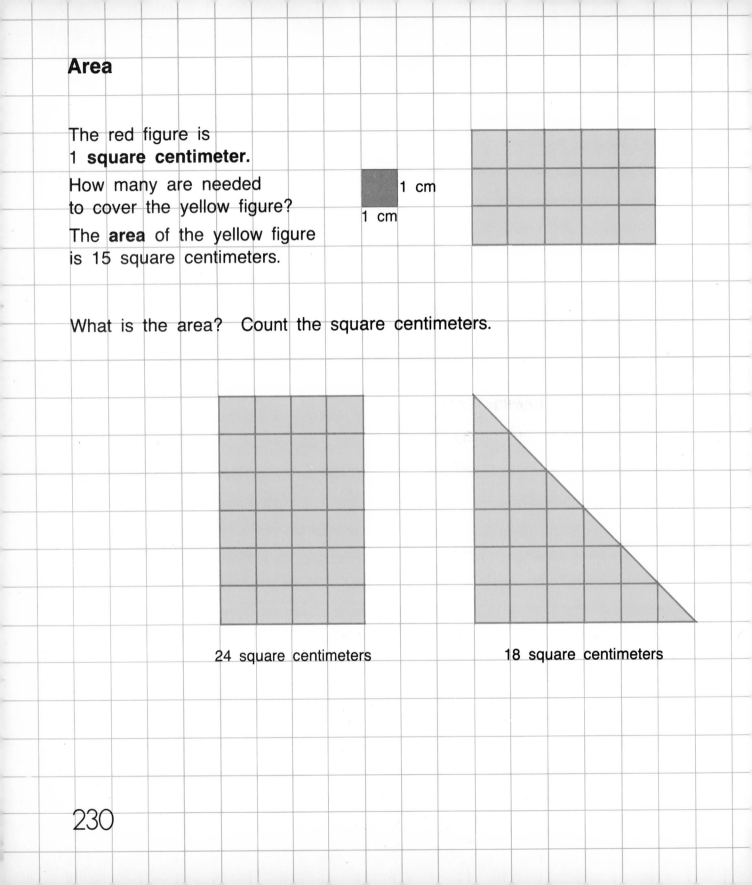

1 cm

1 cm

What is the area? Count the square centimeters.

24 square centimeters

18 square centimeters

230

Find the area in square centimeters.

1.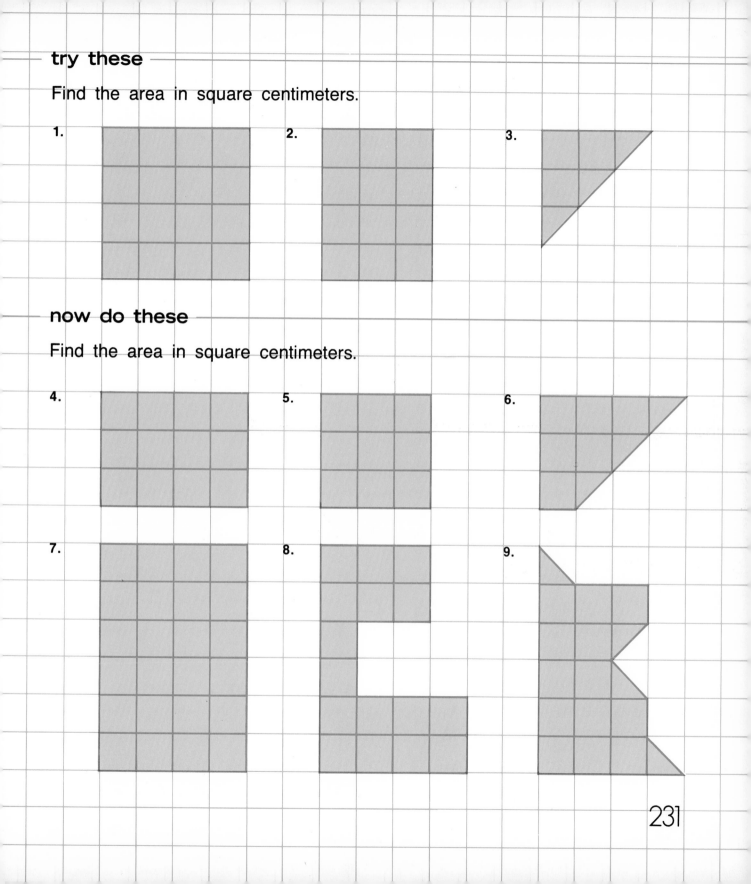

2.

3.

now do these

Find the area in square centimeters.

4.

5.

6.

7.

8.

9.

231

Area and Rectangles

This figure is a rectangle.
Count to find the area.
The area is 12 square centimeters.

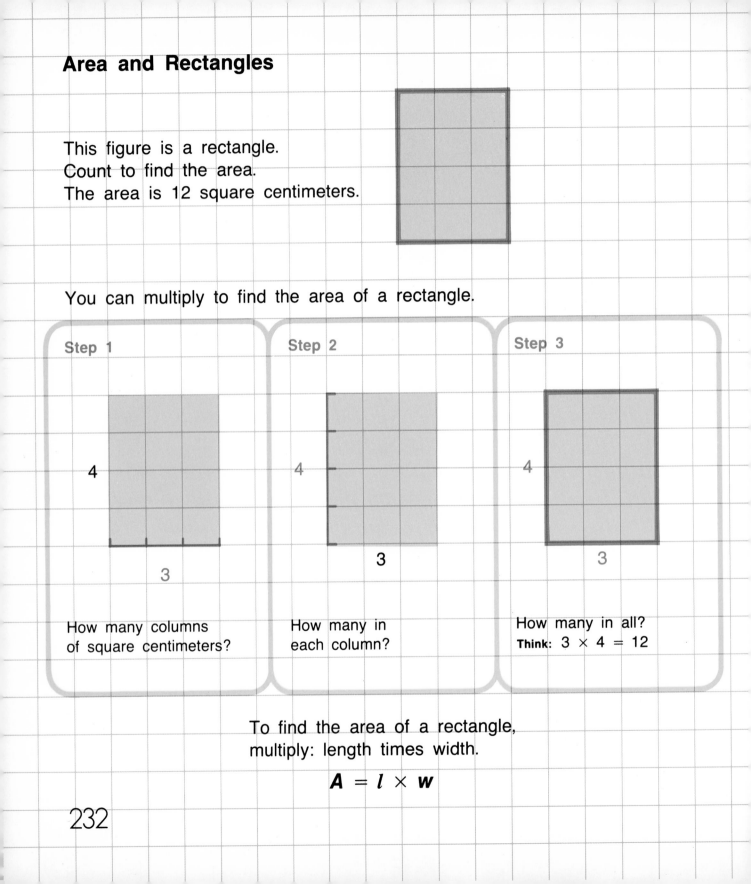

You can multiply to find the area of a rectangle.

Step 1

4

3

How many columns
of square centimeters?

Step 2

4

3

How many in
each column?

Step 3

4

3

How many in all?
Think: 3 × 4 = 12

To find the area of a rectangle,
multiply: length times width.

$$A = l \times w$$

Multiply to find the area in square centimeters.

1.

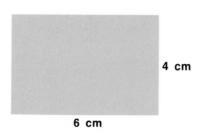

4 cm

6 cm

2.

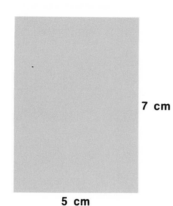

7 cm

5 cm

3.

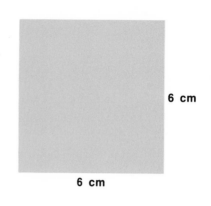

6 cm

6 cm

now do these

Multiply to find the area in square centimeters.

4.

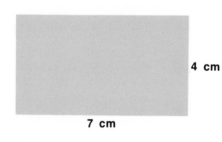

4 cm

7 cm

5.

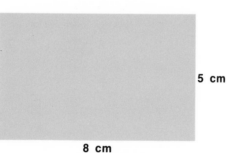

5 cm

8 cm

6.

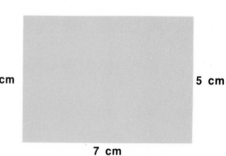

5 cm

7 cm

Multiply to find the area in square millimeters.

7.

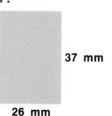

37 mm

26 mm

8.

42 mm

68 mm

9.

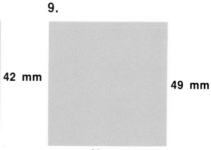

49 mm

49 mm

Area and Right Triangles

Step 1

This figure is a right triangle.

It is a triangle with a square corner.

4 cm

3 cm

Step 2

Draw another right triangle the same size.

You now have a rectangle.

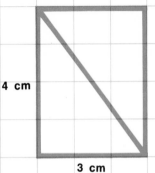

4 cm

3 cm

Step 3

Find the area of the rectangle.

3 × 4 = 12

12 square centimeters

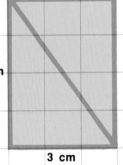

4 cm

3 cm

Step 4

The area of the triangle is $\frac{1}{2}$ the area of the rectangle.

$\frac{1}{2}$ **of 12 = 6**

6 square centimeters

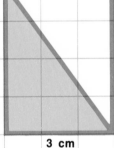

4 cm

3 cm

To find the area of a right triangle, multiply: length of the base times height. Then find $\frac{1}{2}$ of the product.

$$A = \tfrac{1}{2} \text{ of } (b \times h)$$

height

base

234

try these

Find the area in square centimeters.

1.

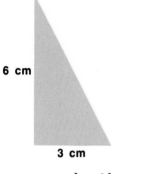

6 cm

3 cm

2.

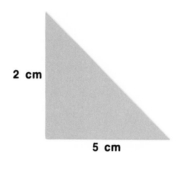

2 cm

5 cm

3.

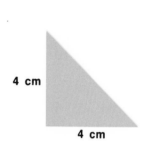

4 cm

4 cm

now do these

Find the area in square centimeters.

4.

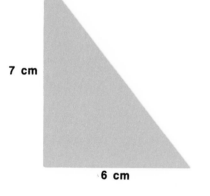

7 cm

6 cm

5.

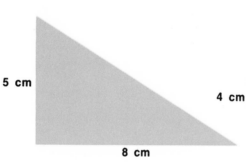

5 cm

8 cm

6.

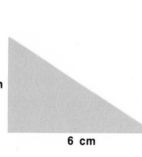

4 cm

6 cm

Find the area in square millimeters.

7.

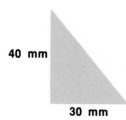

40 mm

30 mm

8.

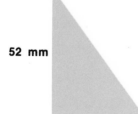

52 mm

40 mm

9.

47 mm

62 mm

Volume

The red cube is
1 **cubic centimeter.**
How many are needed
to fill the box?

Your answer will be
the **volume** of the box.

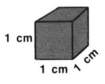

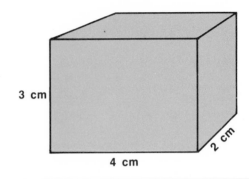

3 cm

4 cm

2 cm

Step 1

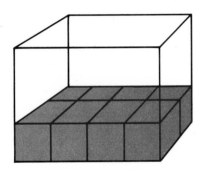

Find how many will make one layer.

Think: 4 rows of 2.

$4 \times 2 = 8$

Step 2

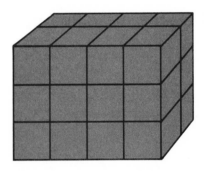

Find how many layers.
Then find how many in all.

Think: 3 layers of 8.

$3 \times 8 = 24$

The volume of the box is
24 cubic centimeters.

To find the volume of a box,
multiply: length times width times height.

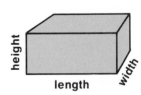

height

length

width

$$V = l \times w \times h$$

236

Find the volume in cubic centimeters.

1.

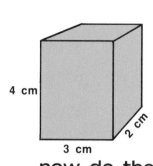

4 cm

3 cm

2 cm

2.

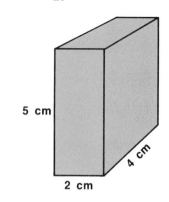

5 cm

2 cm

4 cm

3.

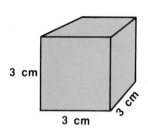

3 cm

3 cm

3 cm

now do these

Find the volume in cubic centimeters.

4.

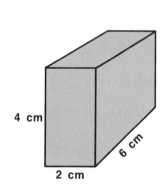

4 cm

2 cm

6 cm

5.

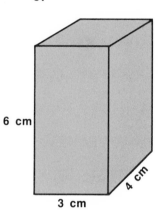

6 cm

3 cm

4 cm

6.

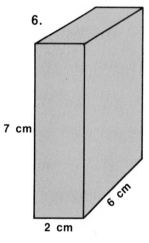

7 cm

2 cm

6 cm

Find the volume in cubic millimeters.

7.

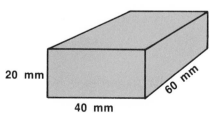

20 mm

40 mm

60 mm

8.

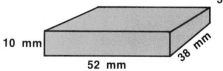

10 mm

52 mm

38 mm

9.

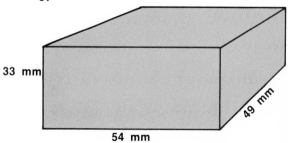

33 mm

54 mm

49 mm

237

Milliliter and Liter

It takes 1 **milliliter** of water
to fill 1 cubic centimeter.

The volume of a metric cup is
250 cubic centimeters.
It takes 250 milliliters
of water to fill a metric cup.

The volume of the pitcher is
1000 cubic centimeters.
It takes 4 metric cups of water
to fill the pitcher.
It takes 1000 milliliters
to fill the pitcher.
The pitcher holds 1 **liter.**

1000 milliliters (ml) = 1 liter (*l*)

try these

One of the measures is correct.   Which one?

1.

25 ml
250 ml
2500 ml

2.

36 ml
360 ml
3600 ml

3.

1 *l*
10 *l*
100 *l*

4.

4 *l*
40 *l*
400 *l*

now do these

One of the measures is correct.   Which one?

5.

1 *l*
1 ml

6.

500 *l*
500 ml

7.
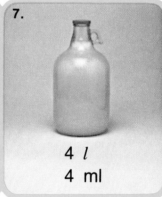

4 *l*
4 ml

8.
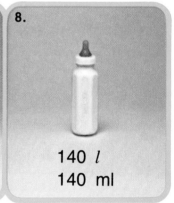

140 *l*
140 ml

TAKE YOUR MEDICINE

Doctors often prescribe medicine in cubic centimeters rather than milliliters. How would they prescribe these amounts?

A.
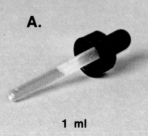

1 ml

B.

8 ml

C.

12 ml

239

Gram and Kilogram

A **gram** is a unit that is
used to weigh things.
A cubic centimeter of
water weighs 1 gram.

This pitcher holds 1000
cubic centimeters of water.
1000 cubic centimeters weigh 1000 grams.
The water weighs 1 **kilogram.**

1000 grams (g) = 1 kilogram (kg)

---

try these

Which unit would you use to measure?
Write GRAM or KILOGRAM.

1.

2.

3.

4.

now do these

One of the measures is correct. Which one?

5.

5 g
5 kg

6.

3 g
3 kg

7.

1 g
1 kg

8.

312 g
312 kg

9.

315 g
315 kg

10.

6 g
6 kg

11.

500 g
500 kg

12.

32 g
32 kg

THIS IS PRETTY DEEP

The dimensions of the pool are
1200 cm by 500 cm by 200 cm.
The pool is filled with water.
How many kilograms does the water weigh?

Test

Complete.

1. 4 cm = _?_ mm (p. 224) 2. 63 cm = _?_ mm (p. 224) 3. _?_ cm = 280 mm (p. 224)

4. _?_ cm = 13 m (p. 226) 5. 4000 mm = _?_ m (p. 226) 6. _?_ m = 16 km (p. 226)

Which unit would you use to measure?
Write CENTIMETER, METER, or KILOMETER.

7. Length of a room. (p. 226)

8. Length of a school building. (p. 226)

9. Length of a pencil. (p. 226)

10. Distance between New York and London. (p. 226)

11. Find the perimeter in centimeters. (p. 228)

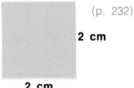

2 cm 3 cm 3 cm

12. Find the volume in cubic centimeters. (p. 236)

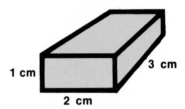

1 cm 3 cm 2 cm

Find the area in square centimeters.

13. (p. 232)

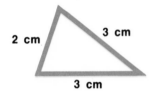

2 cm 2 cm

14. (p. 234)

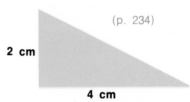

2 cm 4 cm

One of the measures is correct. Which one?

15.   28 ml (p. 238) 280 ml 2800 ml

16.   3 _l_ (p. 238) 30 _l_ 300 _l_

17.   50 ml (p. 238) 500 ml 5000 ml

18.   4 g (p. 240) 4 kg

19.   248 g (p. 240) 248 kg

20.   908 g (p. 240) 908 kg

242

Keeping up

What number does the 5 name?

1. 135,429,304,236
(p. 6)

2. 343,259,346,221
(p. 6)

3. 249,126,537,204
(p. 6)

Write the fraction.

4. $4\frac{2}{3}$ (p. 198)

5. $6\frac{5}{6}$ (p. 198)

6. $4\frac{1}{4}$ (p. 198)

7. $5\frac{3}{10}$ (p. 198)

Write the mixed numeral.

8. $\frac{63}{10}$ (p. 200, 202)

9. $\frac{19}{4}$ (p. 200, 202)

10. $\frac{39}{8}$ (p. 200, 202)

11. $\frac{23}{6}$ (p. 200, 202)

Add. Write the simplest name for the answer.

12. $4\frac{3}{8}$
$+5\frac{3}{8}$
(p. 204)

13. $7\frac{2}{3}$
$+8\frac{2}{3}$
(p. 206)

14. $5\frac{4}{5}$
$+6\frac{7}{10}$
(p. 208)

15. $7\frac{3}{4}$
$+2\frac{5}{6}$
(p. 208)

Subtract. Write the simplest name for the answer.

16. $8\frac{11}{16}$
$-3\frac{5}{16}$
(p. 204)

17. 6
$-2\frac{2}{3}$
(p. 212)

18. $7\frac{5}{6}$
$-3\frac{3}{4}$
(p. 210)

19. $3\frac{5}{8}$
$-2\frac{5}{6}$
(p. 214)

Multiply.

20. 6846
$\times \quad 9$
(p. 78)

21. 9378
$\times \quad 38$
(p. 84)

22. 768
$\times 906$
(p. 86)

23. 465
$\times 362$
(p. 86)

Divide.

(p. 146)   (p. 144)   (p. 144)   (p. 146)

24. $67\overline{)5499}$

25. $32\overline{)2427}$

26. $74\overline{)4669}$

27. $25\overline{)1085}$

243

Other Standard Units

Another standard unit of length is an **inch**.
The ruler above is marked in inches.
How many inches wide is the palm of your hand?

A larger unit of length is a **foot**.

The table tells you that
12 inches make 1 foot.
How many inches in 2 feet?

> 12 inches (in) = 1 foot (ft)
> 3 feet (ft) = 1 yard (yd)
> 36 inches (in) = 1 yard (yd)

3 feet make 1 **yard.** How many feet in 5 yards?
How many inches in 1 yard? How many inches in 5 yards?

Multiply to complete.

1. 4 ft = _?_ in

2. 12 ft = _?_ in

3. 6 yd = _?_ ft

4. 20 yd = _?_ ft

5. 4 yd = _?_ in

6. 10 yd = _?_ in

Divide to complete.

7. 36 in = _?_ ft

8. 60 in = _?_ ft

9. 9 ft = _?_ yd

10. 27 ft = _?_ yd

11. 108 in = _?_ yd

12. 252 in = _?_ yd

A standard unit of liquid measure is an **ounce.**

There are 8 ounces in 1 **cup.**
How many ounces in 2 cups?

2 cups make 1 **pint.**
How many cups in 2 pints?

2 pints make 1 **quart.**
How many pints in 4 quarts?

4 quarts make 1 **gallon.**
How many pints in 1 gallon?

> 8 ounces (oz) = 1 cup (c)
> 2 cups (c) = 1 pint (pt)
> 2 pints (pt) = 1 quart (qt)
> 4 quarts (qt) = 1 gallon (gal)

Complete. Use the table to help you.

13. ? oz = 1 c   **14.** ? oz = 1 qt   **15.** ? oz = 1 gal

16. ? c = 1 pt   **17.** ? c = 1 qt   **18.** ? c = 1 gal

19. ? pt = 1 gal   **20.** ? qt = 5 gal   **21.** ? pt = 5 gal

Two units of weight are an **ounce** and a **pound.**

16 ounces (oz) = 1 pound (lb)

Complete.

22. ? oz = 2 lb   **23.** ? oz = 5 lb   **24.** ? oz = 25 lb

25. 64 oz = ? lb   **26.** 128 oz = ? lb   **27.** 192 oz = ? lb

Ratio

How many pennies do you see?   How many nickels?
The **ratio** of pennies to nickels is 3 to 2.

Ratio is one way of comparing numbers.
Here are three ways to show the ratio.

$$\textbf{3 to 2} \qquad \textbf{3:2} \qquad \frac{3}{2}$$

There are other ways to compare the coins.

The ratio of nickels to pennies is 2 to 3.
The fraction $\frac{2}{3}$ names this ratio.

The ratio of nickels to coins is 2 to 5.
Which fraction names this ratio, $\frac{2}{5}$ or $\frac{5}{2}$?

The ratio of pennies to coins is 3 to 5.
Which fraction names this ratio, $\frac{3}{5}$ or $\frac{5}{3}$?

try these

Write a fraction for the ratio.

1. dimes to pennies

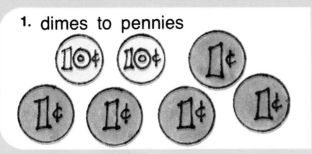

2. dimes to coins.

now do these

Write a fraction for the ratio.

3. dimes to candy bars

4. dimes to candies

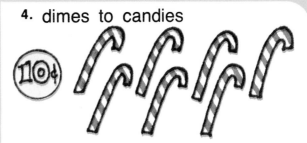

5. carrots to beans

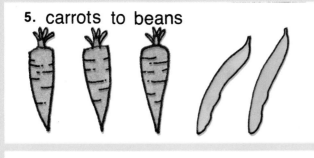

6. beans to carrots

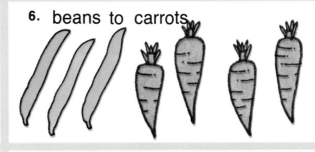

7. cats to mice

8. dogs to cats

247

Equivalent Ratios

There are 3 pennies for each 2 nickels.   The ratio is $\frac{3}{2}$.

There are 6 pennies for each 4 nickels.   The ratio is $\frac{6}{4}$.

$\frac{3}{2}$ and $\frac{6}{4}$ are **equivalent ratios.** $\frac{3}{2} = \frac{6}{4}$

Suppose you know that the ratio of pennies to nickels is $\frac{3}{2}$.
You also know there are 12 pennies.
How many nickels are there?

$$\text{pennies} \longrightarrow \frac{3}{2} = \frac{12}{?} \longleftarrow \text{pennies}$$
$$\text{nickels} \longrightarrow \qquad \longleftarrow \text{nickels}$$

Think:

4 times 3 is 12, so
4 times 2 is 8.

There are 8 nickels.

The ratio of pennies to nickels is $\frac{3}{2}$.
There are 10 nickels.   How many pennies are there?

$$\text{pennies} \longrightarrow \frac{3}{2} = \frac{?}{10} \longleftarrow \text{pennies}$$
$$\text{nickels} \longrightarrow \qquad \longleftarrow \text{nickels}$$

Think:

5 times 2 is 10, so
5 times 3 is 15.

There are 15 pennies.

Complete.

1. $\dfrac{3}{4} = \dfrac{?}{12}$

2. $\dfrac{8}{5} = \dfrac{?}{20}$

3. $\dfrac{3}{5} = \dfrac{9}{?}$

4. $\dfrac{7}{4} = \dfrac{35}{?}$

Solve the problem.

5. The ratio of pennies to dimes is 4 to 7.
   There are 8 pennies.
   How many dimes are there?

6. The ratio of dogs to cats is 2 to 3.
   There are 9 cats.
   How many dogs are there?

now do these

Solve the problem.

7. The ratio of dimes to candy bars is 3 to 2.
   There are 8 candy bars.
   How many dimes are there?

8. The ratio of candies to pennies is 2 to 1.
   There are 12 candies.
   How many pennies are there?

9. The ratio of boys to girls is 5 to 3.
   There are 15 boys.
   How many girls are there?

10. The ratio of girls to boys is 4 to 5.
    There are 20 boys.
    How many girls are there?

THINK ABOUT IT

The ratio of girls to boys is 3 to 2.
A. Are there more girls or more boys?
B. Do you know how many girls there are?
C. Suppose you know there are 12 boys.
   Now do you know how many girls there are?

249

Ratio and Money

The price of fig bars
is 2 for 25¢.
Suppose you want 4.
You can use ratios
to find the cost.

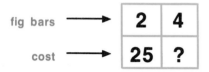

fig bars →

2	4
25	?

$$\frac{2}{25} = \frac{4}{?}$$

cost →

Think: Twice as many bars.
Twice as much money.

Four fig bars cost 50¢.

7 sticks of sugarless
gum cost 10¢.
How many sticks
can you buy for 40¢?

sticks of gum →

7	?
10	40

$$\frac{7}{10} = \frac{?}{40}$$

cost →

Think: 4 times as much money.
4 times as many sticks of gum.

You can buy 28 sticks of gum.

try these

What will they cost?

1. 2 for 10¢
   Buy 6.

2. 3 for 25¢
   Buy 9.

3. 2 for 25¢
   Buy 6.

How many will you get?

4. 4 for 5¢
   Spend 10¢.

5. 2 for 25¢
   Spend 75¢.

6. 2 for 15¢
   Spend 45¢.

now do these

What will they cost?

7. 4 for 50¢
   Buy 12.

8. 3 for 35¢
   Buy 9.

9. 6 for 85¢
   Buy 18.

How many will you get?

10. 3 for 50¢
    Spend $1.50.

11. 3 for $1.00
    Spend $5.00.

12. 5 for $3.00
    Spend $12.00.

251

JUST FOR A CHANGE

A. Linda has only nickels and pennies.
The ratio of nickels to pennies is $\frac{2}{1}$.
She has 11¢.
How many nickels are there?

B. Tina has only dimes and pennies.
The ratio of dimes to pennies is $\frac{2}{3}$.
She has 46¢.
How many dimes are there?

C. Larry has only dimes and nickels.
The ratio of dimes to nickels is $\frac{3}{2}$.
He has 80¢.
How many dimes are there?

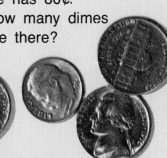

Time, Rate, and Distance

Fred can walk 4 kilometers in 1 hour.
At this rate, how far can he walk in 3 hours?

kilometers ⟶

4	?
1	3

hours ⟶

$$\frac{4}{1} = \frac{?}{3}$$

Think: 3 times as many hours.
3 times as many kilometers.

Fred can walk 12 kilometers in 3 hours.

The speed limit in Fred's state is
85 kilometers per hour.
At this rate, how long will it take to ride
340 kilometers?

kilometers ⟶

85	340
1	?

hours ⟶

$$\frac{85}{1} = \frac{340}{?}$$

Think: 4 times as many kilometers.
4 times as many hours.

It would take 4 hours.

252

How far will you go?

1. 3 km per hour
5 hours

2. 5 km per hour
7 hours

3. 64 km per hour
2 hours

How long will it take?

4. 5 km per hour
20 km

5. 50 km per hour
150 km

6. 65 km per hour
325 km

now do these

How far will you go?

7. 5 km per hour
4 hours

8. 8 km per hour
6 hours

9. 4 km per hour
2 hours

10. 35 km per hour
3 hours

11. 80 km per hour
4 hours

12. 96 km per hour
3 hours

How long will it take?

13. 7 km per hour
21 km

14. 4 km per hour
16 km

15. 15 km per hour
75 km

16. 25 km per hour
200 km

17. 63 km per hour
441 km

18. 85 km per hour
765 km

AN EXPERIMENT

Toss a coin.
The probability that it will
land heads is 1 out of 2.
About how many times can you expect it to land
heads if you toss it 2 times? 4 times? 6 times?
Make a chart.

Now toss a penny.

Compare the results with your chart.

tails   heads

tosses	2	4	6	8	10
heads	1				

Test

Write a fraction for the ratio.

1. apples to oranges (p. 246)

2. pennies to nickels (p. 246)

Complete.

3. $\frac{2}{3} = \frac{?}{21}$ (p. 248)

4. $\frac{8}{6} = \frac{?}{18}$ (p. 248)

5. $\frac{7}{10} = \frac{?}{40}$ (p. 248)

6. $\frac{1}{2} = \frac{5}{?}$ (p. 248)

7. $\frac{3}{5} = \frac{12}{?}$ (p. 248)

8. $\frac{9}{4} = \frac{54}{?}$ (p. 248)

What will they cost?

9. 4 for 15¢ (p. 250)
Buy 16.

10. 5 for 75¢ (p. 250)
Buy 15.

11. 6 for $1.25 (p. 250)
Buy 12.

How many will you get?

12. 7 for 50¢ (p. 250)
Spend $2.00.

13. 3 for $1.00 (p. 250)
Spend $4.00.

14. 4 for $1.20 (p. 250)
Spend $3.60.

How far will you go?

15. 9 km per hour (p. 252)
4 hours

16. 65 km per hour (p. 252)
3 hours

17. 21 km per hour (p. 252)
7 hours

How long will it take?

18. 6 km per hour (p. 252)
30 km

19. 55 km per hour (p. 252)
165 km

20. 82 km per hour (p. 252)
656 km

Keeping up

1. Find the perimeter of figure **A.** (p. 228)

2. Find the area of figure **A.** (p. 232)

3. Find the volume of figure **B.** (p. 236)

4. Which is longer, 39 mm or 4 cm? (p. 224)

5. Which is farther, 2405 m or 3 km? (p. 226)

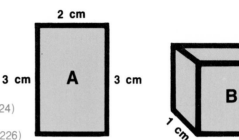

Write the fraction.

6. $5\frac{3}{4}$ (p. 198)

7. $2\frac{7}{8}$ (p. 198)

8. $6\frac{7}{10}$ (p. 198)

9. $3\frac{5}{8}$ (p. 198)

Write the mixed numeral.

10. $\frac{35}{8}$ (p. 200, 202)

11. $\frac{41}{6}$ (p. 200, 202)

12. $\frac{26}{3}$ (p. 200, 202)

13. $\frac{17}{3}$ (p. 200, 202)

Add. Write the simplest name for the answer.

14. $3\frac{5}{8}$
$+7\frac{1}{8}$
(p. 204)

15. $6\frac{3}{4}$
$+5\frac{1}{3}$
(p. 206)

16. $2\frac{3}{8}$
$+9\frac{5}{6}$
(p. 208)

17. $8\frac{3}{4}$
$+\ \ \frac{5}{6}$
(p. 208)

Subtract. Write the simplest name for the answer.

18. $12\frac{9}{10}$
$-\ 9\frac{7}{10}$
(p. 204)

19. 24
$-18\frac{3}{4}$
(p. 212)

20. $8\frac{2}{3}$
$-5\frac{3}{5}$
(p. 210)

21. $15\frac{3}{4}$
$-\ 7\frac{7}{8}$
(p. 214)

Divide.

(p. 144)

22. $34\overline{)2349}$

(p. 146)

23. $47\overline{)3817}$

(p. 146)

24. $68\overline{)2934}$

(p. 144)

25. $52\overline{)4730}$

255

Scale Drawing

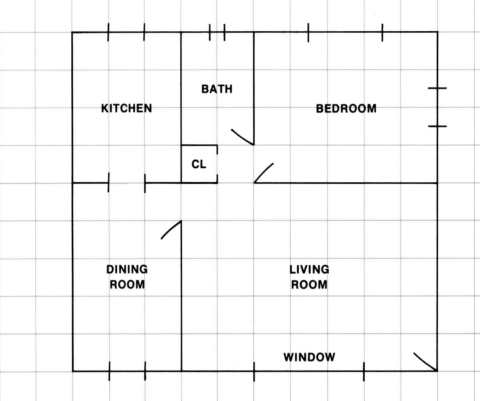

Marsha made a **scale drawing** of her apartment.
Each centimeter on the drawing represents 1 meter.

Measure the drawing of the kitchen.
The drawing measures 4 cm by 3 cm.
So, the dimensions of the kitchen are 4 m by 3 m.

Find the dimensions of each room.

How wide are the doors?
How long is the window in the living room?

13 Geometry

Shapes Around Us

There are shapes all around us.
How many can you find and name?

The Vocabulary of Geometry

This is a model of a **line segment.**
A line segment is straight.
It has two **endpoints.**
Call it line segment *AB*
or line segment *BA.*

This is a model of a **line.**
A line has no endpoints.
The arrowheads show that
it goes on forever in both
directions.
Call it line *CD* or line *DC.*

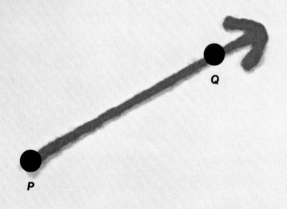

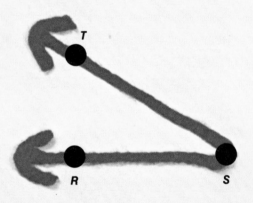

A **ray** is part of a line.
It has one endpoint.
It goes on forever
in one direction only.
Call it ray *PQ.*
(Name the endpoint first.)

These two rays have the
same endpoint.
They form an **angle.**
The endpoint is the **vertex.**
Call it angle *RST*
or angle *TSR.*

258

try these

Write a name for the figure.

1.

2.

3.
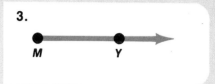

now do these

Name the figure.

4.
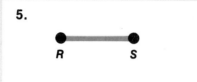

5.
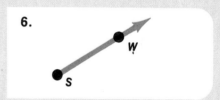

6.
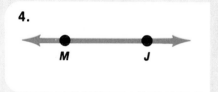

7.
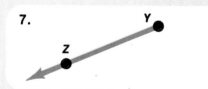

8.

9.
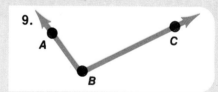

Draw the figure.

10. Draw points *A* and *B*.   Then draw line segment *AB*.

11. Draw points *C* and *D*.   Then draw line *CD*.

12. Draw points *E* and *F*.   Then draw ray *FE*.

Draw points *X* and *Y*.   Then answer the question.

13. How many line segments can you draw
   with points *X* and *Y* as endpoints?

14. How many lines can you draw through points *X* and *Y*?

15. How many lines can you draw through point *X*?

Congruent Line Segments

Congruent line segments have the same length.
Construct a line segment congruent to line segment AB.

A   B

Step 1

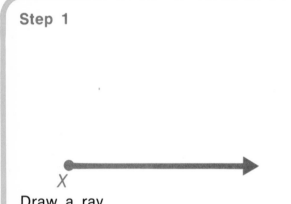
X

Draw a ray.
Name the endpoint X.

Step 2

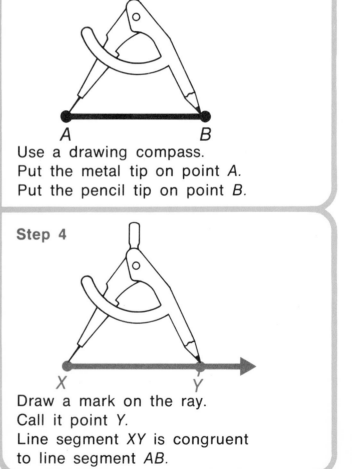
A   B

Use a drawing compass.
Put the metal tip on point A.
Put the pencil tip on point B.

Step 3

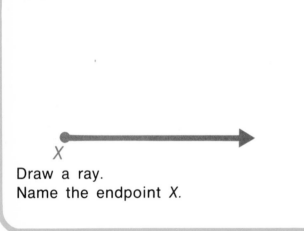
X

Keep the same compass opening.
Put the metal tip on point X.

Step 4

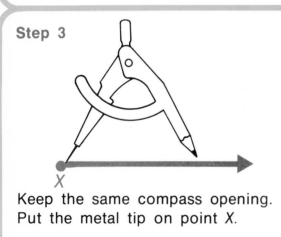
X   Y

Draw a mark on the ray.
Call it point Y.
Line segment XY is congruent
to line segment AB.

Construct a congruent line segment.

1.

2.

Construct a congruent line segment.

3.

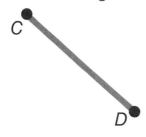

4.

5.

6.

CONGRUENT SIDES

Name the congruent line segments in the figure.

A.

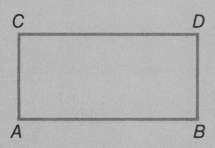

B.

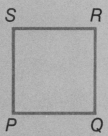

Right, Acute, and Obtuse Angles

An index card has
4 square corners.
Each is a **right angle.**

Jenny used an index
card to test angle *ABC.*

Is angle *ABC* a right angle?

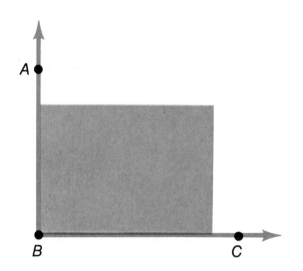

Jenny used her right angle tester on these angles.

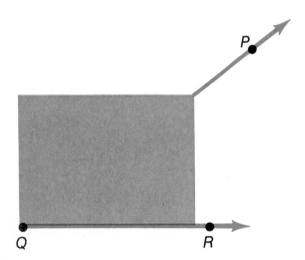

Angle *PQR* is smaller than
a right angle.

An angle smaller than
a right angle is an
acute angle.

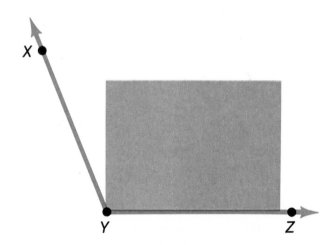

Angle *XYZ* is larger than
a right angle.

An angle larger than
a right angle is an
obtuse angle.

262

try these
Write RIGHT, ACUTE, or OBTUSE.

1.

2.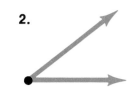

3.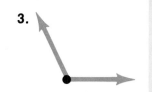

4.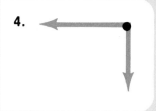

now do these
Write RIGHT, ACUTE, or OBTUSE.

5.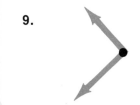

6.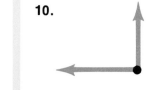

7.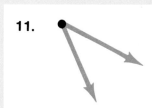

8.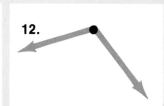

9.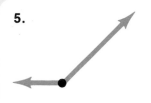

10.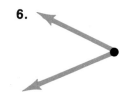

11.

12.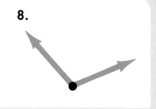

AN ANGLE ON TIME

The hands on a clock often form an angle.
The hands on this clock form a right angle.

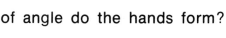

Which kind of angle do the hands form?

A.

B.

C.

D.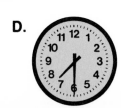

263

Using a Protractor

The unit of measure for an angle is the **degree** (**1°.**)

UNIT ANGLE   One Degree

You use a **protractor** to measure angles.
Place the protractor so the arrowhead is on the vertex.
The edge is on one of the rays.
Look where the other ray crosses the protractor.
The measure of angle *ABC* is 50 degrees (50°).

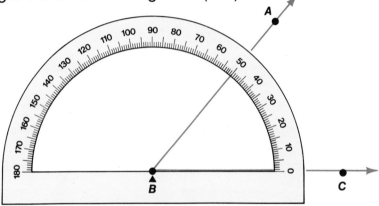

The measure of angle *DEF* is 140 degrees (140°).

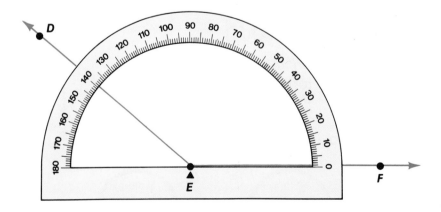

264

Measure the angle.

1.
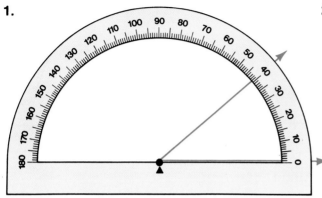

2.
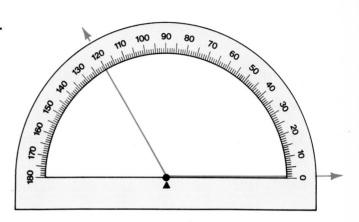

Measure the angle.

3.
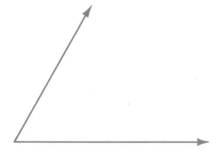

4.

5.
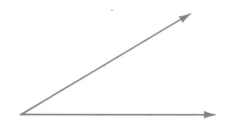

6.
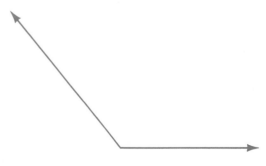

265

Which Scale Do You Use?

Angle *ABC* is a right angle.
The measure of a right angle is 90°.

So, the measure of an acute angle is less than 90°.

The measure of an obtuse angle is greater than 90° and less than 180°.

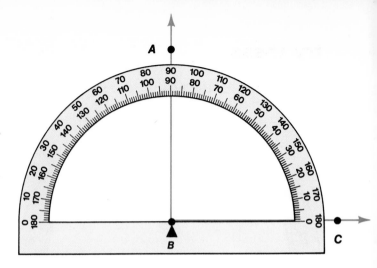

Angle *XYZ* is an acute angle.

Its measure is less than 90°.

Use the scale on which the number is less than 90.

The measure of angle *XYZ* is 45°.

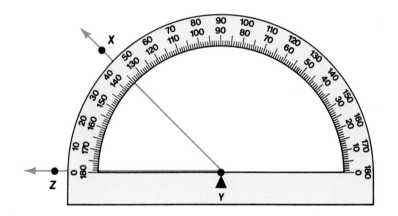

Angle *DEF* is an obtuse angle.

Its measure is greater than 90° and less than 180°.

Use the scale on which the number is greater than 90.

The measure of angle *DEF* is 120°.

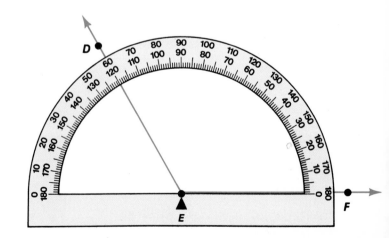

266

Write ACUTE or OBTUSE. Measure the angle.

1.

2.

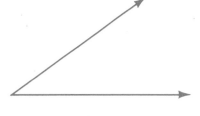

Write ACUTE or OBTUSE. Measure the angle.

3.

4.

5.

6.

THREE ANGLES

Measure each angle.
Add the measures.
What is the sum?

Draw other triangles.
Measure the 3 angles.
Add the measures.
What is the sum every time?

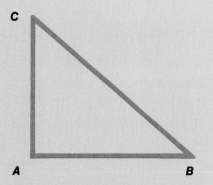

267

Congruent Angles

Congruent angles have the same measure.
Construct an angle congruent to angle *ABC*.

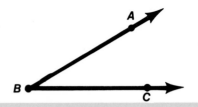

Step 1

Draw a ray.

Step 2

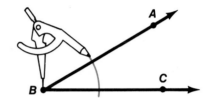

Put the metal tip on point *B*.
Draw a mark through both rays.

Step 3

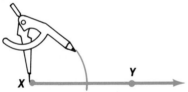

Keep the same compass opening.
Put the metal tip on point *X*.
Draw a mark.

Step 4

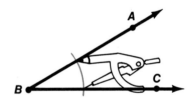

Open the compass so the tips
are on the points where the
mark crosses the rays.

Step 5

Keep the same compass opening.
Put the metal tip on the point
where the mark crosses the ray.
Draw another mark.

Step 6

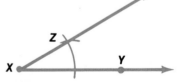

Draw ray *XZ*.
Angle *ZXY* is congruent to angle *ABC*.

Trace the angle. Then construct a congruent angle.

1.

2.

Trace the angle. Then construct a congruent angle.

3.

4.

5.

6.

CAN YOU DO IT?

You can construct congruent line segments.
You can construct congruent angles.
Now try to construct a triangle congruent
to this one.

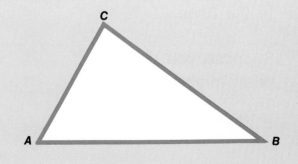

Parallel and Perpendicular Lines

Lines that are always
the same distance apart
are **parallel lines.**

Parallel lines can never meet.
The rails of a train track
are parallel.

Suppose they were not.
What would happen?

Lines that meet to
form right angles
are **perpendicular lines.**

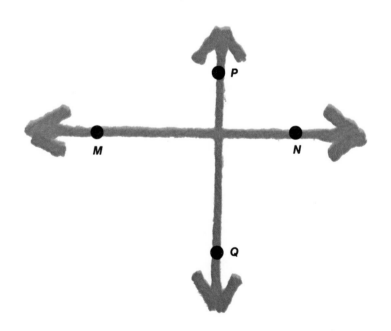

Most of the time you
stand perpendicular
to the floor.

Suppose you did not.
What might happen?

Write PARALLEL, PERPENDICULAR, or NEITHER.

1.

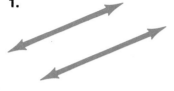

2.

3.

Write PARALLEL, PERPENDICULAR, or NEITHER.

4.

5.

6.

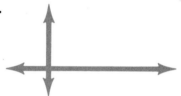

7.

8.

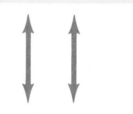

9.

Which segments are parallel? Which are perpendicular?

10.

11.

12.

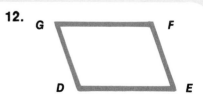

271

Polygons

A **simple closed path** begins and ends at the same point. It does not cross over itself.

Is it a simple closed path?

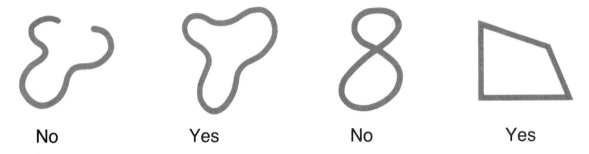

No   Yes   No   Yes

A **polygon** is a simple closed path made up of line segments only.

Names are given to polygons according to the number of sides or number of angles they have.

Triangle   **Quadrilateral**   **Pentagon**   **Hexagon**   **Octagon**

Some quadrilaterals are more special.

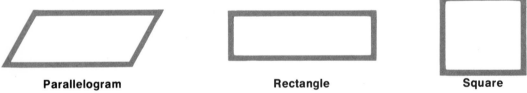

Parallelogram   **Rectangle**   **Square**

The sides that do not meet are parallel and congruent.

The sides that do not meet are parallel and congruent. The sides that meet are perpendicular.

A special kind of rectangle. All sides are congruent.

272

Is it a simple closed path?   Write YES or NO.

1.

2.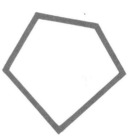

3.

Name the polygon.

4.

5.

6.

Name the polygon.

7.

8.

9.

Name the quadrilateral.

10.

11.

12.

273

Congruent Polygons

Congruent polygons have the same size and shape.
These two polygons are congruent.

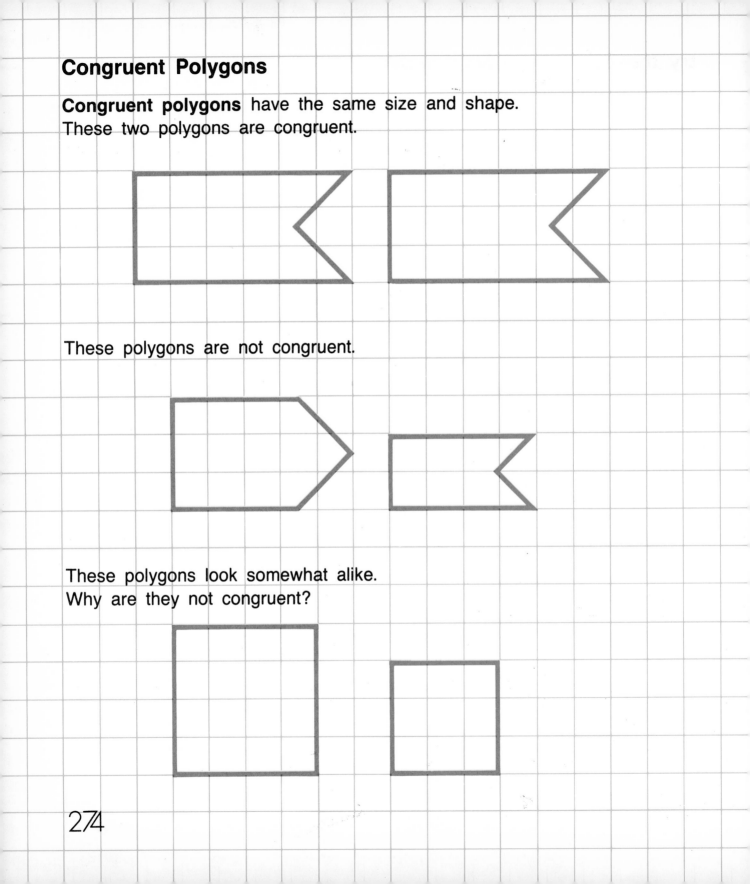

These polygons are not congruent.

These polygons look somewhat alike.
Why are they not congruent?

Are they congruent? Write YES or NO.

1.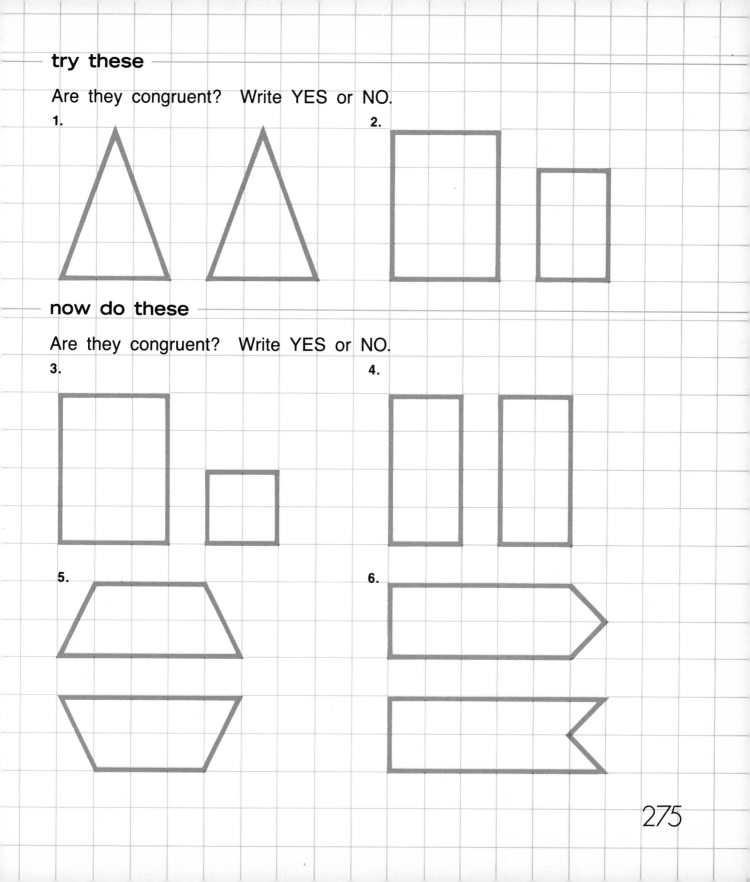

2.

now do these

Are they congruent? Write YES or NO.

3.

4.

5.

6.

Similar Polygons

Similar polygons have the same shape.
These two polygons are similar.

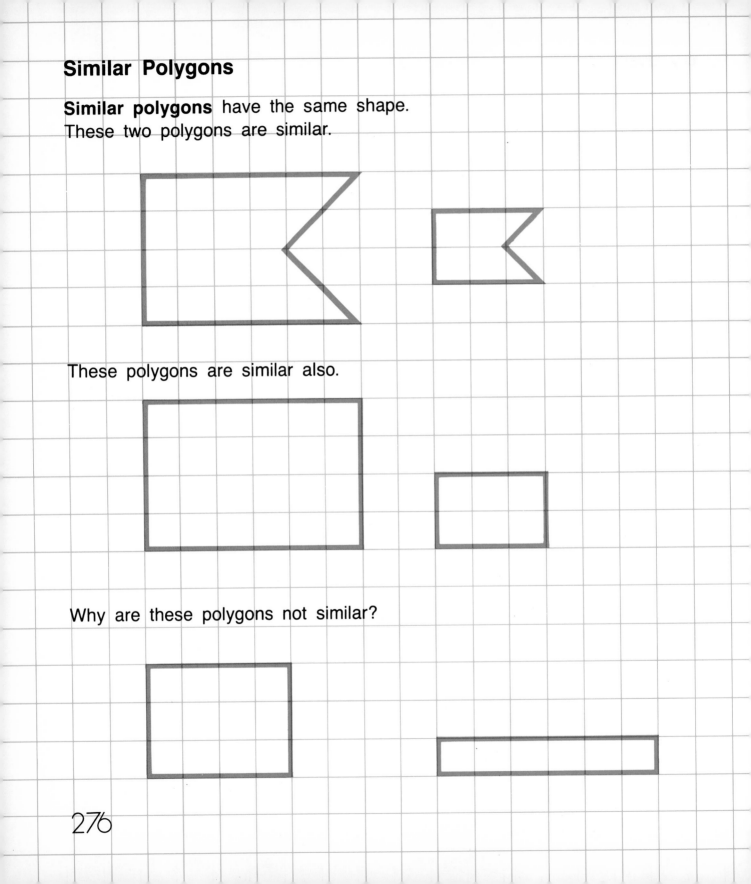

These polygons are similar also.

Why are these polygons not similar?

Are they similar? Write YES or NO.

1.

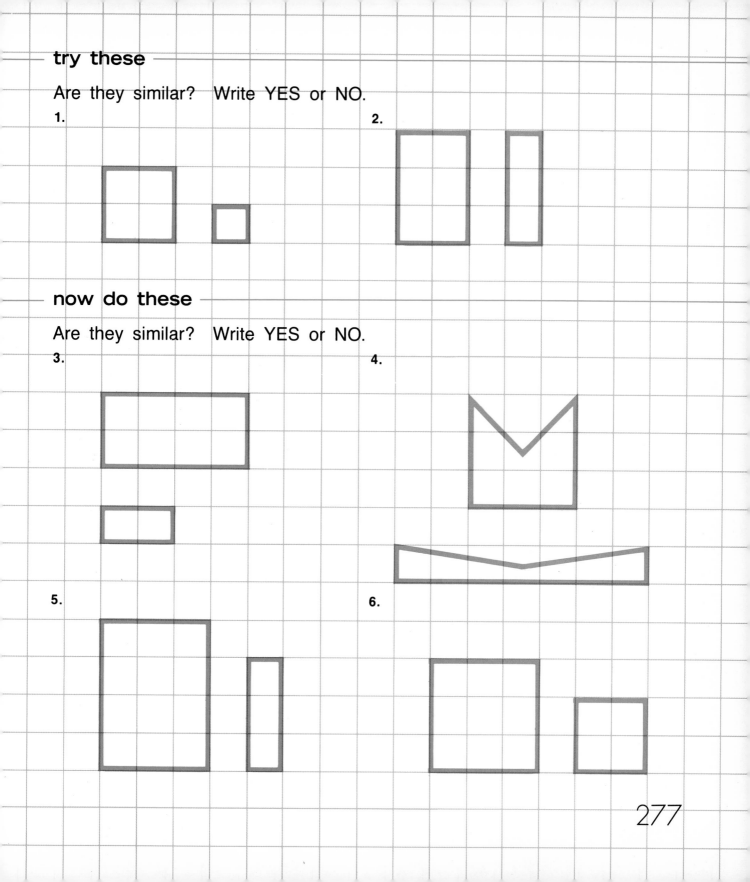

2.

now do these

Are they similar? Write YES or NO.

3.

4.

5.

6.

Constructing a Circle

Step 1

Use your compass.
Put the metal tip on a point.
Swing the pencil around to
construct a simple closed path.

Step 2

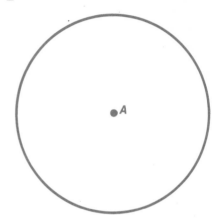

You have constructed a **circle**.
Point *A* is the **center**.
This is circle *A*.

Step 3

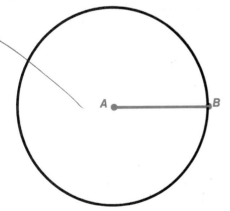

Draw a line segment that joins
the center and a point on
the circle.
You have drawn a **radius**.
How many more could you draw?

Step 4

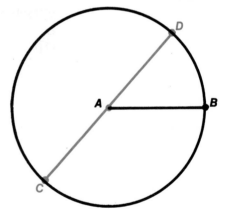

Draw a line segment through
the center that joins two
points on the circle.
You have drawn a **diameter**.
How many more could you draw?

278

Draw a line segment with the length given.
Use it as a radius to construct a circle.

1. 3 cm   2. 4 cm   3. 5 cm   4. 6 cm

now do these

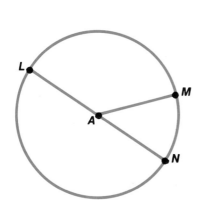 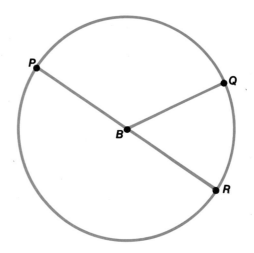

5. In circle *A*, how long is radius *AN*? radius *AM*?
6. If you drew another radius for circle *A*, how long would it be?
7. How long is diameter *LN*?
8. How is the length of diameter *LN* related to the length of radius *LA*?

9. In circle *B*, how long is radius *BR*? radius *BQ*?
10. If you drew another radius for circle *B*, how long would it be?
11. How long is diameter *PR*?
12. How is the length of diameter *PR* related to the length of radius *PB*?

13. Which circle has the longer radius?
14. Which is the larger circle?

279

Three Dimensions

Here are some shapes that you have seen before.

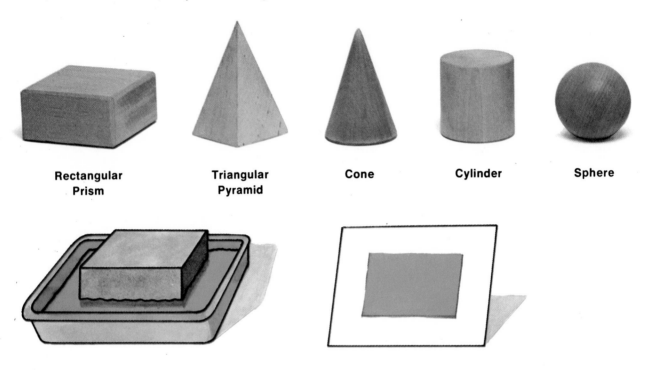

Rectangular Prism   Triangular Pyramid   Cone   Cylinder   Sphere

The flat surfaces are **faces.**
Dip a rectangular prism
into poster paint.
Make a print.

The print is shaped
like a rectangle.
So, what shape does
the face have?

Which shape would make the print?

A.   B.   C.

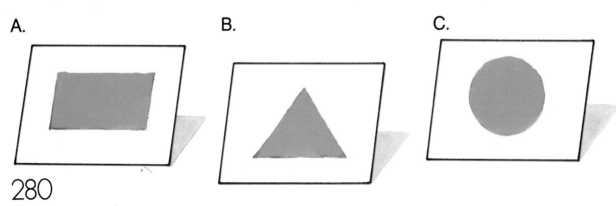

Name the shape of the object.

1.

2.

3.

4.

5.

6.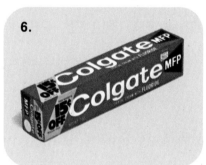

4.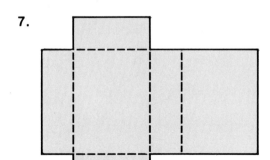

6.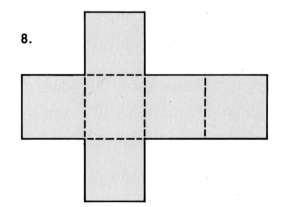

now do these

Trace the pattern. Cut it out.
Fold along the dotted lines. Tape the edges together.
What shape did you make?

7.

8.

281

Test

Name the figure.

1.
(p. 258)
X   Y

2. (p. 258)
A   B

3. (p. 258)
G   H

Write RIGHT, ACUTE, or OBTUSE.

4. (p. 262)

5. (p. 262)

6. (p. 262)

Write PARALLEL, PERPENDICULAR, or NEITHER.

7. (p. 270)

8. (p. 270)

9. (p. 270)

Measure the angle.

10. (p. 264)

11. (p. 264)

Name the polygon.

12. (p. 272)

13. (p. 272)

Name the quadrilateral.

14. (p. 272)

15. (p. 272)

Name the shape.

16. (p. 280)

17. (p. 280)

18. In circle *D*, how long is radius *DC*? (p. 278)

19. In circle *D*, how long is diameter *AB*? (p. 278)

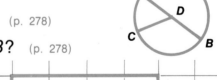

Write YES or NO.

20. Are the polygons congruent? (p. 274)
Are they similar? (p. 276)

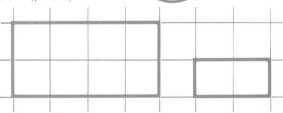

Keeping up

How far will you go

1. in 8 hours at a rate of 79 km per hour? (p. 252)

2. in 6 hours at a rate of 87 km per hour? (p. 252)

What will they cost?

3. Apples are 2 for 19¢. Buy 6. (p. 250)

4. Oranges are 3 for 38¢. Buy 12. (p. 250)

5. Find the volume of the box. (p. 236)

6. Find the area of the blue part of the box. (p. 234)

7. Find the perimeter of the red part of the box. (p. 228)

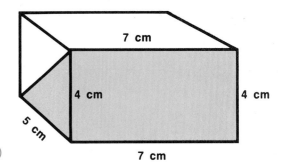

8. Which is heavier, 2360 g or 3 kg? (p. 240)

9. Which is more, 3 *l* or 3572 ml? (p. 238)

Add.

10. 43,625 +21,013 (p. 28)	11. 89,400 + 5,667 (p. 32)	12. 55,830 +42,749 (p. 32)	13. 37,897 + 976 (p. 32)

Subtract.

14. 94,653 −73,542 (p. 48)	15. 62,400 − 8,245 (p. 56)	16. 34,621 −17,849 (p. 54)	17. 72,000 − 978 (p. 56)

283

Slides, Turns, and Flips

Trace shape **A**.
Slide the tracing
to fit over **B**.
Are **A** and **B** congruent?

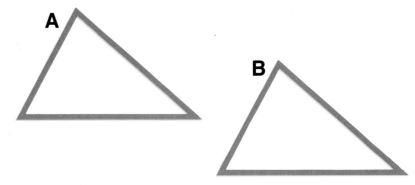

Trace shape **C**.
Turn and slide
the tracing to
fit over **D**.
Are **C** and **D** congruent?

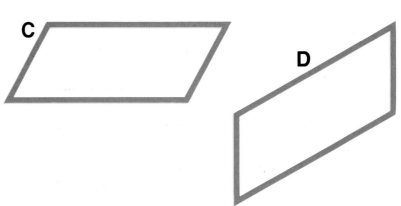

Does it show just a slide or a slide and a turn?

1.

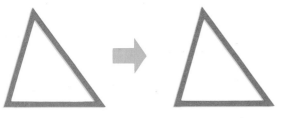

2.

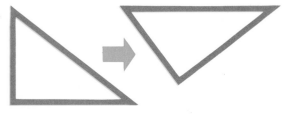

3.

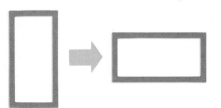

4.

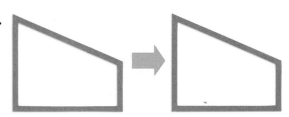

Trace shape **E.**
Cut it out.
Flip it over and
slide to fit on **F.**
Are **E** and **F** congruent?

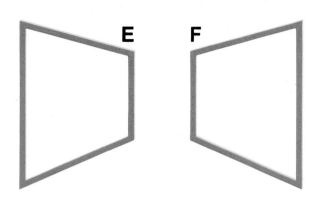

Do you have to flip? Write YES or NO.

5.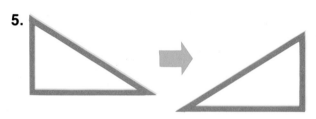

6.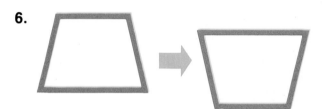

7.

8.

Write the letter to tell where the piece fits.
You can slide, turn, and flip.

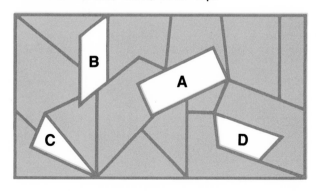

9.    **10.**

11.    **12.**

14 Decimals

Tenths

One pie is cut into 10 pieces of the same size. Each piece is one tenth of the whole pie.

$$\frac{1}{10} = 0.1$$

fraction   decimal

You can write decimals to name tenths.
Read the fractions. Then read the decimals.

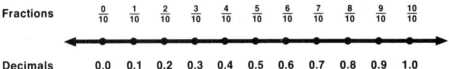

Fractions	$\frac{0}{10}$	$\frac{1}{10}$	$\frac{2}{10}$	$\frac{3}{10}$	$\frac{4}{10}$	$\frac{5}{10}$	$\frac{6}{10}$	$\frac{7}{10}$	$\frac{8}{10}$	$\frac{9}{10}$	$\frac{10}{10}$
Decimals	0.0	0.1	0.2	0.3	0.4	0.5	0.6	0.7	0.8	0.9	1.0

427 students are on a school picnic.
Each student eats a piece of pie.
They eat $42\frac{7}{10}$ pies.
You can use place value to show tenths.

tens	ones	tenths
4	2	7

Where is the decimal point?
In what place is the digit 2?
In what place is the 4? the 7?

286

Write the decimal.

1. $\frac{3}{10}$ 2. $\frac{9}{10}$ 3. $1\frac{7}{10}$ 4. $6\frac{1}{10}$ 5. $17\frac{2}{10}$

now do these

Write the decimal.

6. $\frac{1}{10}$ 7. $\frac{4}{10}$ 8. $\frac{5}{10}$ 9. $3\frac{8}{10}$ 10. $5\frac{2}{10}$

11. $8\frac{3}{10}$ 12. $9\frac{7}{10}$ 13. $21\frac{4}{10}$ 14. $78\frac{7}{10}$ 15. $86\frac{9}{10}$

Write the fraction or the mixed numeral.

16. 0.4   17. 0.2   18. 0.5   19. 7.8   20. 5.2

21. 3.4   22. 8.5   23. 16.3   24. 45.6   25. 87.9

What part is red? Write the decimal.

26.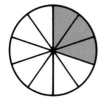

27.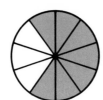

28.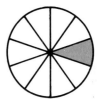

ODOMETERS

An odometer tells how far a car has gone.
This car has gone 5 tenths of a kilometer.

How far has the car gone?

0.5 km

A. | 0 | 0 | 0 | 0 | 0 | 9 |

B. | 0 | 0 | 0 | 0 | 1 | 0 |

C. | 0 | 0 | 0 | 0 | 7 | 6 |

D. | 0 | 0 | 0 | 1 | 4 | 8 |

E. | 0 | 0 | 0 | 2 | 0 | 3 |

F. | 0 | 0 | 1 | 4 | 8 | 7 |

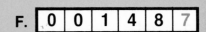

287

Hundredths

100 pennies are worth 1 dollar.
Each cent is $\frac{1}{100}$ of a dollar.
The decimal for $\frac{1}{100}$ is 0.01.
1 is in the hundredths place.

$$\frac{1}{100} = 0.01$$

There are 100 pennies here.
A ring is drawn around 32.
$\frac{32}{100}$ of the pennies are inside.

$$\frac{32}{100} = 0.32$$

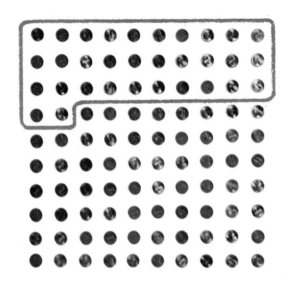

Suppose you have 3 dollar
bills and 17 pennies.
That is worth $3\frac{17}{100}$ dollars.
The decimal for $3\frac{17}{100}$ is 3.17.

$$3\frac{17}{100} = 3.17$$

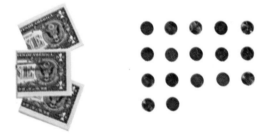

You can use place value to show hundredths.
The decimal for $476\frac{28}{100}$ is 476.28.

hundreds	tens	ones	tenths	hundredths
4	7	6	2	8

Where is the decimal point?
In what place is the digit 6?
In what place is the 7? the 2? the 4? the 8?

288

Write the decimal.

1. $\frac{65}{100}$ 2. $\frac{90}{100}$ 3. $1\frac{17}{100}$ 4. $24\frac{46}{100}$ 5. $35\frac{4}{100}$

Write the decimal.

6. $\frac{6}{10}$ 7. $\frac{50}{100}$ 8. $\frac{37}{100}$ 9. $\frac{3}{10}$ 10. $\frac{2}{100}$

11. $1\frac{2}{100}$ 12. $3\frac{40}{100}$ 13. $6\frac{8}{10}$ 14. $7\frac{85}{100}$ 15. $2\frac{7}{100}$

16. $34\frac{5}{10}$ 17. $29\frac{60}{100}$ 18. $43\frac{8}{100}$ 19. $150\frac{7}{10}$ 20. $651\frac{59}{100}$

Write the fraction or mixed numeral.

21. 0.3   22. 0.35   23. 0.72   24. 0.03   25. 0.07

26. 4.65   27. 3.7   28. 8.03   29. 6.11   30. 9.87

31. 24.5   32. 62.04   33. 12.08   34. 352.9   35. 747.28

THE METRIC WAY

The paper clip is 34 millimeters long.
A millimeter is $\frac{1}{10}$ of a centimeter.
So, the paper clip is 3.4 centimeters long.

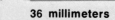

centimeters

How many centimeters long is it?

A.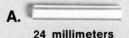
24 millimeters

B.
18 millimeters

C.
36 millimeters

D.
30 millimeters

E.
28 millimeters

F.
20 millimeters

289

Thousandths

There are 1000 bulbs in the sign.
125 burned out last month.
What part had to be replaced?

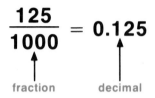

$$\frac{125}{1000} = 0.125$$

fraction   decimal

5 is in the thousandths place.
In what place is the digit 2?
In what place is the 1?

You can use place value
to show thousandths.

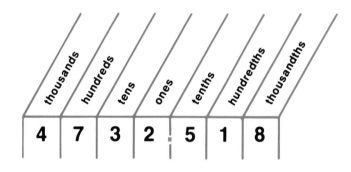

thousands	hundreds	tens	ones	tenths	hundredths	thousandths
4	7	3	2	5	1	8

In what place is the digit 8? the 4?
In what place is the 1? the 7?
In what place is the 5? the 3?

Read the numeral. ⟶ Four thousand, seven hundred thirty-two and
five hundred eighteen thousandths.

Write. ⟶ **4732.518**

290

Write the decimal.

1. $\frac{463}{1000}$

2. $4\frac{172}{1000}$

3. $29\frac{42}{1000}$

4. $37\frac{5}{1000}$

now do these

Write the decimal.

5. $\frac{238}{1000}$

6. $\frac{4}{10}$

7. $\frac{2}{100}$

8. $\frac{8}{1000}$

9. $2\frac{9}{10}$

10. $6\frac{52}{100}$

11. $48\frac{399}{1000}$

12. $83\frac{5}{1000}$

13. $406\frac{40}{100}$

14. $888\frac{43}{1000}$

15. $2431\frac{900}{1000}$

16. $1876\frac{3}{1000}$

Write the fraction or the mixed numeral.

17. 0.4

18. 0.05

19. 0.006

20. 0.186

21. 6.098

22. 8.5

23. 3.650

24. 39.007

25. 67.83

26. 82.387

27. 904.081

28. 700.004

THE METRIC WAY

This book is 23 centimeters wide.
A centimeter is $\frac{1}{100}$ of a meter.
So, the book is 0.23 meter wide.

How many meters is the measurement?

A. 42 centimeters
B. 54 centimeters
C. 70 centimeters
D. 136 centimeters
E. 248 centimeters
F. 975 centimeters
G. 1426 centimeters
H. 2374 centimeters
I. 6140 centimeters

291

Place Value

A digit in different places names different numbers.
The chart shows how 3 can name seven different numbers.

thousands	hundreds	tens	ones	tenths	hundredths	thousandths	
3	0	0	0 .				→ three thousand
	3	0	0 .				→ three hundred
		3	0 .				→ thirty
			3 .				→ three
			0 .	3			→ three tenths
			0 .	0	3		→ three hundredths
			0 .	0	0	3	→ three thousandths

Each place in a numeral has a value

■ 10 times the value of the place at its right.

■ $\frac{1}{10}$ the value of the place at its left.

292

In what place is the red digit?

1. 21.760   2. 85.365   3. 29.246

What number does the red digit name?

4. 35.689   5. 32.478   6. 20.304

now do these

In what place is the red digit?

7. 26.498   8. 35.789   9. 53.987

10. 247.633   11. 9357.249   12. 1175.321

What number does the red digit name?

13. 87.234   14. 38.423   15. 97.876

16. 463.489   17. 9836.984   18. 9658.357

In which numeral does the digit 3 have the greater value?

19. 23   20. 9.438   21. 12.536

    2.3   6.345   1.253

THE METRIC WAY

It is 32 meters from Angela's house
to Alfred's house.
A meter is $\frac{1}{1000}$ of a kilometer.
So, their houses are 0.032 kilometer apart.

How many kilometers is the measurement?
A. 4 meters   B. 8 meters   C. 26 meters   D. 73 meters
E. 257 meters   F. 142 meters   G. 1489 meters   H. 2735 meters

293

Comparing Decimals

It is 28.7 kilometers from Hushtown to Newville.
It is 28.4 kilometers from Hushtown to Crabby Corners.
Which town is farther from Hushtown?
　　　　Compare as you would whole numbers.

$$28.7 > 28.4$$

Newville is farther from Hushtown.

Use > or < to compare.

6.75 ● 6.71	**36.8 ● 39.4**	**8.362 ● 8.367**
6.75 is greater than 6.71	36.8 is less than 39.4	8.362 is less than 8.367
6.75 > 6.71	**36.8 < 39.4**	**8.362 < 8.367**

Write > or <.
1. 2.39 ● 2.47
2. 63.4 ● 63.7
3. 5.74 ● 5.73
4. 8.272 ● 8.262
5. 43.81 ● 47.23
6. 36.817 ● 36.815

now do these

Write > or <.
7. 16.7 ● 16.9
8. 2.036 ● 2.034
9. 42.83 ● 42.80
10. 85.6 ● 83.7
11. 3.48 ● 3.63
12. 9.431 ● 9.432
13. 73.42 ● 76.63
14. 9.6 ● 9.3
15. 8.473 ● 8.491
16. 27.48 ● 27.27
17. 34.099 ● 34.098
18. 86.4 ● 87.8
19. 63.932 ● 63.678
20. 77.894 ● 79.996
21. 40.612 ● 40.321

Which is greater?
22. 47.6 cm or 47.3 cm
23. 1.8 km or 2.7 km
24. 17.5 cm or 17.2 cm
25. 2.52 m or 2.25 m
26. 16.3 km or 17.3 km
27. 15.4 cm or 14.3 cm

A CHALLENGE

1 meter ⟷ 100 centimeters

1 centimeter ⟷ $\frac{1}{100}$ meter

Which is greater?

342 cm or 3.36 m

You can change cm to m:

342 cm = 3.42 m

Now compare:

3.42 m or 3.36 m

Or change m to cm:

3.36 m = 336 cm

Now compare:

342 cm or 336 cm

Either way, you can see that 342 cm is greater.

Which is greater?
A. 128 cm or 1.26 m
B. 345 cm or 3.49 m
C. 520 cm or 6.82 m
D. 28 cm or 1.29 m
E. 420 cm or 0.42 m
F. 647 cm or 6.09 m

Addition

You have 3.24 liters of yellow paint.
You have 2.57 liters of blue paint. Mix them.
How many liters of green paint do you get?

Step 1

```
    1
  3.24
+ 2.57
------
     1
```

Line up the decimal points.
Add the hundredths.

Step 2

```
    1
  3.24
+ 2.57
------
    81
```

Add the tenths.

Step 3

```
    1
  3.24
+ 2.57
------
  5.81
```

Add the ones.
Write the decimal point in the answer.

You get 5.81 liters of green paint.

Add: 7.583 + 4.928.

Step 1

```
    1
  7.583
+ 4.928
-------
      1
```

Line up the decimal points.
Add the thousandths.

Step 2

```
   1 1
  7.583
+ 4.928
-------
     11
```

Add the hundredths.

Step 3

```
  1 11
  7.583
+ 4.928
-------
    511
```

Add the tenths.

Step 4

```
  1 11
  7.583
+ 4.928
-------
 12.511
```

Add the ones.
Write the decimal point.

296

Copy and complete.

1.
```
  1 1 1
  6.789
 +4.567
  .356
```

2.
```
  1 1
  0.89
 +9.34
  .23
```

3.
```
   1
  75.67
 + 2.70
   37
```

4.
```
   1
  0.96
 +0.08
   4
```

5.
```
    1
  60.87
 +30.69
      6
```

Add.

6.
```
  0.329
 +0.468
```

7.
```
  3.45
 +7.89
```

8.
```
  0.279
 +9.865
```

9.
```
  30.72
 + 4.93
```

10.
```
  42.45
 +38.36
```

Add.

11.
```
  23.7
 +45.8
```

12.
```
  6.76
 +9.48
```

13.
```
  82.46
 + 2.29
```

14.
```
  35.82
 +67.63
```

15.
```
  5.629
 +4.836
```

16.
```
  6.734
 +5.923
```

17.
```
  6.003
 +4.798
```

18.
```
  42.39
 + 8.78
```

19.
```
  0.07
 +9.96
```

20.
```
  27.23
 +95.97
```

21.
```
  4.256
 +2.879
```

22.
```
  93.07
 + 2.95
```

23.
```
  3.879
 +2.603
```

24.
```
  80.08
 +40.95
```

25.
```
  0.06
 +0.09
```

26.
```
  7.54
 +2.39
```

27.
```
  0.92
 +0.83
```

28.
```
  15.28
 + 4.79
```

29.
```
  6.08
 +3.59
```

30.
```
  0.698
 +0.758
```

31.
```
  43.79
 +65.28
```

32.
```
  735.9
 +423.6
```

33.
```
  2.435
 +6.897
```

34.
```
  13.4
 +14.9
```

35.
```
  48.64
 +61.38
```

297

Subtraction

There are 2.73 liters of milk in a pitcher.
Janet pours out 1.38 liters.
How much milk is left in the pitcher?

Step 1

$$\begin{array}{r} {\scriptstyle 6\ 13} \\ 2.\cancel{7}\cancel{3} \\ -1.38 \\ \hline 5 \end{array}$$

Line up the decimal points.
Subtract the hundredths.

Step 2

$$\begin{array}{r} {\scriptstyle 6\ 13} \\ 2.\cancel{7}\cancel{3} \\ -1.38 \\ \hline 35 \end{array}$$

Subtract the tenths.

Step 3

$$\begin{array}{r} {\scriptstyle 6\ 13} \\ 2.\cancel{7}\cancel{3} \\ -1.38 \\ \hline 1.35 \end{array}$$

Subtract the ones.
Write the decimal point in the answer.

There are 1.35 liters of milk left.

Subtract: 8.372 − 2.914.

Step 1

$$\begin{array}{r} {\scriptstyle 6\ 12} \\ 8.3\cancel{7}\cancel{2} \\ -2.914 \\ \hline 8 \end{array}$$

Line up the decimal points. Subtract the thousandths.

Step 2

$$\begin{array}{r} {\scriptstyle 6\ 12} \\ 8.3\cancel{7}\cancel{2} \\ -2.914 \\ \hline 58 \end{array}$$

Subtract the hundredths.

Step 3

$$\begin{array}{r} {\scriptstyle 7\ 13\ 6\ 12} \\ 8.\cancel{3}\cancel{7}\cancel{2} \\ -2.914 \\ \hline 458 \end{array}$$

Subtract the tenths.

Step 4

$$\begin{array}{r} {\scriptstyle 7\ 13\ 6\ 12} \\ 8.\cancel{3}\cancel{7}\cancel{2} \\ -2.914 \\ \hline 5.458 \end{array}$$

Subtract the ones. Write the decimal point.

Copy and complete.

				10 10		9 9

1. $\quad\quad$ 6 13
    9.7̸3̸
    −4.39
    ‾‾‾‾‾‾
    $\quad$.34

2. $\quad$ 8 $\quad$13
    6̸9̸.3̸
    −37.7
    ‾‾‾‾‾‾
    $\quad$1.6

3. $\quad\quad$ 6 15
    84.7̸5̸
    −73.68
    ‾‾‾‾‾‾‾
    $\quad\quad$7

4. $\quad$ 10 10
    $\quad$3 0̸ 1̸ 13
    4̸.1̸2̸3̸
    −0.568
    ‾‾‾‾‾‾
    $\quad$.555

5. $\quad$ 9   9
    $\quad$5 1̸0̸ 1̸0̸ 10
    6̸0̸.0̸0̸
    − 3.42
    ‾‾‾‾‾‾
    $\quad\quad$8

Subtract.

6. 3.06
    −1.27
    ‾‾‾‾‾

7. 0.215
    −0.194
    ‾‾‾‾‾‾

8. 46.23
    − 5.45
    ‾‾‾‾‾‾

9. 7.273
    −3.485
    ‾‾‾‾‾‾

10. 49.76
    −15.48
    ‾‾‾‾‾‾

Subtract.

11. 9.654
    −3.728
    ‾‾‾‾‾‾

12. 8.35
    −6.29
    ‾‾‾‾‾

13. 7.453
    −6.819
    ‾‾‾‾‾‾

14. 6.493
    −2.658
    ‾‾‾‾‾‾

15. 86.07
    − 5.86
    ‾‾‾‾‾‾

16. 5.473
    −4.728
    ‾‾‾‾‾‾

17. 6.364
    −5.857
    ‾‾‾‾‾‾

18. 59.23
    − 6.45
    ‾‾‾‾‾‾

19. 8.06
    −3.97
    ‾‾‾‾‾

20. 32.4
    −11.9
    ‾‾‾‾‾

21. 6.530
    −1.713
    ‾‾‾‾‾‾

22. 4.23
    −2.17
    ‾‾‾‾‾

23. 4.06
    −2.35
    ‾‾‾‾‾

24. 8.19
    −7.26
    ‾‾‾‾‾

25. 8.396
    −5.488
    ‾‾‾‾‾‾

26. 5.13
    −3.29
    ‾‾‾‾‾

27. 7.03
    −2.09
    ‾‾‾‾‾

28. 8.374
    −2.837
    ‾‾‾‾‾‾

29. 82.27
    −61.56
    ‾‾‾‾‾‾

30. 98.64
    − 5.29
    ‾‾‾‾‾‾

31. 95.00
    −42.59
    ‾‾‾‾‾‾

32. 178.4
    − 96.7
    ‾‾‾‾‾‾

33. 8.790
    −4.236
    ‾‾‾‾‾‾

34. 6.40
    −2.38
    ‾‾‾‾‾

35. 64.29
    −32.86
    ‾‾‾‾‾‾

299

more than one step

Harold and Susan are architects. They are planning a playground. They want to buy safe equipment. Flat-board swings cost $7.25 each. Animal-form swings cost $150 each. They plan for 6 flat-board swings and 5 animal-form swings. How much will they cost?

It takes more than one step to solve this problem.

First, multiply to find the cost for each kind of swing.

$$\begin{array}{r} \$7.25 \\ \times\ \ \ \ 6 \\ \hline \$43.50 \end{array} \qquad \begin{array}{r} \$150 \\ \times\ \ \ \ 5 \\ \hline \$750 \end{array}$$

Then, add to find the total cost of all the swings.

$$\begin{array}{r} \$750.00 \\ +\ \ \ 43.50 \\ \hline \$793.50 \end{array}$$

The swings will cost $793.50.

What steps must you take to solve the problem?

1. Swing chains cost $12.50 per meter. The chains for a flat swing must be 3 meters long. Each swing needs 2 chains. How much will chain cost for one swing?

2. They need 20 loads of brick to build a field house. Brick A sells for $130 a load. Brick B sells for $140 a load. How much will be saved if they buy Brick A?

300

Solve the problem.

3. Small slides cost $98.75 each.
Large slides cost $180.00 each.
Susan orders 2 of each. How
much will they cost?

4. The playground will have 2 baseball
diamonds. The bags for first, second,
and third base cost $8.75 each.
How much will the bags cost for
both diamonds?

5. The backstop for a baseball field
costs $3000. A side wing costs
$2000. What will be the cost for a
backstop and two side wings?

6. The field house has one window
with 3 panes. Plate glass costs
$6.23 for each pane. It may break.
Unbreakable window material
costs $18.45 for each pane.
How much more will it cost
to make the window unbreakable?

Test

Write the decimal.

1. $\frac{8}{10}$ (p. 286)

2. $2\frac{73}{100}$ (p. 288)

3. $24\frac{35}{1000}$ (p. 290)

Write the fraction or mixed numeral.

4. 3.3 (p. 286)

5. 18.91 (p. 288)

6. 0.783 (p. 290)

In what place is the red digit?

7. 1035.794 (p. 292)

8. 28.643 (p. 292)

9. 1156.102 (p. 292)

What number does the red digit name?

10. 86.415 (p. 292)

11. 13.297 (p. 292)

12. 1023.506 (p. 292)

Write > or <.

13. 25.031 ● 25.130 (p. 294)

14. 6.72 ● 6.59 (p. 294)

15. 2.10 ● 1.99 (p. 294)

Add.

16. 8.63
    +9.89
    (p. 296)

17. 0.138
    +0.947
    (p. 296)

18. 84.65
    + 7.85
    (p. 296)

19. 5.944
    +4.867
    (p. 296)

20. 0.400
    +6.865
    (p. 296)

Subtract.

21. 88.5
    −16.7
    (p. 298)

22. 6.37
    −2.84
    (p. 298)

23. 35.92
    −24.68
    (p. 298)

24. 87.0
    − 3.1
    (p. 298)

25. 63.00
    − 8.99
    (p. 298)

bonus

Solve the problem.

26. There are 4.88 liters of water in one pail. There are 6.07 liters in another pail. How many liters are there in all? (p. 296)

27. You have 7.43 liters of paint. You use 3.85 liters. How many liters do you have left? (p. 298)

302

Keeping up

1. Which two triangles are congruent? (p. 274)
2. Which two rectangles are similar? (p. 276)
3. Which polygons have parallel line segments? (p. 270)
4. Which polygons have right angles? (p. 262)
5. Which have acute angles? (p. 262)

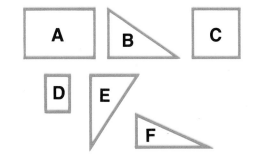

Complete.

6. 3 boxes weigh 325 g, so 12 boxes weigh _?_ g. (p. 248)

7. 4 jars hold 223 ml, so 28 jars hold _?_ ml. (p. 248)

Add.

8. 643
  + 97
  (p. 32)

9. 888
  +769
  (p. 32)

10. 4783
  + 349
  (p. 32)

11. 9045
  +5685
  (p. 32)

Subtract.

12. 834
  −797
  (p. 54)

13. 500
  − 89
  (p. 56)

14. 5623
  −3589
  (p. 54)

15. 8000
  − 752
  (p. 56)

Multiply.

16. 890
  × 70
  (p. 80)

17. 678
  ×987
  (p. 86)

18. 580
  ×790
  (p. 86)

19. 725
  ×478
  (p. 86)

Divide.

20. (p. 146) 36)2998

21. (p. 144) 74)1819

22. (p. 146) 26)2198

23. (p. 144) 64)2443

303

Symmetry

Trace the drawing.
Cut it out.
Fold along the red line.
Do the parts match?

The figure is
symmetric.

The red line is a
line of symmetry.

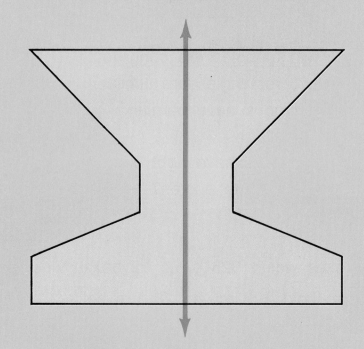

Each figure below has two lines of symmetry.
One is shown.
Trace the figure.   Show the other line of symmetry.

1.   **2.**

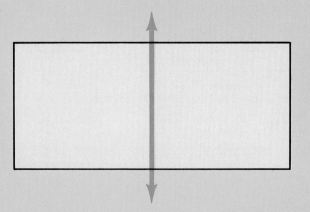

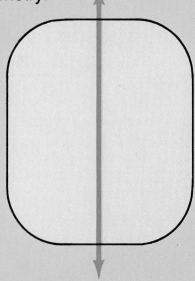

Trace the figure. Draw lines of symmetry.

3.

4.

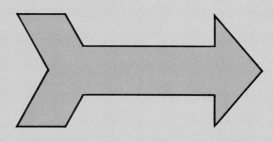

5.

6.

Trace the drawing.
Then complete it to make it symmetric.

7.

8.

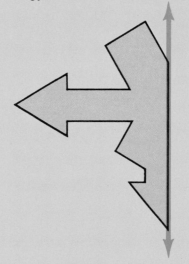

15 Multiplying Fractions

Finding Parts

What number is $\frac{1}{4}$ of $\frac{1}{2}$?

Cut the cake into 2 fair shares.

$\frac{1}{2}$ cake

Cut the half into 4 fair shares.

$\frac{1}{4}$ of $\frac{1}{2}$ cake

1 piece is 1 of 8 fair shares.

$\frac{1}{4}$ of $\frac{1}{2}$ is $\frac{1}{8}$.

What number is $\frac{2}{3}$ of $\frac{1}{4}$?

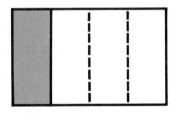

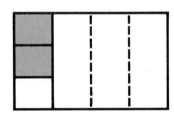

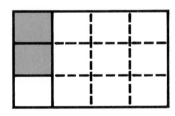

$\frac{1}{4}$ cake

$\frac{2}{3}$ of $\frac{1}{4}$ cake

$\frac{2}{3}$ of $\frac{1}{4}$ is $\frac{2}{12}$.

What number is $\frac{3}{4}$ of $\frac{2}{3}$?

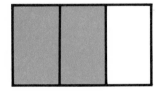

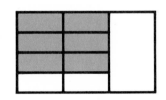

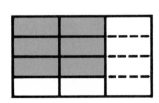

$\frac{2}{3}$ cake

$\frac{3}{4}$ of $\frac{2}{3}$ cake

$\frac{3}{4}$ of $\frac{2}{3}$ is $\frac{6}{12}$.

306

Use the drawing to complete the sentence.

1.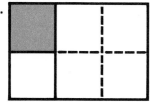

$\frac{1}{2}$ of $\frac{1}{3}$ is ___?___

2.

$\frac{1}{3}$ of $\frac{3}{4}$ is ___?___

3.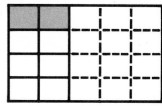

$\frac{1}{4}$ of $\frac{2}{5}$ is ___?___

now do these

Use the drawing to complete the sentence.

4.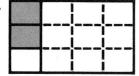

$\frac{2}{3}$ of $\frac{1}{4}$ = ___?___

5.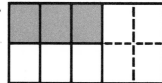

$\frac{1}{2}$ of $\frac{3}{5}$ = ___?___

6.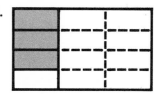

$\frac{3}{4}$ of $\frac{1}{3}$ = ___?___

7.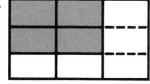

$\frac{2}{3}$ of $\frac{2}{3}$ = ___?___

8.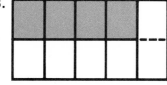

$\frac{1}{2}$ of $\frac{4}{5}$ = ___?___

9.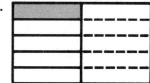

$\frac{1}{5}$ of $\frac{1}{2}$ = ___?___

10.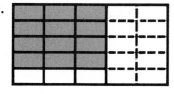

$\frac{4}{5}$ of $\frac{3}{5}$ = ___?___

11.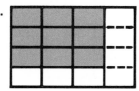

$\frac{3}{4}$ of $\frac{3}{4}$ = ___?___

12.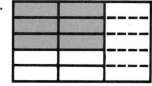

$\frac{3}{5}$ of $\frac{2}{3}$ = ___?___

307

Multiplication

You can make a drawing
to complete the sentence.

$$\frac{3}{4} \text{ of } \frac{3}{5} = ?$$

The drawing shows:

$$\frac{3}{4} \text{ of } \frac{3}{5} = \frac{9}{20}$$

You can also multiply to find the answer: $\frac{3}{4} \times \frac{3}{5}$.

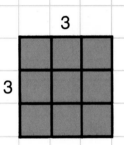

3

3

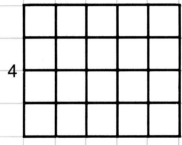

5

4

Multiply the numerators
to find how many
parts are red.

$$3 \times 3 = 9$$

Multiply the denominators
to find how many
parts in all.

$$4 \times 5 = 20$$

To multiply with fractions $\longrightarrow$ $\frac{3}{4} \times \frac{3}{5} = ?$

Step 1 Multiply the numerators. $\longrightarrow$ $\frac{3}{4} \times \frac{3}{5} = \frac{9}{}$

Step 2 Multiply the denominators. $\longrightarrow$ $\frac{3}{4} \times \frac{3}{5} = \frac{9}{20}$

308

Multiply. Write the simplest name for the answer.

1. $\frac{1}{8} \times \frac{2}{3} = $ _?_

2. $\frac{1}{2} \times \frac{4}{5} = $ _?_

3. $\frac{2}{5} \times \frac{1}{4} = $ _?_

now do these

Multiply. Write the simplest name for the answer.

4. $\frac{3}{5} \times \frac{2}{3} = $ _?_

5. $\frac{5}{6} \times \frac{3}{4} = $ _?_

6. $\frac{3}{9} \times \frac{1}{2} = $ _?_

7. $\frac{3}{4} \times \frac{1}{9} = $ _?_

8. $\frac{5}{9} \times \frac{3}{5} = $ _?_

9. $\frac{6}{7} \times \frac{1}{2} = $ _?_

10. $\frac{4}{5} \times \frac{2}{10} = $ _?_

11. $\frac{1}{2} \times \frac{4}{9} = $ _?_

12. $\frac{2}{3} \times \frac{3}{6} = $ _?_

13. $\frac{7}{8} \times \frac{2}{5} = $ _?_

14. $\frac{3}{5} \times \frac{4}{7} = $ _?_

15. $\frac{2}{3} \times \frac{3}{10} = $ _?_

16. $\frac{7}{8} \times \frac{5}{7} = $ _?_

17. $\frac{1}{10} \times \frac{5}{6} = $ _?_

18. $\frac{1}{8} \times \frac{4}{7} = $ _?_

19. $\frac{2}{3} \times \frac{3}{8} = $ _?_

20. $\frac{6}{10} \times \frac{5}{12} = $ _?_

21. $\frac{3}{4} \times \frac{4}{5} = $ _?_

22. $\frac{5}{8} \times \frac{2}{3} = $ _?_

23. $\frac{3}{4} \times \frac{3}{8} = $ _?_

24. $\frac{4}{5} \times \frac{5}{6} = $ _?_

25. $\frac{3}{4} \times \frac{3}{4} = $ _?_

26. $\frac{5}{8} \times \frac{3}{5} = $ _?_

27. $\frac{5}{6} \times \frac{3}{8} = $ _?_

28. $\frac{4}{5} \times \frac{3}{5} = $ _?_

29. $\frac{5}{6} \times \frac{2}{3} = $ _?_

30. $\frac{5}{8} \times \frac{7}{8} = $ _?_

Fractions and Whole Numbers

John practices the guitar
$\frac{3}{4}$ hour every day.
He does this 6 days a week.

How many hours does
he practice each week?

$$6 \times \frac{3}{4} = ?$$

Step 1 Rename the whole number.
Use a fraction. ⟶ $\frac{6}{1} \times \frac{3}{4}$

Step 2 Multiply the numerators. ⟶ $\frac{6}{1} \times \frac{3}{4} = \frac{18}{}$

Step 3 Multiply the denominators. ⟶ $\frac{6}{1} \times \frac{3}{4} = \frac{18}{4}$

Step 4 You can write a mixed
numeral for the answer. ⟶ $\frac{6}{1} \times \frac{3}{4} = \frac{18}{4} = 4\frac{1}{2}$

John practices $4\frac{1}{2}$ hours a week.

Multiply. Write the simplest name for the answer.

1. $4 \times \frac{3}{4} = $ _?_

2. $6 \times \frac{2}{8} = $ _?_

3. $\frac{2}{5} \times 7 = $ _?_

now do these

Multiply. Write the simplest name for the answer.

4. $3 \times \frac{4}{5} = $ _?_

5. $9 \times \frac{5}{6} = $ _?_

6. $8 \times \frac{2}{3} = $ _?_

7. $\frac{2}{3} \times 4 = $ _?_

8. $7 \times \frac{4}{6} = $ _?_

9. $5 \times \frac{5}{8} = $ _?_

10. $9 \times \frac{2}{4} = $ _?_

11. $\frac{3}{5} \times 6 = $ _?_

12. $\frac{4}{6} \times 8 = $ _?_

13. $\frac{3}{4} \times 7 = $ _?_

14. $3 \times \frac{5}{6} = $ _?_

15. $\frac{5}{8} \times 4 = $ _?_

16. $3 \times \frac{3}{8} = $ _?_

17. $\frac{3}{4} \times 5 = $ _?_

18. $6 \times \frac{5}{6} = $ _?_

19. $\frac{2}{6} \times 5 = $ _?_

20. $4 \times \frac{3}{6} = $ _?_

21. $\frac{3}{4} \times 3 = $ _?_

TRIANGLE NUMBERS

Find the next three numbers in the pattern.

1   3   6   10   15

311

Fractions and Mixed Numerals

Alice owns a bakery.
She works $7\frac{1}{2}$ hours every day.
$\frac{3}{4}$ of this time she bakes.
The rest of the time she
serves customers.
How many hours a day
does she bake?

$$\frac{3}{4} \times 7\frac{1}{2} = ?$$

Step 1 Rename the mixed numeral.
Use a fraction. $\longrightarrow$ $\frac{3}{4} \times \frac{15}{2}$

Step 2 Multiply the numerators. $\longrightarrow$ $\frac{3}{4} \times \frac{15}{2} = \frac{45}{}$

Step 3 Multiply the denominators. $\longrightarrow$ $\frac{3}{4} \times \frac{15}{2} = \frac{45}{8}$

Step 4 You can write a mixed
numeral for the answer. $\longrightarrow$ $\frac{3}{4} \times \frac{15}{2} = \frac{45}{8} = 5\frac{5}{8}$

Alice bakes for $5\frac{5}{8}$ hours every day.

312

Multiply. Write the simplest name for the answer.

1. $3\frac{2}{3} \times \frac{5}{6} = \underline{\ ?\ }$

2. $\frac{2}{5} \times 5\frac{1}{2} = \underline{\ ?\ }$

3. $2\frac{1}{3} \times \frac{3}{4} = \underline{\ ?\ }$

now do these

Multiply. Write the simplest name for the answer.

4. $\frac{3}{4} \times 4\frac{1}{4} = \underline{\ ?\ }$

5. $9\frac{1}{3} \times \frac{2}{6} = \underline{\ ?\ }$

6. $8\frac{1}{2} \times \frac{3}{4} = \underline{\ ?\ }$

7. $\frac{3}{5} \times 6\frac{1}{3} = \underline{\ ?\ }$

8. $\frac{7}{8} \times 7\frac{1}{4} = \underline{\ ?\ }$

9. $\frac{3}{4} \times 8\frac{2}{3} = \underline{\ ?\ }$

10. $\frac{5}{8} \times 4\frac{2}{3} = \underline{\ ?\ }$

11. $5\frac{1}{3} \times \frac{5}{6} = \underline{\ ?\ }$

12. $\frac{3}{8} \times 3\frac{1}{2} = \underline{\ ?\ }$

13. $\frac{4}{5} \times 9\frac{1}{2} = \underline{\ ?\ }$

14. $6\frac{1}{2} \times \frac{2}{6} = \underline{\ ?\ }$

15. $\frac{2}{5} \times 8\frac{1}{4} = \underline{\ ?\ }$

16. $2\frac{1}{4} \times \frac{5}{8} = \underline{\ ?\ }$

17. $\frac{5}{8} \times 9\frac{3}{4} = \underline{\ ?\ }$

18. $3\frac{3}{4} \times \frac{2}{6} = \underline{\ ?\ }$

19. $\frac{3}{5} \times 7\frac{1}{2} = \underline{\ ?\ }$

20. $3\frac{1}{3} \times \frac{3}{5} = \underline{\ ?\ }$

21. $\frac{7}{8} \times 4\frac{1}{2} = \underline{\ ?\ }$

22. $8\frac{3}{4} \times \frac{3}{5} = \underline{\ ?\ }$

23. $\frac{5}{6} \times 9\frac{2}{3} = \underline{\ ?\ }$

24. $\frac{2}{5} \times 7\frac{2}{3} = \underline{\ ?\ }$

25. $\frac{4}{5} \times 3\frac{1}{4} = \underline{\ ?\ }$

26. $2\frac{1}{2} \times \frac{2}{3} = \underline{\ ?\ }$

27. $\frac{4}{5} \times 5\frac{3}{4} = \underline{\ ?\ }$

28. $\frac{7}{8} \times 9\frac{1}{4} = \underline{\ ?\ }$

29. $6\frac{1}{4} \times \frac{4}{5} = \underline{\ ?\ }$

30. $\frac{2}{3} \times 8\frac{1}{3} = \underline{\ ?\ }$

Mixed Numerals

Chris and Leslie are baking.
The recipe calls for $2\frac{1}{2}$
cups of flour.
Chris and Leslie want
$1\frac{1}{2}$ times as much
as the recipe makes.

How much flour should
they use?

$$1\frac{1}{2} \times 2\frac{1}{2} = ?$$

Step 1   Rename the mixed numerals.
Use fractions. $\longrightarrow$ $\dfrac{3}{2} \times \dfrac{5}{2}$

Step 2   Multiply the numerators. $\longrightarrow$ $\dfrac{3}{2} \times \dfrac{5}{2} = \dfrac{15}{}$

Step 3   Multiply the denominators. $\longrightarrow$ $\dfrac{3}{2} \times \dfrac{5}{2} = \dfrac{15}{4}$

Step 4   You can write a mixed
numeral for the answer. $\longrightarrow$ $\dfrac{3}{2} \times \dfrac{5}{2} = \dfrac{15}{4} = 3\frac{3}{4}$

They should use $3\frac{3}{4}$ cups of flour.

314

Multiply. Write the simplest name for the answer.

1. $2\frac{1}{2} \times 1\frac{2}{3} = \underline{\ ?\ }$

2. $4\frac{1}{2} \times 1\frac{7}{8} = \underline{\ ?\ }$

3. $3\frac{1}{2} \times 1\frac{2}{6} = \underline{\ ?\ }$

now do these

Multiply. Write the simplest name for the answer.

4. $3\frac{1}{3} \times 1\frac{3}{5} = \underline{\ ?\ }$

5. $2\frac{1}{3} \times 1\frac{7}{8} = \underline{\ ?\ }$

6. $4\frac{2}{3} \times 3\frac{5}{8} = \underline{\ ?\ }$

7. $1\frac{4}{5} \times 2\frac{3}{4} = \underline{\ ?\ }$

8. $3\frac{2}{3} \times 2\frac{5}{6} = \underline{\ ?\ }$

9. $2\frac{2}{3} \times 2\frac{3}{4} = \underline{\ ?\ }$

10. $2\frac{1}{4} \times 2\frac{2}{6} = \underline{\ ?\ }$

11. $4\frac{2}{3} \times 2\frac{2}{5} = \underline{\ ?\ }$

12. $1\frac{3}{8} \times 3\frac{2}{3} = \underline{\ ?\ }$

13. $3\frac{1}{3} \times 2\frac{5}{6} = \underline{\ ?\ }$

14. $2\frac{1}{3} \times 1\frac{3}{5} = \underline{\ ?\ }$

15. $4\frac{1}{4} \times 1\frac{3}{4} = \underline{\ ?\ }$

16. $3\frac{1}{4} \times 3\frac{4}{5} = \underline{\ ?\ }$

17. $3\frac{1}{2} \times 2\frac{3}{8} = \underline{\ ?\ }$

18. $2\frac{1}{3} \times 3\frac{5}{6} = \underline{\ ?\ }$

19. $4\frac{3}{4} \times 2\frac{3}{8} = \underline{\ ?\ }$

20. $2\frac{3}{5} \times 4\frac{1}{2} = \underline{\ ?\ }$

21. $3\frac{3}{4} \times 1\frac{2}{6} = \underline{\ ?\ }$

SQUARE NUMBERS

Find the next three numbers in the pattern.

1   4   9   16   25

315

add or multiply?

Joanne and John want to help save electricity. This will help
them to save money. They find out the cost of running each appliance.
Should they add or can they multiply to solve each problem?

Problem

It costs 24¢ to run the refrigerator
each day. It costs $\frac{2}{5}$¢ per day
to run the clock. What does it cost
each day to run these two appliances?

Solution

You are joining groups. The addends
are different. So, you add.

$$24 + \frac{2}{5} = 24\frac{2}{5}$$

It costs $24\frac{2}{5}$¢ per day.

Problem

Their family watches TV
about 16 hours a week. Each
hour costs $2\frac{2}{3}$¢. What does
it cost for a week of TV?

Solution

You are joining groups. The addends
are equal. So, you can multiply.

$$16 \times 2\frac{2}{3} = 42\frac{2}{3}$$

It costs about $42\frac{2}{3}$¢ per week.

How would you solve? Write ADD or MULTIPLY.

1. It costs $4\frac{7}{10}$¢ to run the
   dishwasher each time. How
   much would it cost to run
   the dishwasher 15 times?

2. It costs $4\frac{3}{5}$¢ per hour to use
   their iron. How much would
   it cost to use the iron for
   5 hours?

3. It costs $2\frac{2}{3}$¢ per hour for the
   TV. It costs $4\frac{3}{5}$¢ per hour
   to run the iron. How much
   does an hour of ironing and
   watching TV cost?

4. It costs $\frac{4}{5}$¢ per hour for a 100-watt
   light bulb. A 60-watt bulb costs
   $\frac{1}{2}$¢ per hour. How much would
   it cost to keep one of each
   kind of bulb lighted for an hour?

Solve the problem.

5. It costs $4\frac{3}{5}$¢ to use the iron for one hour. How much would it cost to use the iron for $2\frac{1}{2}$ hours?

6. Their clock uses $\frac{2}{5}$¢ of electricity each day. How much does it cost to run the clock for a 30-day month?

7. Their washing machine costs $1\frac{9}{10}$¢ per load. The drier costs 24¢ per load. How much does it cost to wash and dry each load?

8. A 100-watt bulb costs $\frac{4}{5}$¢ per hour. Joanne keeps one on for 8 hours. How much does this cost?

9. A 60-watt bulb costs $\frac{1}{2}$¢ per hour. A 25-watt bulb costs $\frac{1}{5}$¢ per hour. They each burn for one hour. How much does this cost?

10. The vacuum cleaner uses 5¢ worth of electricity per hour. Their color TV uses $2\frac{2}{3}$¢ worth per hour. It takes John 1 hour to vacuum their home. How much does it cost if he watches TV at the same time?

Test

Use the drawing to complete the sentence.

1.

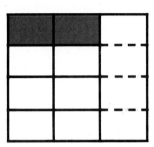

$\frac{1}{4}$ of $\frac{2}{3}$ = __?__ (p. 306)

2.

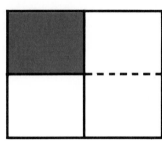

$\frac{1}{2}$ of $\frac{1}{2}$ = __?__ (p. 306)

3.

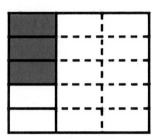

$\frac{3}{5}$ of $\frac{1}{3}$ = __?__ (p. 306)

4.

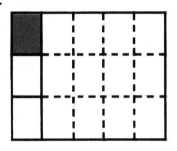

$\frac{1}{3}$ of $\frac{1}{5}$ = __?__ (p. 306)

5.

$\frac{4}{5}$ of $\frac{3}{4}$ = __?__ (p. 306)

Multiply. Write the simplest name for the answer.

6. $\frac{1}{2} \times \frac{2}{9}$ = __?__ (p. 308)   **7.** $\frac{4}{7} \times \frac{2}{10}$ = __?__ (p. 308)   **8.** $\frac{5}{6} \times \frac{7}{8}$ = __?__ (p. 308)

9. $7 \times \frac{2}{4}$ = __?__ (p. 310)   **10.** $3 \times \frac{5}{6}$ = __?__ (p. 310)   **11.** $\frac{3}{8} \times 6$ = __?__ (p. 310)

12. $\frac{4}{7} \times 4$ = __?__ (p. 310)   **13.** $7\frac{3}{4} \times \frac{3}{8}$ = __?__ (p. 312)   **14.** $\frac{1}{4} \times 7\frac{2}{3}$ = __?__ (p. 312)

15. $\frac{4}{5} \times 6\frac{1}{2}$ = __?__ (p. 312)   **16.** $6\frac{3}{4} \times \frac{1}{3}$ = __?__ (p. 312)   **17.** $3\frac{4}{5} \times 4\frac{3}{6}$ = __?__ (p. 314)

18. $5\frac{3}{4} \times 7\frac{3}{4}$ = __?__ (p. 314)   **19.** $5\frac{5}{8} \times 3\frac{1}{6}$ = __?__ (p. 314)   **20.** $9\frac{2}{4} \times 7\frac{4}{6}$ = __?__ (p. 314)

318

Keeping up

Add.

1. 5.734
+7.632

2. 4.08
+2.96
(p. 296)

3. 0.08
+9.95
(p. 296)

4. 23.27
+ 8.94
(p. 296)

Subtract.

5. 7.473
−3.629
(p. 298)

6. 8.23
−5.45
(p. 298)

7. 9.06
−4.97
(p. 298)

8. 42.407
−11.843
(p. 298)

9. Find the perimeter of figure **A.** (p. 228)

10. Find the area of figure **A.**   234)

11. Find the volume of figure **B.** (p. 236)

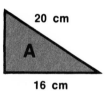

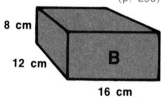

Add.   Write the simplest name for the answer.

12. $8\frac{3}{4}$
$+7\frac{5}{6}$
(p. 208)

13. $4\frac{5}{6}$
$+ \frac{7}{8}$
(p. 208)

14. $7\frac{2}{3}$
$+2\frac{8}{9}$
(p. 208)

15. $16\frac{4}{7}$
$+ 4\frac{3}{4}$
(p. 208)

Subtract.   Write the simplest name for the answer.

16. $3\frac{3}{8}$
$- \frac{5}{6}$
(p. 214)

17. 5
$-2\frac{3}{4}$
(p. 212)

18. $7\frac{1}{3}$
$-2\frac{4}{9}$
(p. 214)

19. $18\frac{1}{2}$
$-12\frac{7}{10}$
(p. 214)

Multiply.

20. 243
× 62
(p. 82)

21. 802
× 55
(p. 82)

22. 968
×407
(p. 86)

23. 605
×463
(p. 86)

Divide.

(p. 144)   (p. 144)   (p. 146)   (p. 146)

24. 34)2686   **25.** 23)1326   **26.** 38)3116   **27.** 47)3240

319

Some Are and Some Are Not

There are 24 pages of coins in one of Angela's coin albums.
6 pages contain old pennies.
8 pages contain old nickels.
How many pages contain <u>neither</u> pennies <u>nor</u> nickels?

1. Find the number of pages of pennies and nickels. ⟶ **6 + 8 = 14**

2. Find the number of pages of other kinds of coins. ⟶ **24 − 14 = 10**

10 pages contain neither pennies nor nickels.

Solve the problem.

1. 36 pages in a coin album.
   3 pages contain two-cent pieces.
   8 pages contain one-cent pieces.
   How many pages contain neither two-cent nor one-cent pieces?

2. 148 pages in a coin album.
   36 pages contain silver dimes.
   28 pages contain silver dollars.
   How many pages contain neither silver dimes nor silver dollars?

3. 378 coins in a collection.
   45 are Indian-head pennies.
   52 are buffalo nickels.
   25 are eagle pennies.
   How many are not Indian-head pennies, buffalo nickels, nor eagle pennies?

4. 580 coins in a collection.
   83 are two-cent pieces.
   28 are half-cent pieces.
   10 are one-cent pieces.
   How many are not two-cent pieces, half-cent pieces, nor one-cent pieces?

Try These Answers

Unit 1 **2.** **1.** 2 thousands   4 hundreds   3 tens   9 ones

5. **1.** 267 **2.** 583 **3.** 3624 **4.** 9401 **5.** 4006 **6.** 300 **7.** 900 **8.** 400 **9.** 5000

10. 2000		70	30	+ 6	800
900		+ 8	+ 7		20
+ 40					+ 1

7. **1.** 300 **2.** 30 **3.** 3000 **4.** 300,000 **5.** 30,000

9. **1.** 46 thousand, 172 **2.** 94 thousand, 625 **3.** 212 thousand, 874
4. 6 million, 371 thousand, 192 **5.** 18 million, 721 thousand, 965
6. 783 million, 192 thousand, 841

11. **1.** 7 billion, 116 million, 295 thousand, 101 **2.** 8 billion, 671 thousand, 842
3. 24 billion, 172 million, 142 **4.** 19 billion, 764 million, 963 thousand, 400
5. 162 billion, 792 million, 100 thousand, 631 **6.** 834 billion, 117 million,
345 thousand, 104

13. **1.** > **2.** < **3.** < **4.** <

15. **1.** 40 **2.** 30 **3.** 300 **4.** 300

Unit 2 **19.** **1.** 18 **2.** 14 **3.** 14 **4.** 10 **5.** 13 **6.** 12 **7.** 11 **8.** 13 **9.** 14 **10.** 12 **11.** 13 **12.** 16

21. **1.** 17 **2.** 17 **3.** 7 **4.** 17 **5.** 17 **6.** 16

22. **1.** 8, 12, 14, 11

27. **1.** 90	**2.** 90	**3.** 70	**4.** 60	**5.** 60	**6.** 30
+70	+30	+50	+70	+90	+90
160	120	120	130	150	120

28. **1.** 1127 **2.** 1358 **3.** 1269 **4.** 727 **5.** 989 **6.** 499

30. **1.** 5 tens 6 ones, 56 **2.** 9 tens 9 ones, 99 **3.** 6 tens 4 ones, 64
4. 8 tens 1 one, 81 **5.** 4 tens 0 ones, 40

33. **1.** 763 **2.** 827 **3.** 656 **4.** 1104 **5.** 1053 **6.** 808 **7.** 945 **8.** 1002 **9.** 990 **10.** 1844

34. **1.** 1802 **2.** 1043 **3.** 1476 **4.** 1972 **5.** 2686

Unit 3 **41.** **1.** 4 **2.** 8 **3.** 8 **4.** 9 **5.** 9 **6.** 8 **7.** 8 **8.** 8 **9.** 6 **10.** 9 **11.** 9 **12.** 9

42. **1.** $10 - 7 = 3$ **2.** $14 - 5 = 9$ **3.** $6 + 7 = 13$ **4.** $8 + 3 = 11$

5. $3 + 5 = 8$	**6.** $9 + 4 = 13$	**7.** $5 + 7 = 12$	**8.** $6 + 4 = 10$
$5 + 3 = 8$	$4 + 9 = 13$	$7 + 5 = 12$	$4 + 6 = 10$
$8 - 3 = 5$	$13 - 4 = 9$	$12 - 5 = 7$	$10 - 6 = 4$
$8 - 5 = 3$	$13 - 9 = 4$	$12 - 7 = 5$	$10 - 4 = 6$

47.

	1.	2.	3.	4.	5.	6.
	90	80	60	60	40	60
	−80	−60	−30	−40	−20	−20
	10	20	30	20	20	40

48. 1. 24 2. 141 3. 303 4. 105 5. 87 6. 516

50. 1. 48 2. 50 3. 63 4. 31 5. 60 6. 42 7. 19 8. 26 9. 17

53. 1. 23 2. 6 3. 49 4. 335 5. 341 6. 8 7. 44 8. 51 9. 41 10. 380

54. 1. 278 2. 174 3. 364 4. 596 5. 46 6. 733 7. 195 8. 197 9. 179 10. 559 11. 199 12. 633

57. 1. 325 2. 154 3. 705 4. 7 5. 97 6. 93 7. 509 8. 126 9. 758 10. 84

58. 1. $2.75 2. $5.16 3. $7.40 4. $33.75 5. $61.62 6. $1.13 7. $3.25 8. $1.07 9. $11.01 10. $3.37

Unit 4

67. 1. 48 2. 42 3. 54 4. 24 5. 30 6. 28 7. 72 8. 56 9. 42 10. 54 11. 32 12. 27

69. 1. 54 2. 54 3. 8 4. 18 5. 18 6. 0

72. 1. 560 2. 400 3. 5400 4. 4900 5. 48,000

75. 1. 336 2. 1175 3. 2367 4. 115 5. 3192 6. 2030 7. 174 8. 288 9. 92 10. 192 11. 268 12. 275

77. 1. 783 2. 138 3. 304 4. 1638 5. 2660 6. 4525 7. 408 8. 711 9. 602 10. 2076 11. 1416 12. 3384

79. 1. 19,744 2. 18,474 3. 23,002 4. 23,025 5. 21,105 6. 21,388 7. 14,958 8. 35,052 9. 63,240 10. 32,053

81. 1. 70 2. 180 3. 460 4. 700 5. 840 6. 320 7. 700 8. 1800 9. 4600 10. 7000 11. 8400 12. 3200 13. 1260 14. 4270 15. 3440 16. 15,900 17. 31,200 18. 17,500

83. 1. 7644 2. 5762 3. 2352 4. 78,182 5. 39,060 6. 63,510 7. 1104 8. 3393 9. 1904 10. 29,274 11. 40,488 12. 27,680

84. 1. 438,885 2. 176,581 3. 91,723 4. 557,764 5. 527,296 6. 347,328 7. 442,475 8. 537,600 9. 313,973 10. 533,304

87. 1. 283,824 2. 279,500 3. 118,638 4. 145,920 5. 295,872 6. 248,263 7. 130,464 8. 66,768 9. 410,400 10. 24,969 11. 502,818 12. 109,278

Unit 5

93. 1. About the same 2. 1970 3. Decrease

95. 1. Irons 2. Blenders 3. Can openers 4. Toasters

97. 1. Feb., May, Aug., Nov., Dec. 2. Mar., Apr., June, July, Sept. 3. Oct.

99. 1. Bank 2. Post Office 3. Drug Store 4. East 2, North 5 5. East 4, North 9 6. East 2, North 2

101. 1. A 2. B 3. H 4. F 5. Z 6. (5, 2) 7. (4, 1) 8. (1, 7) 9. (4, 6) 10. (6, 4)

Unit 6 105. 1. 8 2. 8 3. 6 4. 7 5. 9 6. 7 7. 8 8. 9 9. 5 10. 8 11. 6 12. 9

107. 1. $12 \div 4 = 3$ 2. $18 \div 2 = 9$ 3. $6 \times 5 = 30$ 4. $3 \times 5 = 15$ 5. $7 \times 4 = 28$
$5 \times 3 = 15$ $4 \times 7 = 28$
6. $9 \times 5 = 45$ $15 \div 5 = 3$ $28 \div 4 = 7$
$5 \times 9 = 45$ $15 \div 3 = 5$ $28 \div 7 = 4$
$45 \div 5 = 9$
$45 \div 9 = 5$

111. 1. 8 r3 2. 7 r3 3. 5 r2 4. 7 r1 5. 5 r3 6. 6 r2

113. 1. 30 2. 30 3. 80 4. 70 5. 30 6. 40 7. 90 8. 30 9. 60 10. 30

115. 1. 85 r1 2. 65 r3 3. 24 r2 4. 36 r1 5. 27 6. 55 r5 7. 94 r5 8. 87 r3 9. 84 r7 10. 68

117. 1. 63 2. 68 r3 3. 79 r2 4. 33 r1 5. 65 6. 74 r2 7. 14 r1 8. 26 r2 9. 48 r3 10. 42 r6

119. 1. 18 2. 43 3. 33

121. 1. 400 2. 400 3. 800 4. 200 5. 800 6. 400 7. 400 8. 700 9. 300 10. 800

123. 1. 264 r5 2. 450 3. 902 4. 552 5. 756 r1 6. 936 7. 469 8. 762 r3 9. 840 r3 10. 447 r6

Unit 7 131. 1. 2 2. 3 3. 6 4. 3 5. 3

133. 1. 3 r25 2. 4 r27 3. 7 r24 4. 3 r42 5. 6 r16 6. 9 r24 7. 9 r13 8. 3 r44 9. 5 r75
10. 6 r24

135. 1. 7 r10 2. 5 r4 3. 2 r11 4. 8 5. 3 r12 6. 5 r18 7. 3 r6 8. 3 r13 9. 8 10. 6 r4

137. 1. Yes 2. Yes 3. No 4. Yes 5. No 6. 7 r18 7. 7 r41 8. 6 r49 9. 8 r9 10. 6 r45

139. 1. 5 r29 2. 6 r21 3. 8 r39 4. 6 r25 5. 9 r20 6. 4 r29 7. 8 r43 8. 7 r36 9. 8 r43
10. 5 r34

141. 1. No 2. No 3. Yes 4. No 5. Yes 6. 9 7. 7 r2 8. 6 r13 9. 7 r11 10. 8 r14

143. 1. 31 r28 2. 26 r5 3. 36 r7 4. 40 r37 5. 47 r8 6. 24 r7 7. 72 r55 8. 32 r9

145. 1. Yes 2. No 3. Yes 4. No 5. 74 6. 69 7. 58 r10 8. 78 r21

147. 1. No 2. No 3. Yes 4. No 5. 61 r10 6. 71 r3 7. 72 8. 72 r43

149. 1. 119 2. 132 r7 3. 213 r6 4. 207 r19 5. 112 r7 6. 112 7. 241 r9 8. 114 r2

Unit 8 157. 1. Yes 2. Yes 3. No 4. No 5. Yes

159. 1. 1 2. 2 3. 1 4. 2 5. 1, 2, 3, 6 6. 1, 2, 5, 10 7. 1, 3 8. 1, 2, 4, 8, 16

161. 1. 1, 2, 3, 4, 6, 9, 12, 18, 36 2. 1, 2, 3, 4, 6, 8, 12, 24 3. 1, 2, 3, 6, 9, 18
4. 1, 2, 3, 4, 6, 12 5. 1, 2, 3, 6 6. 1, 2, 3, 6 7. 12 8. 6 9. 6

163. 1. 4, 8, 12, 16, 20 2. 5, 10, 15, 20, 25 3. 7, 14, 21, 28, 35 4. 9, 18, 27, 36, 45
5. 18, 36, 54, 72, 90 6. 20 7. 35 8. 18 9. 28 10. 36

Unit 9 169. 1. $\frac{1}{2}$ 2. $\frac{1}{4}$ 3. $\frac{3}{4}$ 4. $\frac{1}{8}$

171. 1. $\frac{3}{5}$ 2. $\frac{1}{3}$ 3. $\frac{3}{4}$

173. 1. 2 2. 10

175. 1. $\frac{2}{6}$ 2. $\frac{2}{10}$ 3. $\frac{4}{6}$ 4. $\frac{6}{8}$ 5. $\frac{10}{16}$ 6. $\frac{15}{20}$ 7. $\frac{10}{20}$ 8. $\frac{25}{30}$ 9. $\frac{15}{40}$ 10. $\frac{20}{50}$

177. 1. $\frac{2}{4}$ 2. $\frac{2}{6}$ 3. $\frac{4}{8}$ 4. $\frac{6}{10}$

179. 1. $\frac{2}{4}$ 2. $\frac{3}{8}$ 3. $\frac{1}{4}$ 4. $\frac{3}{5}$ 5. $\frac{5}{16}$ 6. $\frac{9}{16}$ 7. 4 8. 2 9. 4 10. $\frac{1}{4}$ 11. $\frac{1}{2}$ 12. $\frac{3}{4}$ 13. $\frac{5}{6}$ 14. $\frac{4}{5}$ 15. $\frac{4}{5}$

181. 1. 8 2. 10 3. 18 4. 30 5. $\frac{6}{8}, \frac{5}{8}$ 6. $\frac{4}{10}, \frac{3}{10}$ 7. $\frac{15}{18}, \frac{2}{18}$ 8. $\frac{21}{30}, \frac{16}{30}$

183. 1. $\frac{7}{8}$ 2. $\frac{2}{3}$ 3. $\frac{1}{2}$ 4. $\frac{1}{2}$ 5. $\frac{1}{2}$ 6. $\frac{1}{2}$

185. 1. 8 2. 15 3. 24 4. $\frac{7}{8}$ 5. $\frac{11}{15}$ 6. $\frac{13}{24}$

187. 1. 8 2. 16 3. 24 4. $\frac{3}{8}$ 5. $\frac{7}{16}$ 6. $\frac{19}{24}$

189. 1. $\frac{5}{8}$ 2. $\frac{2}{3}$ 3. $\frac{4}{5}$ 4. $\frac{9}{10}$ 5. $\frac{11}{12}$ 6. $\frac{11}{12}$ 7. $\frac{1}{16}$ 8. $\frac{1}{4}$ 9. $\frac{1}{15}$ 10. $\frac{11}{24}$ 11. $\frac{1}{12}$ 12. $\frac{1}{15}$

Unit 10

195. 1. 3 2. 4 3. 7 4. 4 5. $\frac{12}{3}$ 6. $\frac{56}{8}$ 7. $\frac{18}{6}$ 8. $\frac{20}{5}$

197. 1. $7\frac{5}{6}$ 2. $4\frac{1}{2}$ 3. $7\frac{3}{4}$ 4. $5\frac{7}{8}$ 5. $3\frac{9}{10}$ 6. $6\frac{2}{3}$ 7. $2\frac{5}{16}$ 8. $12\frac{1}{4}$

199. 1. $\frac{7}{2}$ 2. $\frac{13}{3}$ 3. $\frac{9}{5}$ 4. $\frac{19}{8}$ 5. $\frac{5}{3}$ 6. $\frac{19}{4}$ 7. $\frac{21}{8}$ 8. $\frac{11}{3}$ 9. $\frac{5}{3}$ 10. $\frac{12}{5}$

201. 1. $1\frac{1}{8}$ 2. $3\frac{1}{2}$ 3. $2\frac{2}{3}$ 4. $2\frac{3}{8}$ 5. $2\frac{1}{3}$ 6. $4\frac{1}{3}$ 7. $1\frac{4}{5}$ 8. $4\frac{3}{4}$ 9. $3\frac{1}{4}$ 10. $3\frac{2}{5}$

203. 1. $2\frac{1}{3}$ 2. $3\frac{3}{5}$ 3. $7\frac{1}{2}$ 4. $5\frac{3}{8}$ 5. $6\frac{1}{6}$ 6. $9\frac{4}{9}$ 7. $5\frac{1}{2}$ 8. $6\frac{3}{4}$ 9. $4\frac{3}{8}$ 10. $5\frac{2}{3}$ 11. $9\frac{1}{2}$ 12. $6\frac{1}{4}$

205. 1. $9\frac{3}{5}$ 2. $8\frac{1}{2}$ 3. $17\frac{2}{5}$ 4. $9\frac{3}{8}$ 5. $13\frac{2}{3}$ 6. $8\frac{1}{2}$ 7. $3\frac{1}{5}$ 8. $6\frac{5}{8}$ 9. $1\frac{1}{5}$ 10. $5\frac{1}{3}$

207. 1. $9\frac{2}{5}$ 2. 12 3. $16\frac{1}{3}$ 4. 15 5. $14\frac{1}{5}$ 6. $6\frac{1}{4}$ 7. $9\frac{1}{4}$ 8. $22\frac{1}{5}$

209. 1. $15\frac{1}{12}$ 2. $18\frac{7}{12}$ 3. $11\frac{7}{10}$ 4. $11\frac{11}{12}$ 5. $18\frac{3}{10}$ 6. $19\frac{11}{14}$ 7. $14\frac{1}{8}$ 8. $22\frac{5}{8}$

211. 1. $2\frac{1}{6}$ 2. $5\frac{3}{8}$ 3. $5\frac{2}{15}$ 4. $1\frac{3}{10}$ 5. $4\frac{5}{12}$ 6. $5\frac{1}{24}$ 7. $5\frac{7}{20}$ 8. $7\frac{5}{16}$

213. 1. $3\frac{1}{2}$ 2. $2\frac{1}{8}$ 3. $3\frac{2}{3}$ 4. $4\frac{1}{2}$ 5. $4\frac{3}{5}$ 6. $4\frac{1}{4}$ 7. $7\frac{2}{3}$ 8. $1\frac{1}{2}$

215. 1. $6\frac{3}{4}$ 2. $1\frac{7}{12}$ 3. $3\frac{7}{10}$ 4. $6\frac{5}{8}$ 5. $5\frac{7}{12}$ 6. $2\frac{11}{15}$ 7. $5\frac{7}{8}$

Unit 11

223. 1. 7 cm 2. 10 cm 3. 11 cm
225. 1. 98 mm 2. 120 mm
227. 1. Centimeter 2. Meter 3. Kilometer 4. Centimeter 5. Meter 6. Kilometer
229. 1. 11 cm 2. 144 cm
231. 1. 16 square centimeters 2. 12 square centimeters 3. $4\frac{1}{2}$ square centimeters
233. 1. 24 square centimeters 2. 35 square centimeters 3. 36 square centimeters
235. 1. 9 square centimeters 2. 5 square centimeters 3. 8 square centimeters
237. 1. 24 cubic centimeters 2. 40 cubic centimeters 3. 27 cubic centimeters
239. 1. 250 ml 2. 360 ml 3. 1 *l* 4. 4 *l*
240. 1. Gram 2. Kilogram 3. Gram 4. Kilogram

Unit 12   **247.** 1. $\frac{2}{5}$ 2. $\frac{2}{7}$

           249. 1. $\frac{9}{12}$ 2. $\frac{32}{20}$ 3. $\frac{9}{15}$ 4. $\frac{35}{20}$ 5. 14 6. 6

           251. 1. 30¢ 2. 75¢ 3. 75¢ 4. 8 5. 6 6. 6

           253. 1. 15 km 2. 35 km 3. 128 km 4. 4 hours 5. 3 hours 6. 5 hours

Unit 13   **259.** 1. Angle *XYZ* or *ZYX* 2. Line *PB* or *BP* 3. Ray *MY*

           261. See construction on page 260.

           263. 1. Right 2. Acute 3. Obtuse 4. Right

           265. 1. 40° 2. 120°

           267. 1. Acute, 80° 2. Obtuse, 105°

           269. See construction on page 268.

           271. 1. Parallel 2. Neither 3. Perpendicular

           273. 1. No 2. Yes 3. Yes 4. Triangle 5. Quadrilateral 6. Pentagon

           275. 1. Yes 2. No

           277. 1. Yes 2. No

           279. See construction on page 278.

           281. 1. Sphere 2. Cone 3. Cylinder 4. Rectangular prism 5. Triangular pyramid 6. Rectangular prism

Unit 14   **287.** 1. 0.3 2. 0.9 3. 1.7 4. 6.1 5. 17.2

           289. 1. 0.65 2. 0.90 3. 1.17 4. 24.46 5. 35.04

           291. 1. 0.463 2. 4.172 3. 29.042 4. 37.005

           293. 1. Hundredths 2. Tenths 3. Thousandths 4. 0.009 5. 0.07 6. 0.3

           295. 1. < 2. < 3. > 4. > 5. < 6. >

           297. 1. 11.356 2. 10.23 3. 78.37 4. 1.04 5. 91.56 6. 0.797 7. 11.34 8. 10.144 9. 35.65 10. 80.81

           299. 1. 5.34 2. 31.6 3. 11.07 4. 3.555 5. 56.58 6. 1.79 7. 0.021 8. 40.78 9. 3.788 10. 34.28

Unit 15   **307.** 1. $\frac{1}{6}$ 2. $\frac{3}{12}$ 3. $\frac{2}{20}$

           309. 1. $\frac{1}{12}$ 2. $\frac{2}{5}$ 3. $\frac{1}{10}$

           311. 1. 3 2. $1\frac{1}{2}$ 3. $2\frac{4}{5}$

           313. 1. $3\frac{1}{18}$ 2. $2\frac{1}{5}$ 3. $1\frac{3}{4}$

           315. 1. $4\frac{1}{6}$ 2. $8\frac{7}{16}$ 3. $4\frac{2}{3}$

Practice Sets

Practice Sets

Set 1 p. 12

Write > or <.

1. 68 < 86
2. 1437 ● 1451
3. 12,960 ● 12,965
4. 30,400 ● 28,250
5. 473,130 ● 456,262
6. 528,047 ● 528,937
7. 7,420,000 ● 7,450,000
8. 8,000,000 ● 7,999,999

Set 2 p. 14

Write the approximation to the nearest ten.

1. 76   80
2. 23
3. 739
4. 1608

Write the approximation to the nearest hundred.

5. 472   500
6. 916
7. 2130
8. 42,256

Write the approximation to the nearest thousand.

9. 2145   2000
10. 7804
11. 16,032
12. 79,722

Write the approximation to the nearest ten thousand.

13. 46,273   50,000
14. 92,508
15. 129,420
16. 865,000

Set 3 p. 26

Estimate.   Use the nearest tens.

1. 36   40
   +45 +50
        ───
         90
2. 20
   +86
3. 85
   +14
4. 67
   +61
5. 41
   +83
6. 93
   +37

7. 18
   +20
8. 52
   +75
9. 74
   +82
10. 38
    +69
11. 94
    +58
12. 71
    +35

Estimate.   Use the nearest hundreds.

13. 218   200
    +501 +500
          ────
           700
14. 496
    +550
15. 761
    +948
16. 830
    +323
17. 157
    +445
18. 604
    +760

19. 982
    +137
20. 525
    +874
21. 979
    +212
22. 303
    +670
23. 147
    +296
24. 550
    +899

328

Set 4 p. 28

Add.

1. 243
   +430
   673

2. 108
   +440

3. 825
   +323

4. 691
   + 8

5. 570
   + 19

6. 3500
   +9270

7. 7931
   +8061

8. 4426
   + 470

9. 6843
   + 36

10. 1554
    +9414

11. 21,300
    + 2,305

12. 63,224
    +81,035

13. 89,515
    +90,103

14. 76,737
    + 1,102

15. 97,896
    + 102

Set 5 p. 32

Add.

1. 423
   +238
   661

2. 198
   +421

3. 570
   + 66

4. 797
   + 45

5. 612
   +789

6. 1580
   +6385

7. 4256
   +5809

8. 725
   +1975

9. 5247
   +5972

10. 9419
    +9598

11. 12,708
    +34,890

12. 31,976
    + 714

13. 96,655
    + 6,829

14. 70,893
    +89,395

15. 59,287
    +40,597

Set 6 p. 34

Add.

1. 17
   8
   +21
   46

2. 26
   95
   +89

3. 64
   55
   + 9

4. 128
   410
   + 58

5. 275
   9
   + 78

6. 242
   427
   +117

7. 601
   698
   +936

8. 1076
   727
   + 59

9. 3615
   3270
   +1908

10. 7163
    8378
    +9459

11. 35
    7
    80
    +54

12. 58
    79
    46
    +18

13. 97
    400
    238
    76
    +178

14. 2936
    1706
    4127
    8915
    +6002

15. 1209
    789
    1445
    67
    + 140

Set 7 p. 46

Estimate. Use the nearest tens.

1. 86   90
   −12   −10
         ───
          80

2. 54
   −26

3. 20
   −13

4. 77
   −39

5. 85
   −40

6. 32
   −15

7. 93
   −28

8. 68
   −41

9. 91
   −64

10. 42
    −13

11. 59
    −17

12. 75
    −45

Estimate. Use the nearest hundreds.

13. 617   600
    −303   −300
           ────
            300

14. 453
    −272

15. 798
    −546

16. 289
    −125

17. 944
    −581

18. 863
    −754

19. 805
    −569

20. 371
    −139

21. 698
    −288

22. 536
    −412

23. 900
    −130

24. 550
    −325

Set 8 p. 48

Subtract.

1. 963
   −823
   ────
    140

2. 504
   −202

3. 182
   − 61

4. 759
   −509

5. 874
   − 70

6. 6630
   −6400

7. 9378
   −7130

8. 8945
   − 343

9. 5487
   − 70

10. 7268
    −4004

11. 55,186
    −41,125

12. 82,793
    − 2,602

13. 49,691
    −32,160

14. 98,677
    −   312

15. 84,985
    −81,155

Set 9 p. 52

Subtract.

1. 46
   − 8
   ──
   38

2. 38
   −19

3. 82
   − 7

4. 60
   −25

5. 95
   −86

6. 408
   −162

7. 145
   − 19

8. 1384
   − 357

9. 8015
   −7911

10. 9706
    −3410

11. 78,218
    −64,050

12. 98,756
    −   219

13. 25,277
    −18,074

14. 83,409
    − 2,805

15. 36,804
    −33,482

330

Set 10 p. 54

Subtract.

1. 468 − 189 279	**2.** 720 − 54	**3.** 153 − 95	**4.** 985 − 888	**5.** 257 − 168
6. 541 − 169	**7.** 870 − 198	**8.** 714 − 565	**9.** 2360 − 570	**10.** 1210 − 1088
11. 6322 − 5862	**12.** 1763 − 898	**13.** 4525 − 2867	**14.** 9740 − 8782	**15.** 6652 − 1659

Set 11 p. 56

Subtract.

1. 400 − 215 185	**2.** 208 − 109	**3.** 501 − 64	**4.** 800 − 739	**5.** 900 − 537
6. 105 − 87	**7.** 700 − 298	**8.** 904 − 856	**9.** 2500 − 146	**10.** 1507 − 259
11. 7031 − 4212	**12.** 3706 − 869	**13.** 4700 − 3738	**14.** 6200 − 2183	**15.** 7305 − 6706

Set 12 p. 58

Add.

1. $2.39 + .52 $2.91	**2.** $4.00 + 7.98	**3.** $7.66 + 3.08	**4.** $25.98 + 2.57	**5.** $67.02 + 89.48
6. $1.78 .95 + 2.39	**7.** $9.24 1.53 + 6.75	**8.** $ 6.47 27.25 + 9.50	**9.** $27.30 16.42 + 39.09	**10.** $16.95 .85 + 9.73

Subtract.

11. $2.56 − 1.02 $1.54	**12.** $1.75 − .26	**13.** $5.80 − 1.99	**14.** $6.08 − 1.49	**15.** $5.00 − 2.66
16. $10.00 − 5.25	**17.** $37.45 − 19.08	**18.** $68.20 − 5.99	**19.** $25.00 − 9.50	**20.** $34.00 − 16.25

331

Multiply.

1. 20 × 4 80	**2.** 60 × 3	**3.** 90 × 4	**4.** 30 × 5	**5.** 50 × 4
6. 400 × 4	**7.** 700 × 2	**8.** 600 × 5	**9.** 300 × 9	**10.** 500 × 7
11. 6000 × 2	**12.** 2000 × 8	**13.** 5000 × 8	**14.** 7000 × 9	**15.** 4000 × 8

Multiply.

1. 23 × 2 46	**2.** 18 × 3	**3.** 63 × 6	**4.** 15 × 5	**5.** 75 × 4	**6.** 23 × 8
7. 122 × 4	**8.** 318 × 4	**9.** 409 × 5	**10.** 509 × 3	**11.** 815 × 7	**12.** 478 × 9
13. 926 × 9	**14.** 629 × 7	**15.** 475 × 8	**16.** 528 × 6	**17.** 792 × 5	**18.** 387 × 7

Multiply.

1. 3252 × 3 9756	**2.** 1905 × 2	**3.** 4103 × 8	**4.** 7015 × 6	**5.** 5112 × 9
6. 8125 × 5	**7.** 1294 × 7	**8.** 9245 × 6	**9.** 3549 × 4	**10.** 7753 × 5
11. 40,148 × 2	**12.** 61,037 × 6	**13.** 54,006 × 4	**14.** 27,814 × 7	**15.** 82,075 × 8
16. $301.79 × 3	**17.** $826.39 × 8	**18.** $700.15 × 9	**19.** $123.69 × 9	**20.** $916.20 × 5

Set 16 p. 80

Multiply.

1. 32 ×10 320	**2.** 29 ×30	**3.** 52 ×60	**4.** 38 ×50	**5.** 80 ×90	**6.** 46 ×40
7. 45 ×100	**8.** 79 ×600	**9.** 72 ×200	**10.** 96 ×100	**11.** 90 ×900	**12.** 94 ×500
13. 84 ×300	**14.** 55 ×700	**15.** 82 ×400	**16.** 23 ×900	**17.** 20 ×500	**18.** 25 ×800

Set 17 p. 82

Multiply.

1. 41 ×24 984	**2.** 18 ×83	**3.** 23 ×15	**4.** 60 ×37	**5.** 56 ×42	**6.** 78 ×28
7. 78 ×45	**8.** 91 ×16	**9.** 27 ×92	**10.** 96 ×70	**11.** 93 ×94	**12.** 78 ×83
13. 126 × 91	**14.** 405 × 85	**15.** 260 × 14	**16.** 703 × 73	**17.** 396 × 52	**18.** 568 × 61
19. 409 × 82	**20.** 359 × 59	**21.** 145 × 47	**22.** 950 × 24	**23.** 618 × 66	**24.** 626 × 87

Set 18 p. 84

Multiply.

1. 2108 × 51 107,508	**2.** 3325 × 46	**3.** 8024 × 72	**4.** 1516 × 48	**5.** 7038 × 17
6. 4080 × 28	**7.** 7508 × 90	**8.** 3675 × 65	**9.** 4009 × 34	**10.** 3270 × 37
11. 4695 × 14	**12.** 9985 × 72	**13.** 6758 × 33	**14.** 8025 × 86	**15.** 7050 × 95

Set 19 p. 86

Multiply.

1. 614 ×124 76,136	2. 223 ×618	3. 190 ×320	4. 714 ×255	5. 900 ×519	6. 384 ×209
7. 934 ×136	8. 750 ×460	9. 818 ×771	10. 703 ×192	11. 718 ×845	12. 504 ×607
13. 698 ×108	14. 542 ×256	15. 400 ×705	16. 675 ×683	17. 188 ×413	18. 792 ×759

Set 20 p. 110

Divide.

7 r1 1. 2)15	2. 9)21	3. 7)51	4. 3)19	5. 2)11	6. 6)27
7. 8)78	8. 7)60	9. 3)25	10. 4)33	11. 5)33	12. 6)55
13. 4)38	14. 5)49	15. 5)27	16. 8)51	17. 6)40	18. 9)80
19. 6)47	20. 2)19	21. 8)68	22. 3)28	23. 9)85	24. 7)47

Set 21 p. 112

Divide.

20 1. 3)60	2. 7)70	3. 2)80	4. 6)120	5. 4)280
6. 9)540	7. 5)300	8. 8)320	9. 4)160	10. 6)480
11. 7)560	12. 5)450	13. 2)140	14. 8)720	15. 9)630
16. 3)270	17. 6)420	18. 5)200	19. 9)450	20. 8)400

334

Set 22 p. 116

Divide.

1. 6)76   _12 r4_
2. 3)89
3. 5)95
4. 8)600
5. 2)155

6. 4)130
7. 7)657
8. 2)161
9. 9)190
10. 6)199

11. 7)378
12. 3)250
13. 4)295
14. 8)724
15. 5)399

16. 4)362
17. 9)509
18. 5)418
19. 7)444
20. 9)898

Set 23 p. 118

Find the mean.

1. 9, 7, 5   _7_
2. 2, 6, 8, 8
3. 1, 9, 6, 5, 4

4. 13, 9, 20
5. 8, 12, 13, 7
6. 22, 22, 15, 45, 36

7. 120, 88, 95
8. 87, 128, 140, 93
9. 100, 98, 85, 92, 75

10. 75, 60, 83, 78
11. 133, 210, 140, 210, 187
12. 28, 19, 46, 62, 30, 55

13. 123, 168, 105, 152
14. 64, 100, 78, 85, 73
15. 18, 20, 34, 40, 18, 18, 34

Set 24 p. 120

Divide.

1. 3)600   _200_
2. 9)900
3. 2)800
4. 4)2400
5. 5)1500

6. 7)2100
7. 9)3600
8. 6)4200
9. 2)1200
10. 5)4000

11. 3)2700
12. 8)7200
13. 7)6300
14. 4)2000
15. 9)5400

16. 8)4800
17. 5)4500
18. 6)5400
19. 4)3600
20. 9)6300

335

Set 25 p. 122

Divide.

1. $3\overline{)942}$ 314

2. $6\overline{)795}$ **3.** $4\overline{)900}$ **4.** $2\overline{)519}$ **5.** $8\overline{)990}$

6. $4\overline{)2186}$ **7.** $5\overline{)1888}$ **8.** $7\overline{)4907}$ **9.** $6\overline{)1970}$ **10.** $3\overline{)1915}$

11. $2\overline{)1541}$ **12.** $6\overline{)3908}$ **13.** $3\overline{)1607}$ **14.** $8\overline{)7560}$ **15.** $9\overline{)2875}$

16. $7\overline{)3009}$ **17.** $5\overline{)4755}$ **18.** $6\overline{)5000}$ **19.** $2\overline{)1605}$ **20.** $9\overline{)7259}$

21. $4\overline{)1563}$ **22.** $9\overline{)4504}$ **23.** $5\overline{)3968}$ **24.** $8\overline{)5845}$ **25.** $7\overline{)6000}$

Set 26 p. 122

Divide.

1. $3\overline{)\$6.24}$ $2.08

2. $7\overline{)\$9.73}$ **3.** $2\overline{)\$5.70}$ **4.** $5\overline{)\$4.55}$ **5.** $8\overline{)\$14.80}$

6. $9\overline{)\$27.36}$ **7.** $6\overline{)\$51.00}$ **8.** $6\overline{)\$35.94}$ **9.** $4\overline{)\$32.20}$ **10.** $7\overline{)\$33.25}$

Set 27 p. 130

Divide.

1. $10\overline{)30}$ 3

2. $10\overline{)90}$ **3.** $10\overline{)100}$ **4.** $10\overline{)280}$ **5.** $10\overline{)360}$

6. $20\overline{)60}$ **7.** $40\overline{)40}$ **8.** $30\overline{)240}$ **9.** $90\overline{)180}$ **10.** $50\overline{)100}$

11. $30\overline{)180}$ **12.** $20\overline{)140}$ **13.** $50\overline{)200}$ **14.** $60\overline{)120}$ **15.** $20\overline{)180}$

16. $80\overline{)400}$ **17.** $40\overline{)160}$ **18.** $90\overline{)810}$ **19.** $50\overline{)350}$ **20.** $60\overline{)300}$

Set 28 p. 132

Divide.

1. 20)68 3 r8
2. 50)72
3. 30)95
4. 40)88
5. 70)91

6. 30)217
7. 60)195
8. 20)112
9. 80)233
10. 40)166

11. 20)183
12. 70)211
13. 90)235
14. 50)283
15. 60)280

16. 80)407
17. 60)400
18. 30)160
19. 90)408
20. 40)300

21. 80)505
22. 50)499
23. 80)650
24. 70)500
25. 90)815

Set 29 p. 134

Divide.

1. 33)268 8 r4
2. 92)276
3. 54)275
4. 21)110
5. 72)440

6. 84)509
7. 71)500
8. 22)154
9. 41)382
10. 63)260

11. 44)100
12. 34)204
13. 51)409
14. 82)271
15. 73)382

16. 31)280
17. 64)450
18. 23)138
19. 92)850
20. 73)602

21. 42)175
22. 61)567
23. 94)470
24. 53)379
25. 81)666

Set 30 p. 136

Divide.

1. 23)135 5 r20
2. 41)160
3. 62)500
4. 84)498
5. 52)354

6. 81)725
7. 33)297
8. 22)150
9. 91)545
10. 74)146

11. 71)636
12. 64)249
13. 53)155
14. 44)309
15. 34)200

16. 21)190
17. 92)454
18. 64)125
19. 31)189
20. 72)718

21. 42)368
22. 51)405
23. 63)309
24. 82)572
25. 93)725

337

Set 31 p. 138

Divide.

1. 5 r15
   27)150
2. 49)208
3. 65)215
4. 87)549
5. 19)160

6. 38)375
7. 56)428
8. 76)175
9. 35)160
10. 78)500

11. 46)266
12. 88)200
13. 25)120
14. 57)508
15. 39)308

16. 66)654
17. 18)100
18. 75)263
19. 69)512
20. 37)95

21. 28)250
22. 89)542
23. 45)206
24. 76)756
25. 57)510

Set 32 p. 140

Divide.

1. 4 r2
   36)146
2. 75)375
3. 17)160
4. 28)182
5. 49)396

6. 57)423
7. 66)200
8. 85)175
9. 39)352
10. 38)114

11. 35)149
12. 67)140
13. 29)174
14. 18)172
15. 16)83

16. 47)382
17. 76)684
18. 58)192
19. 89)268
20. 65)520

21. 26)55
22. 48)360
23. 79)476
24. 56)284
25. 87)350

Set 33 p. 142

Divide.

1. 36 r18
   20)738
2. 50)695
3. 60)1872
4. 30)1900

5. 40)3247
6. 70)4009
7. 30)788
8. 90)4036

9. 60)5198
10. 50)4119
11. 20)1260
12. 40)3920

13. 30)2733
14. 60)4000
15. 40)599
16. 70)5950

17. 20)1936
18. 80)7590
19. 50)3900
20. 90)7096

338

Set 34 p. 144

Divide.

1. $22\overline{)1230}$ 55 r20
2. $41\overline{)2442}$
3. $63\overline{)1134}$
4. $81\overline{)6609}$

5. $52\overline{)3328}$
6. $73\overline{)4300}$
7. $64\overline{)3150}$
8. $91\overline{)4672}$

9. $44\overline{)3408}$
10. $23\overline{)1978}$
11. $32\overline{)2311}$
12. $83\overline{)6615}$

13. $84\overline{)5800}$
14. $62\overline{)5063}$
15. $42\overline{)3780}$
16. $74\overline{)3624}$

17. $24\overline{)1208}$
18. $72\overline{)5000}$
19. $53\overline{)1537}$
20. $92\overline{)6470}$

Set 35 p. 146

Divide.

1. $28\overline{)686}$ 24 r14
2. $68\overline{)4860}$
3. $57\overline{)2396}$
4. $16\overline{)864}$

5. $49\overline{)1578}$
6. $55\overline{)4188}$
7. $77\overline{)5484}$
8. $69\overline{)4296}$

9. $65\overline{)6204}$
10. $56\overline{)4720}$
11. $39\overline{)3600}$
12. $76\overline{)6324}$

13. $18\overline{)1572}$
14. $45\overline{)2899}$
15. $56\overline{)4088}$
16. $59\overline{)5340}$

17. $55\overline{)4126}$
18. $35\overline{)3185}$
19. $19\overline{)1714}$
20. $38\overline{)3200}$

Set 36 p. 148

Divide.

1. $27\overline{)3564}$ 132
2. $86\overline{)9614}$
3. $31\overline{)7260}$
4. $62\overline{)9052}$

5. $59\overline{)8825}$
6. $44\overline{)9376}$
7. $29\overline{)5945}$
8. $76\overline{)9000}$

9. $33\overline{)6975}$
10. $75\overline{)9825}$
11. $46\overline{)9962}$
12. $85\overline{)9820}$

13. $28\overline{)9562}$
14. $92\overline{)9752}$
15. $32\overline{)9984}$
16. $45\overline{)6605}$

17. $58\overline{)9000}$
18. $74\overline{)8024}$
19. $84\overline{)9420}$
20. $18\overline{)4788}$

339

Set 37 p. 160

Find the greatest common factor.

1. 4, 20 4   **2.** 10, 15   **3.** 6, 8   **4.** 20, 8   **5.** 12, 3

6. 15, 45   **7.** 28, 16   **8.** 6, 15   **9.** 18, 30   **10.** 45, 18

11. 24, 32   **12.** 36, 72   **13.** 30, 45   **14.** 12, 30   **15.** 24, 96

Set 38 p. 162

Find the least common multiple.

1. 3, 5 15   **2.** 4, 6   **3.** 6, 9   **4.** 8, 10   **5.** 10, 40

6. 5, 15   **7.** 9, 24   **8.** 4, 14   **9.** 10, 35   **10.** 12, 18

11. 4, 22   **12.** 8, 18   **13.** 20, 35   **14.** 9, 15   **15.** 16, 20

Set 39 p. 172

Complete the sentence.

1. $\frac{1}{2}$ of 16 = _?_ 8   **2.** $\frac{1}{3}$ of 9 = _?_   **3.** $\frac{1}{10}$ of 50 = _?_

4. $\frac{1}{4}$ of 32 = _?_   **5.** $\frac{1}{2}$ of 24 = _?_   **6.** $\frac{1}{5}$ of 30 = _?_

7. $\frac{1}{3}$ of 18 = _?_   **8.** $\frac{1}{8}$ of 32 = _?_   **9.** $\frac{1}{4}$ of 36 = _?_

10. $\frac{1}{6}$ of 24 = _?_   **11.** $\frac{1}{8}$ of 40 = _?_   **12.** $\frac{1}{10}$ of 80 = _?_

13. $\frac{3}{8}$ of 8 = _?_   **14.** $\frac{5}{6}$ of 18 = _?_   **15.** $\frac{3}{4}$ of 36 = _?_

16. $\frac{2}{3}$ of 24 = _?_   **17.** $\frac{3}{5}$ of 25 = _?_   **18.** $\frac{5}{6}$ of 36 = _?_

19. $\frac{2}{3}$ of 9 = _?_   **20.** $\frac{3}{4}$ of 8 = _?_   **21.** $\frac{3}{10}$ of 60 = _?_

22. $\frac{2}{5}$ of 10 = _?_   **23.** $\frac{5}{8}$ of 48 = _?_   **24.** $\frac{9}{10}$ of 50 = _?_

Set 40 pp. 176, 178

Make the fractions equivalent.

1. $\frac{1}{2} = \frac{?}{12}$ 6
2. $\frac{1}{6} = \frac{?}{18}$
3. $\frac{1}{3} = \frac{?}{9}$
4. $\frac{1}{4} = \frac{?}{8}$

5. $\frac{2}{3} = \frac{?}{12}$
6. $\frac{3}{4} = \frac{?}{16}$
7. $\frac{3}{5} = \frac{?}{15}$
8. $\frac{2}{3} = \frac{?}{18}$

Write the simplest name.

9. $\frac{2}{4}$ $\frac{1}{2}$
10. $\frac{4}{6}$
11. $\frac{3}{9}$
12. $\frac{2}{10}$
13. $\frac{6}{15}$
14. $\frac{4}{12}$

15. $\frac{2}{16}$
16. $\frac{16}{20}$
17. $\frac{3}{12}$
18. $\frac{10}{16}$
19. $\frac{20}{25}$
20. $\frac{16}{36}$

Set 41 p. 180

Find the least common denominator. Rename the fractions.

1. $\frac{1}{4}, \frac{1}{2}$ $\frac{1}{4}, \frac{2}{4}$
2. $\frac{1}{3}, \frac{3}{4}$
3. $\frac{2}{5}, \frac{7}{10}$
4. $\frac{3}{4}, \frac{1}{6}$

5. $\frac{2}{3}, \frac{4}{5}$
6. $\frac{5}{6}, \frac{5}{9}$
7. $\frac{3}{8}, \frac{3}{10}$
8. $\frac{7}{10}, \frac{5}{12}$

9. $\frac{1}{3}, \frac{5}{12}$
10. $\frac{3}{5}, \frac{1}{7}$
11. $\frac{1}{4}, \frac{9}{10}$
12. $\frac{2}{3}, \frac{1}{15}$

Set 42 p. 182

Add. Write the simplest name for the answer.

1. $\frac{1}{3} + \frac{1}{3} = \underline{\ ?\ }$ $\frac{2}{3}$
2. $\frac{1}{5} + \frac{2}{5} = \underline{\ ?\ }$
3. $\frac{3}{8} + \frac{2}{8} = \underline{\ ?\ }$

4. $\frac{4}{8} + \frac{3}{8} = \underline{\ ?\ }$
5. $\frac{1}{9} + \frac{2}{9} = \underline{\ ?\ }$
6. $\frac{4}{10} + \frac{1}{10} = \underline{\ ?\ }$

7. $\frac{8}{15} + \frac{4}{15} = \underline{\ ?\ }$
8. $\frac{2}{10} + \frac{6}{10} = \underline{\ ?\ }$
9. $\frac{1}{12} + \frac{5}{12} = \underline{\ ?\ }$

Subtract. Write the simplest name for the answer.

10. $\frac{3}{4} - \frac{1}{4} = \underline{\ ?\ }$ $\frac{1}{2}$
11. $\frac{4}{5} - \frac{2}{5} = \underline{\ ?\ }$
12. $\frac{2}{3} - \frac{1}{3} = \underline{\ ?\ }$

13. $\frac{8}{9} - \frac{2}{9} = \underline{\ ?\ }$
14. $\frac{5}{6} - \frac{3}{6} = \underline{\ ?\ }$
15. $\frac{7}{8} - \frac{1}{8} = \underline{\ ?\ }$

16. $\frac{8}{15} - \frac{4}{15} = \underline{\ ?\ }$
17. $\frac{7}{10} - \frac{4}{10} = \underline{\ ?\ }$
18. $\frac{15}{16} - \frac{3}{16} = \underline{\ ?\ }$

Add.

1. $\frac{1}{2} + \frac{1}{4} = \underline{\ ?\ }$ $\frac{3}{4}$

2. $\frac{1}{5} + \frac{1}{3} = \underline{\ ?\ }$

3. $\frac{1}{6} + \frac{1}{8} = \underline{\ ?\ }$

4. $\frac{1}{5} + \frac{1}{6} = \underline{\ ?\ }$

5. $\frac{1}{9} + \frac{2}{3} = \underline{\ ?\ }$

6. $\frac{3}{8} + \frac{1}{2} = \underline{\ ?\ }$

7. $\frac{1}{8} + \frac{3}{4} = \underline{\ ?\ }$

8. $\frac{4}{15} + \frac{2}{5} = \underline{\ ?\ }$

9. $\frac{1}{6} + \frac{1}{2} = \underline{\ ?\ }$

Subtract.

10. $\frac{1}{2} - \frac{1}{4} = \underline{\ ?\ }$ $\frac{1}{4}$

11. $\frac{1}{4} - \frac{1}{6} = \underline{\ ?\ }$

12. $\frac{7}{8} - \frac{1}{2} = \underline{\ ?\ }$

13. $\frac{3}{4} - \frac{3}{10} = \underline{\ ?\ }$

14. $\frac{2}{3} - \frac{1}{2} = \underline{\ ?\ }$

15. $\frac{1}{2} - \frac{2}{5} = \underline{\ ?\ }$

16. $\frac{5}{12} - \frac{1}{4} = \underline{\ ?\ }$

17. $\frac{5}{6} - \frac{2}{9} = \underline{\ ?\ }$

18. $\frac{1}{3} - \frac{1}{6} = \underline{\ ?\ }$

Add.

1. $\frac{1}{2}$ $+\frac{3}{10}$ $\frac{4}{5}$

2. $\frac{1}{8}$ $+\frac{5}{6}$

3. $\frac{3}{10}$ $+\frac{1}{3}$

4. $\frac{3}{8}$ $+\frac{5}{12}$

5. $\frac{1}{16}$ $+\frac{3}{4}$

6. $\frac{2}{5}$ $+\frac{1}{10}$

Subtract.

7. $\frac{1}{2}$ $-\frac{3}{10}$ $\frac{1}{5}$

8. $\frac{9}{16}$ $-\frac{1}{4}$

9. $\frac{2}{3}$ $-\frac{5}{8}$

10. $\frac{11}{15}$ $-\frac{1}{3}$

11. $\frac{7}{12}$ $-\frac{3}{8}$

12. $\frac{8}{15}$ $-\frac{2}{5}$

Write the numeral for a whole number.

1. $\frac{5}{5} = \underline{\ ?\ }$ 1

2. $\frac{8}{2} = \underline{\ ?\ }$

3. $\frac{18}{3} = \underline{\ ?\ }$

4. $\frac{42}{6} = \underline{\ ?\ }$

5. $\frac{10}{10} = \underline{\ ?\ }$

Write the fraction.

6. $\frac{?}{12} = 1$ 12

7. $\frac{?}{2} = 5$

8. $\frac{?}{4} = 3$

9. $\frac{?}{10} = 2$

10. $\frac{?}{5} = 5$

Set 46 pp. 198, 202

Write the fraction.

1. $1\frac{1}{3}$ $\frac{4}{3}$ **2.** $1\frac{1}{5}$ **3.** $2\frac{1}{6}$ **4.** $4\frac{1}{8}$ **5.** $3\frac{1}{4}$ **6.** $1\frac{2}{5}$

7. $5\frac{3}{4}$ **8.** $1\frac{3}{8}$ **9.** $4\frac{5}{8}$ **10.** $3\frac{4}{5}$ **11.** $7\frac{2}{3}$ **12.** $2\frac{5}{6}$

Write the mixed numeral.

13. $\frac{3}{2}$ $1\frac{1}{2}$ **14.** $\frac{5}{4}$ **15.** $\frac{19}{3}$ **16.** $\frac{8}{5}$ **17.** $\frac{21}{8}$ **18.** $\frac{14}{5}$

19. $\frac{26}{3}$ **20.** $\frac{23}{4}$ **21.** $\frac{17}{2}$ **22.** $\frac{46}{5}$ **23.** $\frac{17}{10}$ **24.** $\frac{29}{6}$

Set 47 p. 204

Add. Write the simplest name for the answer.

1. $3\frac{1}{4}$ **2.** $7\frac{2}{5}$ **3.** $4\frac{1}{3}$ **4.** $6\frac{2}{8}$ **5.** 2

$+5\frac{1}{4}$ $+7\frac{1}{5}$ $+3\frac{1}{3}$ $+8\frac{1}{8}$ $+5\frac{3}{4}$

$8\frac{1}{2}$

6. $4\frac{7}{10}$ **7.** $6\frac{2}{3}$ **8.** $9\frac{1}{8}$ **9.** $8\frac{4}{5}$ **10.** $9\frac{1}{10}$

$+6\frac{1}{10}$ $+4$ $+6\frac{6}{8}$ $+4$ $+8\frac{6}{10}$

Subtract. Write the simplest name for the answer.

11. $6\frac{2}{3}$ **12.** $12\frac{4}{5}$ **13.** $10\frac{2}{4}$ **14.** $7\frac{3}{4}$ **15.** $15\frac{7}{8}$

$-1\frac{1}{3}$ $-7\frac{2}{5}$ $-8\frac{1}{4}$ -2 $-5\frac{3}{8}$

$5\frac{1}{3}$

16. $6\frac{1}{2}$ **17.** $16\frac{9}{10}$ **18.** $8\frac{1}{3}$ **19.** $18\frac{13}{16}$ **20.** $25\frac{9}{10}$

$-2\frac{1}{2}$ $-8\frac{3}{10}$ -7 $-5\frac{5}{16}$ $-8\frac{1}{10}$

Set 48 p. 206

Add. Write the simplest name for the answer.

1. $6\frac{3}{8}$ **2.** $4\frac{2}{3}$ **3.** $8\frac{7}{9}$ **4.** $6\frac{3}{4}$ **5.** $4\frac{5}{6}$

$+2\frac{7}{8}$ $+4\frac{2}{3}$ $+7\frac{5}{9}$ $+9\frac{1}{4}$ $+8\frac{5}{6}$

$9\frac{1}{4}$

6. $7\frac{3}{4}$ **7.** $14\frac{7}{10}$ **8.** $4\frac{11}{20}$ **9.** $5\frac{1}{2}$ **10.** $6\frac{2}{3}$

$+11\frac{3}{4}$ $+4\frac{3}{10}$ $+9\frac{19}{20}$ 6 $1\frac{1}{3}$

$+3\frac{1}{2}$ $+4\frac{1}{3}$

Set 49   p. 208

Add.   Write the simplest name for the answer.

1. $2\frac{1}{2}$
$+4\frac{1}{3}$
$6\frac{5}{6}$

2. $6\frac{1}{4}$
$+7\frac{1}{8}$

3. $1\frac{3}{4}$
$+1\frac{1}{2}$

4. $8\frac{2}{5}$
$+6\frac{7}{15}$

5. $6\frac{2}{3}$
$+5\frac{1}{4}$

6. $4\frac{2}{3}$
$+9\frac{3}{5}$

7. $10\frac{3}{4}$
$+\ 5\frac{7}{12}$

8. $6\frac{1}{2}$
$+9\frac{3}{10}$

9. $6\frac{1}{3}$
$+6\frac{11}{12}$

10. $3\frac{1}{10}$
$+4\frac{4}{15}$

Set 50   p. 210

Subtract.   Write the simplest name for the answer.

1. $6\frac{1}{2}$
$-2\frac{1}{4}$
$4\frac{1}{4}$

2. $5\frac{3}{4}$
$-2\frac{3}{5}$

3. $9\frac{4}{5}$
$-6\frac{1}{2}$

4. $4\frac{1}{3}$
$-1\frac{2}{9}$

5. $8\frac{5}{6}$
$-1\frac{1}{3}$

6. $9\frac{7}{10}$
$-9\frac{1}{2}$

7. $8\frac{1}{2}$
$-2\frac{3}{10}$

8. $1\frac{3}{4}$
$-1\frac{1}{10}$

9. $9\frac{1}{2}$
$-4\frac{3}{8}$

10. $7\frac{2}{3}$
$-1\frac{1}{6}$

11. $12\frac{3}{5}$
$-\ 6\frac{3}{10}$

12. $15\frac{7}{8}$
$-\ 3\frac{7}{12}$

13. $10\frac{15}{16}$
$-\ 3\frac{1}{2}$

14. $20\frac{5}{6}$
$-\ 4\frac{3}{4}$

15. $18\frac{11}{14}$
$-\ 9\frac{3}{7}$

Set 51   p. 212

Subtract.   Write the simplest name for the answer.

1. $5\frac{1}{4}$
$-2\frac{3}{4}$
$2\frac{1}{2}$

2. $9\frac{3}{5}$
$-2\frac{4}{5}$

3. $8\frac{1}{3}$
$-3\frac{2}{3}$

4. $10\frac{3}{7}$
$-\ 5\frac{6}{7}$

5. 8
$-3\frac{1}{2}$

6. 18
$-\ 9\frac{2}{3}$

7. $14\frac{4}{9}$
$-\ 3\frac{8}{9}$

8. 10
$-\ 4\frac{3}{5}$

9. $9\frac{7}{10}$
$-6\frac{9}{10}$

10. 8
$-1\frac{5}{8}$

11. $24\frac{3}{10}$
$-\ 8\frac{7}{10}$

12. 14
$-13\frac{1}{4}$

13. $12\frac{1}{5}$
$-\ 6\frac{4}{5}$

14. 16
$-\ 7\frac{3}{10}$

15. $14\frac{7}{20}$
$-\ 5\frac{11}{20}$

344

Set 52 p. 214

Subtract. Write the simplest name for the answer.

1. $7\frac{1}{2}$
$-3\frac{3}{4}$
$\overline{3\frac{3}{4}}$

2. $3\frac{2}{3}$
$-1\frac{5}{6}$

3. $9\frac{1}{4}$
$-3\frac{5}{6}$

4. $6\frac{3}{8}$
$-2\frac{3}{4}$

5. $8\frac{2}{5}$
$-7\frac{1}{2}$

6. $9\frac{1}{10}$
$-7\frac{1}{2}$

7. $7\frac{1}{4}$
$-2\frac{3}{8}$

8. $10\frac{1}{2}$
$-6\frac{2}{3}$

9. $12\frac{2}{5}$
$-3\frac{9}{10}$

10. $9\frac{1}{3}$
$-3\frac{1}{2}$

11. $17\frac{3}{10}$
$-8\frac{9}{20}$

12. $15\frac{1}{2}$
$-8\frac{7}{10}$

13. $9\frac{1}{5}$
$-3\frac{7}{15}$

14. $8\frac{3}{16}$
$-1\frac{1}{2}$

15. $7\frac{5}{8}$
$-4\frac{11}{16}$

Set 53 p. 290

Write the decimal.

1. $\frac{2}{10}$ 0.2
2. $1\frac{83}{100}$
3. $3\frac{17}{1000}$
4. $10\frac{7}{10}$
5. $48\frac{276}{1000}$

6. $\frac{1}{100}$
7. $68\frac{9}{100}$
8. $1\frac{3}{10}$
9. $\frac{6}{10}$
10. $205\frac{16}{100}$

11. $\frac{903}{1000}$
12. $8\frac{9}{10}$
13. $\frac{58}{1000}$
14. $118\frac{1}{10}$
15. $\frac{69}{100}$

Write the fraction or mixed numeral.

16. 0.8 $\frac{8}{10}$
17. 96.24
18. 100.75
19. 4.01
20. 7.5

21. 15.085
22. 44.360
23. 9.167
24. 0.1
25. 56.4

26. 212.9
27. 0.3
28. 0.70
29. 0.466
30. 0.05

Set 54 p. 294

Write > or <.

1. 24.6 < 24.8
2. 2.67 ● 2.68
3. 16.20 ● 16.18

4. 9.054 ● 9.053
5. 10.362 ● 9.987
6. 7.2 ● 7.3

7. 24.66 ● 26.01
8. 33.8 ● 35.6
9. 5.448 ● 5.463

10. 45.09 ● 45.90
11. 37.8 ● 38.2
12. 61.905 ● 61.876

Set 55 p. 296

Add.

1. 2.56 $\underline{+8.17}$ 10.73	**2.** 12.8 $\underline{+\ \ 9.8}$	**3.** 0.07 $\underline{+0.59}$	**4.** 1.26 $\underline{+8.78}$	**5.** 8.79 $\underline{+0.54}$
6. 36.7 $\underline{+16.3}$	**7.** 10.3 $\underline{+99.5}$	**8.** 4.47 $\underline{+8.65}$	**9.** 58.9 $\underline{+80.9}$	**10.** 9.48 $\underline{+7.81}$
11. 1.029 $\underline{+3.088}$	**12.** 0.564 $\underline{+7.277}$	**13.** 37.81 $\underline{+26.97}$	**14.** 281.7 $\underline{+634.8}$	**15.** 5.908 $\underline{+4.650}$
16. 0.329 $\underline{+0.955}$	**17.** 1.435 $\underline{+9.966}$	**18.** 626.4 $\underline{+628.6}$	**19.** 37.59 $\underline{+52.82}$	**20.** 4.658 $\underline{+1.345}$

Set 56 p. 298

Subtract.

1. 4.236 $\underline{-0.085}$ 4.151	**2.** 8.109 $\underline{-0.149}$	**3.** 5.712 $\underline{-0.258}$	**4.** 34.00 $\underline{-\ \ 3.25}$	**5.** 65.1 $\underline{-57.4}$
6. 71.16 $\underline{-38.16}$	**7.** 81.2 $\underline{-53.3}$	**8.** 2.920 $\underline{-1.048}$	**9.** 8.79 $\underline{-0.81}$	**10.** 4.834 $\underline{-1.796}$
11. 3.008 $\underline{-2.904}$	**12.** 69.16 $\underline{-13.78}$	**13.** 3.407 $\underline{-1.817}$	**14.** 79.4 $\underline{-69.7}$	**15.** 24.56 $\underline{-14.89}$
16. 5.28 $\underline{-5.19}$	**17.** 65.8 $\underline{-49.1}$	**18.** 5.035 $\underline{-3.037}$	**19.** 77.9 $\underline{-69.4}$	**20.** 2.82 $\underline{-0.79}$

Set 57 p. 308

Multiply. Write the simplest name for the answer.

1. $\frac{1}{2} \times \frac{3}{4} = \underline{\ ?\ }$ $\frac{3}{8}$ **2.** $\frac{2}{5} \times \frac{2}{5} = \underline{\ ?\ }$ **3.** $\frac{1}{3} \times \frac{1}{3} = \underline{\ ?\ }$

4. $\frac{1}{2} \times \frac{1}{2} = \underline{\ ?\ }$ **5.** $\frac{6}{7} \times \frac{1}{3} = \underline{\ ?\ }$ **6.** $\frac{2}{5} \times \frac{5}{6} = \underline{\ ?\ }$

7. $\frac{8}{9} \times \frac{1}{2} = \underline{\ ?\ }$ **8.** $\frac{3}{10} \times \frac{3}{4} = \underline{\ ?\ }$ **9.** $\frac{1}{2} \times \frac{7}{10} = \underline{\ ?\ }$

10. $\frac{7}{8} \times \frac{2}{3} = \underline{\ ?\ }$ **11.** $\frac{1}{6} \times \frac{1}{6} = \underline{\ ?\ }$ **12.** $\frac{7}{10} \times \frac{5}{6} = \underline{\ ?\ }$

Set 58 p. 310

Multiply. Write the simplest name for the answer.

1. $3 \times \frac{1}{2} = \underline{\ ?\ }$ $1\frac{1}{2}$ **2.** $\frac{1}{3} \times 8 = \underline{\ ?\ }$ **3.** $\frac{3}{4} \times 2 = \underline{\ ?\ }$

4. $\frac{2}{5} \times 5 = \underline{\ ?\ }$ **5.** $\frac{3}{6} \times 7 = \underline{\ ?\ }$ **6.** $3 \times \frac{7}{8} = \underline{\ ?\ }$

7. $9 \times \frac{1}{3} = \underline{\ ?\ }$ **8.** $3 \times \frac{3}{5} = \underline{\ ?\ }$ **9.** $\frac{1}{2} \times 6 = \underline{\ ?\ }$

10. $\frac{2}{3} \times 2 = \underline{\ ?\ }$ **11.** $8 \times \frac{3}{4} = \underline{\ ?\ }$ **12.** $\frac{2}{6} \times 3 = \underline{\ ?\ }$

13. $\frac{5}{6} \times 8 = \underline{\ ?\ }$ **14.** $\frac{3}{5} \times 8 = \underline{\ ?\ }$ **15.** $10 \times \frac{3}{4} = \underline{\ ?\ }$

Set 59 p. 312

Multiply. Write the simplest name for the answer.

1. $\frac{2}{3} \times 6\frac{1}{4} = \underline{\ ?\ }$ $4\frac{1}{6}$ **2.** $3\frac{1}{2} \times \frac{3}{4} = \underline{\ ?\ }$ **3.** $\frac{2}{5} \times 2\frac{1}{4} = \underline{\ ?\ }$

4. $2\frac{1}{8} \times \frac{1}{4} = \underline{\ ?\ }$ **5.** $\frac{5}{6} \times 3\frac{1}{3} = \underline{\ ?\ }$ **6.** $\frac{3}{8} \times 4\frac{1}{2} = \underline{\ ?\ }$

7. $3\frac{1}{3} \times \frac{3}{8} = \underline{\ ?\ }$ **8.** $6\frac{1}{4} \times \frac{3}{4} = \underline{\ ?\ }$ **9.** $6\frac{3}{4} \times \frac{1}{2} = \underline{\ ?\ }$

10. $\frac{1}{2} \times 7\frac{2}{3} = \underline{\ ?\ }$ **11.** $4\frac{1}{6} \times \frac{1}{4} = \underline{\ ?\ }$ **12.** $\frac{2}{3} \times 5\frac{1}{2} = \underline{\ ?\ }$

13. $5\frac{1}{8} \times \frac{2}{3} = \underline{\ ?\ }$ **14.** $5\frac{1}{4} \times \frac{4}{5} = \underline{\ ?\ }$ **15.** $7\frac{1}{2} \times \frac{4}{6} = \underline{\ ?\ }$

Set 60 p. 314

Multiply. Write the simplest name for the answer.

1. $2\frac{1}{3} \times 2\frac{1}{4} = \underline{\ ?\ }$ $5\frac{1}{4}$ **2.** $1\frac{1}{2} \times 3\frac{1}{3} = \underline{\ ?\ }$ **3.** $2\frac{1}{2} \times 1\frac{3}{4} = \underline{\ ?\ }$

4. $1\frac{1}{4} \times 3\frac{1}{4} = \underline{\ ?\ }$ **5.** $2\frac{1}{4} \times 2\frac{1}{6} = \underline{\ ?\ }$ **6.** $2\frac{1}{2} \times 1\frac{1}{8} = \underline{\ ?\ }$

7. $1\frac{5}{6} \times 3\frac{1}{3} = \underline{\ ?\ }$ **8.** $1\frac{1}{3} \times 1\frac{5}{8} = \underline{\ ?\ }$ **9.** $3\frac{1}{2} \times 3\frac{1}{5} = \underline{\ ?\ }$

10. $3\frac{1}{3} \times 2\frac{1}{5} = \underline{\ ?\ }$ **11.** $2\frac{1}{4} \times 2\frac{1}{4} = \underline{\ ?\ }$ **12.** $2\frac{2}{3} \times 1\frac{1}{2} = \underline{\ ?\ }$

13. $4\frac{1}{3} \times 2\frac{2}{5} = \underline{\ ?\ }$ **14.** $1\frac{3}{4} \times 3\frac{1}{8} = \underline{\ ?\ }$ **15.** $2\frac{5}{8} \times 3\frac{1}{2} = \underline{\ ?\ }$

Tables of Measurement

Metric System

Length

10 millimeters = 1 centimeter
100 centimeters = 1 meter
1000 meters = 1 kilometer

10 centimeters = 1 decimeter
10 decimeters = 1 meter
10 meters = 1 dekameter
10 dekameters = 1 hectometer
10 hectometers = 1 kilometer

Area

100 square millimeters = 1 square centimeter
10,000 square centimeters = 1 square meter
10,000 square meters = 1 hectare

Volume

1000 cubic millimeters = 1 cubic centimeter
1,000,000 cubic centimeters = 1 cubic meter

Mass (weight)

1000 milligrams = 1 gram
1000 grams = 1 kilogram
1000 kilograms = 1 metric ton

Capacity

1000 milliliters = 1 liter
1000 liters = 1 kiloliter

United States Customary System

Length

12 inches = 1 foot
3 feet = 1 yard
1760 yards = 1 mile

Area

144 square inches = 1 square foot
9 square feet = 1 square yard
4840 square yards = 1 acre

Volume

1728 cubic inches = 1 cubic foot
27 cubic feet = 1 cubic yard

Weight

16 ounces = 1 pound
2000 pounds = 1 ton

Capacity

8 fluid ounces = 1 cup
2 cups = 1 pint
2 pints = 1 quart
4 quarts = 1 gallon

348

Glossary

Angle Two rays that have the same endpoint. The endpoint is the **vertex** of the angle. Angles can be described according to their measures.

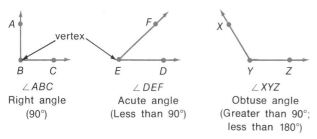

∠ABC
Right angle
(90°)

∠DEF
Acute angle
(Less than 90°)

∠XYZ
Obtuse angle
(Greater than 90°;
less than 180°)

Approximation A number used in the place of an exact number.

Examples: Approximations for 4,454,433:
4,000,000 (nearest million)
4,500,000 (nearest hundred thousand)
4,450,000 (nearest ten thousand)

Area The number of square units needed to cover a given surface.

Examples: Some ways to find area:
rectangle $A = l \times w$
right triangle $A = \frac{1}{2}$ of $(b \times h)$

Circle A simple closed path. All the points on the path are the same distance from a point inside, called the **center.**

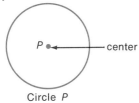

Circle *P*

Congruent angles Angles that have the same measure.

Example: All right angles are congruent.

Congruent line segments Line segments that have the same length.

Example: The four sides of a square are congruent.

Congruent polygons Polygons that have the same size and shape.

Decimal A numeral that uses place value and a **decimal point.** Any digits to the left of the decimal point name a whole number. Digits to the right stand for a fraction.

Example: 4.25, which means $4\frac{25}{100}$.

decimal point

Degree (°) A standard unit used to measure angles.

Example: The measurement of a right angle is 90 degrees, or 90°.

Degree Celsius (°) A standard unit used to measure temperature.

Example: Water boils at 100 degrees Celsius, or 100°C.

Denominator In the fraction $\frac{2}{3}$, 3 is the *denominator.*

Diameter of a circle Any line segment that goes through the center of the circle, and whose endpoints are on the circle.

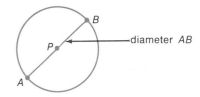

diameter *AB*

Digit Any one of the ten symbols used to write our numerals:

0, 1, 2, 3, 4, 5, 6, 7, 8, 9

Divisible by Divide one whole number by another. If the remainder is 0, then the first number *is divisible by* the second.

Example: 14 is divisible by 2 because $2\overline{)14}$
$\begin{array}{r} 7\,r0 \\ 2\overline{)14} \\ -14 \\ \hline 0 \end{array}$

Equivalent fractions Fractions that name the same number.

Example: $\frac{2}{3}$, $\frac{4}{6}$, $\frac{6}{9}$, $\frac{8}{12}$ are *equivalent fractions.*

Of these, $\frac{2}{3}$ is the **simplest name.**

Equivalent ratios Ratios that show the same comparison.

Example: $\frac{3}{2}$, $\frac{6}{4}$, $\frac{9}{6}$ are *equivalent ratios*.
They are named by **equivalent fractions.**

Even number A whole number whose numeral ends in 0, 2, 4, 6, or 8. An *even number* is divisible by 2.

Examples: 20, 32, 74, 106, 118

Expanded notation A way to show the number named by each digit in a numeral.

Example: These are expanded notations for 6398.

$$\begin{array}{r} 6000 \\ 300 \\ 90 \\ +\ \ \ 8 \end{array} \qquad 6000 + 300 + 90 + 8$$

Factors of a number A whole number is divisible by each of its *factors.* When the factors of different numbers include one or more of the same **(common)** factors, the greatest of these is the **greatest common factor.**

Example: Factors of 8 — 1, 2, 4, 8
Factors of 12 — 1, 2, 3, 4, 6, 12
Common factors of 8 and 12 — 1, 2, 4
Greatest common factor of 8 and 12 — 4
Example: Factors of 7 — 1, 7
Factors of 15 — 1, 3, 5, 15
Common factor of 7 and 15 — 1
Greatest common factor of 7 and 15 — 1

Factor tree When the **prime factors** of a number are multiplied, the product is the number. The prime factors of a number can be found by making a *factor tree.*

Example: These are factor trees for 30. No matter which factor tree is made, the prime factors are the same.

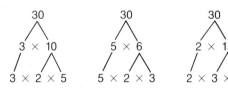

Fraction A numeral that shows how to compare part of a whole (or of a group) with all the parts.

Example: 1 of the 5 fair shares of a pizza is $\frac{1}{5}$ of the pizza.
Example: 5 of the 12 cupcakes are $\frac{5}{12}$ of the cupcakes.
Example: 4 of the 5 tropical fish in a tank are $\frac{4}{5}$ of the fish.

Geometry The study of space and figures in space.

Graph of an ordered pair of numbers A point, located by using two number lines that form right angles.

Example: For the ordered pair of numbers (3, 2): start at 0, go 3 spaces to the right, then go up 2 spaces.

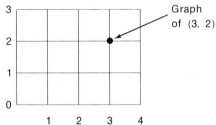

Grouping property of addition (associative property of addition) To add, numbers can be grouped differently. The sum is always the same.

Example: $\underbrace{(3 + 2)}_{5} + 4 = \underline{\ ?\ }$ $\qquad 3 + \underbrace{(2 + 4)}_{6} = \underline{\ ?\ }$
$\qquad\qquad\quad 5\ \ + 4 = 9 \qquad\qquad 3 + \ \ 6\ \ = 9$

Grouping property of multiplication (associative property of multiplication) To multiply, numbers can be grouped differently. The product is always the same.

Example: $\underbrace{(4 \times 3)}_{12} \times 2 = \underline{\ ?\ }$ $\qquad 4 \times \underbrace{(3 \times 2)}_{6} = \underline{\ ?\ }$
$\qquad\qquad\quad 12\ \ \times 2 = 24 \qquad\quad 4 \times \ \ 6\ \ = 24$

Hexagon A polygon that has six sides.

Latitude The measure, in degrees, for north and south distances from the **equator.**

Least common denominator The **least common multiple** of two or more denominators.

Example: 24 is the least common denominator for $\frac{3}{8}$ and $\frac{5}{6}$.

Line A *line* can be thought of as a straight path that never ends. It has no endpoints.

Line of symmetry A line that separates a flat figure into two parts that can be matched exactly.

Line segment Two **endpoints** and the straight (shortest) path between them.

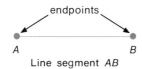

endpoints

A   *B*

Line segment *AB*

Longitude The measure, in degrees, for east and west distances from the **prime meridian.**

Mean The *mean* of a group of numbers is found by dividing the sum of the numbers by the number of addends. The mean can replace each original number to give the same sum.

Example: $8 + 3 + 2 + 7 + 10 = 30$, and $30 \div 5 = 6$.
6 is the mean of these numbers because:
$8 + 3 + 2 + 7 + 10 = 30$, and
$6 + 6 + 6 + 6 + 6 = 30$.

Median The middle number of a group of numbers, when they are arranged in order.

Example: 3 is the median of:

0, 2, 2,   3,   4, 5, 5

Mixed numeral A numeral that uses a name for a whole number and a fraction.

Example: $2\frac{1}{4}$, which means $2 + \frac{1}{4}$.

Multiples of a number When a whole number is multiplied by 1, by 2, by 3, and so on, each product is a *multiple* of the number. Multiples that are the same for two or more numbers are called **common multiples.** The least of these is the **least common multiple.**

Example: Multiples of 2—2, 4, 6, 8, 10, 12, 14, 16, 18, ⋯
Multiples of 3—3, 6, 9, 12, 15, 18, ⋯
Common multiples of 2 and 3—6, 12, 18, ⋯
Least common multiple of 2 and 3—6

Multiplication-addition property (distributive property) To multiply a sum of addends by a number, you may multiply each addend by the number and then add the answers.

Example: This property is used in multiplication. For 6×734, think of 734 as $4 + 30 + 700$. Multiply each addend by 6 and then add the answers.

$$
\begin{array}{r}
734 \\
\times\ 6 \\
\hline
24 \leftarrow 6 \times 4 \\
180 \leftarrow 6 \times 30 \\
+4200 \leftarrow 6 \times 700 \\
\hline
4404
\end{array}
\qquad \text{or} \qquad
\begin{array}{r}
22 \\
734 \\
\times\ 6 \\
\hline
4404
\end{array}
$$

Multiplication property of one (identity property for multiplication) When one of two factors is 1, the product equals the other factor.

Examples: $7 \times 1 = 7$
$1 \times 4 = 4$
$1 \times 1 = 1$

Numerals Names (symbols) for numbers.

Examples: $\frac{3}{4}$; 4.6; 20; XX

Numerator In the fraction $\frac{2}{3}$, 2 is the *numerator.*

Octagon A polygon that has eight sides.

Odd number A whole number whose numeral ends in 1, 3, 5, 7, or 9. When an odd number is divided by 2, the remainder is 1.

Examples: 11, 23, 45, 107, 259

Order property of addition (commutative property of addition) Two numbers can be added in either order. The sums are the same.

Example: $3 + 5 = 8$ and $5 + 3 = 8$.

Order property of multiplication (commutative property of multiplication) Two numbers can be multiplied in either order. The products are the same.

Example: $3 \times 5 = 15$ and $5 \times 3 = 15$.

Parallel lines Lines in the same flat surface that do not cross (intersect).

Parallelogram A quadrilateral. The sides that do not meet are parallel (and congruent).

Pentagon A polygon that has five sides.

351

Perimeter The sum of the lengths of the sides of a polygon.
Example: The perimeter of a triangle is 25 centimeters if the lengths of its sides are 7, 8, and 10 centimeters.

Perpendicular lines Lines that meet to form right angles.

Place value The value of a position (place) for a digit in a numeral. In our system, the value of each place is ten times the value of the place at its right.
Examples: The 2 in 42 names 2.
The 2 in 21 names 20.

Point An exact location. A dot is often drawn to represent a *point.*

Polygon A simple closed path made up of line segments only. The segments are called **sides** of the polygon.

Prime number A whole number greater than 1 that has exactly two different factors: 1 and the number itself.
Example: 19 is a prime number, since 1 and 19 are the only factors of 19.

Probability A number from 0 to 1 that tells how likely it is that a thing will happen.
Example: If there are 2 reds and 1 blue, the probability of drawing a red is 2 out of 3, or $\frac{2}{3}$.

Quadrilateral A polygon that has four sides.

Radius of a circle Any line segment with endpoints that are the center of the circle and a point on the circle.

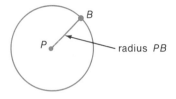

Ratio One way of comparing two numbers.
Example: There are 3 cats and 13 mice. The ratio of cats to mice can be shown as 3 to 13, 3:13, or $\frac{3}{13}$.

Ray A part of a line that has one **endpoint.** It goes on without end in only one direction.

Ray *AB*

Rectangle A quadrilateral. The sides that do not meet are parallel (and congruent). The sides that meet are perpendicular.

Roman numerals A system for naming numbers that does not use place value. The basic symbols are:

I	V	X	L	C	D	M
(1)	(5)	(10)	(50)	(100)	(500)	(1000)

Scale drawing A drawing that pictures the correct shape of something, but not its actual size. The **scale** tells how much actual distance is represented by a unit of length on the drawing.
Examples: Maps and blueprints are scale drawings.

Similar polygons Polygons that have the same shape.

Simple closed path In a flat surface, a path that begins and ends at the same point. It does not cross over (intersect) itself.

Simple closed paths   Not simple closed paths

Simplest name A fraction, when the numerator and the denominator have no common factor greater than 1.
Example: $\frac{3}{5}$ is a simplest name, since the greatest common factor of 3 and 5 is 1.

Square A rectangle that has four congruent sides.

Standard units of measure Units that people, through their government, agree to use when they measure things.
Examples: meter, gram, liter
See also Tables of Measurement, page 348.

Three-dimensional shape Not all of a *three-dimensional shape* is in the same flat surface.

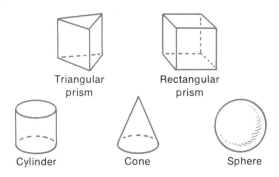

Triangular prism

Rectangular prism

Cylinder

Cone

Sphere

Triangle A polygon that has three sides.

Volume The number of cubic units needed to fill a given space.
Example:
One way to find volume:
rectangular prism $V = l \times w \times h$

Whole number Any one of the numbers 0, 1, 2, 3, 4, 5, 6, and so on. No matter how long you count, you cannot come to the last *whole number.*

Zero property of addition (identity property for addition) When one of two addends is 0, the sum equals the other addend.
Examples: $4 + 0 = 4$
$0 + 6 = 6$
$0 + 0 = 0$

Zero property of multiplication When one of the numbers to be multiplied is 0, the product is 0.
Examples: $0 \times 10 = 0$
$58 \times 0 = 0$
$0 \times 0 = 0$

Zero properties of subtraction When 0 is subtracted from a number, the answer is the number.
Example: $7 - 0 = 7$
When a number is subtracted from itself, the answer is 0.
Example: $7 - 7 = 0$

Table of Symbols

Index

357

C
D
E
F
G
H
I
J